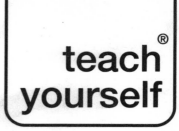

teach® yourself

entrepreneurship

entrepreneurship
alex mcmillan

For over 60 years, more than 50 million people have learnt over 750 subjects the **teach yourself** way, with impressive results.

be where you want to be
with **teach yourself**

For UK order enquiries: please contact Bookpoint Ltd, 130 Milton Park, Abingdon, Oxon, OX14 4SB. Telephone: +44 (0) 1235 827720. Fax: +44 (0) 1235 400454. Lines are open 09.00–17.00, Monday to Saturday, with a 24-hour message answering service. Details about our titles and how to order are available at www.teachyourself.co.uk

For USA order enquiries: please contact McGraw-Hill Customer Services, PO Box 545, Blacklick, OH 43004-0545, USA. Telephone: 1-800-722-4726. Fax: 1-614-755-5645.

For Canada order enquiries: please contact McGraw-Hill Ryerson Ltd, 300 Water St, Whitby, Ontario, L1N 9B6, Canada. Telephone: 905 430 5000. Fax: 905 430 5020.

Long renowned as the authoritative source for self-guided learning – with more than 50 million copies sold worldwide – the **teach yourself** series includes over 500 titles in the fields of languages, crafts, hobbies, business, computing and education.

British Library Cataloguing in Publication Data: a catalogue record for this title is available from the British Library.

Library of Congress Catalog Card Number: on file.

First published in UK 2006 by Hodder Education, 338 Euston Road, London, NW1 3BH.

First published in US 2006 by The McGraw-Hill Companies, Inc.

This edition published 2006.

The **teach yourself** name is a registered trade mark of Hodder Headline.

Typeset by Transet Limited, Coventry, England.
Printed in Great Britain for Hodder Education, a division of Hodder Headline, 338 Euston Road, London, NW1 3BH, by Cox & Wyman Ltd, Reading, Berkshire.

Hodder Headline's policy is to use papers that are natural, renewable and recyclable products and made from wood grown in sustainable forests. The logging and manufacturing processes are expected to conform to the environmental regulations of the country of origin.

Impression number   10 9 8 7 6 5 4 3 2 1
Year   2010 2009 2008 2007 2006

contents

preface

This book works. It delivers what it promises. The owner of it will become a better entrepreneur by reading and completing the exercises.

The book has tips, techniques and secrets that have come from more than 20 years' experience of being an entrepreneur, of reading their biographies, of interviewing them and people who deal with them. It is the end of a long search into the secrets that led to their success. This book will increase your wealth, help you develop your ideas and potential, and change your life for the better. Expect to become more wealthy, satisfied and fulfilled with life.

Covered are many important secrets missing from other less practical works. For example, practical guidance on how to spot opportunities and turn them into profit. Also included are techniques on how to overcome the fear that stops so many would-be entrepreneurs from even starting.

Valuable streetwise tricks and short cuts are included, such as how to grow your business with other people's money, as well as tested techniques from the greatest entrepreneurs in recent history, and from lesser known self-made millionaires. The book shows how they and you too can leverage your enterprise to a new level. It will change the way you think about money, opportunity, potential, security, assets, risk and then your results.

The book is totally practical, interactive with support material and contains a range of accelerated learning techniques.

Alex McMillan's personal mission is to help the entrepreneur, he believes is in all of us, progress and prosper.

He started school in Cyprus during the Eoka uprisings, his father serving with the Royal Air Force. He was educated in Oxford and London where he achieved degrees in Business and Management.

His career has been focused on executive recruitment and training. He is currently a consultant, coach, tutor, motivator and author to entrepreneurs. He is and has been an entrepreneur himself and is currently building an international Club for those ambitious and determined enough to reach the next level in their own business. You can contact the author direct on his website www.clubentrepreneur.co.uk.

Alex's friends consider him to be the eternal optimist with a passionate belief and energy for his next project. He lives with his wife Tracy and three children Alex, Zoe and Naomi in Sussex.

01

what if your entrepreneurial dream happened?

In this chapter you will learn:
- what exactly is an entrepreneur
- how employees and entrepreneurs think differently
- how to be successful in your own business
- what can stop you from becoming an entrepreneur
- the importance of being happy and successful

'Every time something happens, positive or negative, I ask myself, where is the opportunity here?'
Richard Lowden, founder of Eurodrive Car Rental

'Business opportunities are like buses, there's always another one coming.'
Richard Branson, founder of Virgin

A few years from now

You made it. You finally escaped the rat race – built yourself a business to become financially free. You now have the choice to continue and grow or sell out and take a capital gain, enough to retire on.

Imagine now going to estate agents to choose your ideal house with all of the facilities and features you always dreamed about. You tell the agent the location you had in mind: perhaps in this country, perhaps abroad, you know the one. You have waited a while for it to be ready and you are going to pick up the keys now and pay for it in cash. As you walk up the front drive, you feel absolutely fabulous on what you see as the first day of how you always wanted to live with everything you have always wanted. The house is just the material reward; the personal satisfaction of having built a successful business gives you a buzz. You remember all those people who warned you of the risks, told you that you had a good, well-paid, secure job.

The house looks marvellous, you cannot wait to go in. You step in; yes, it looks good, feels good, it even smells good, of newness and quality. It is a beautiful day and the sun is shining. You cannot wait to take a swim in the luxury pool. As each moment passes you can feel your excitement growing.

From your favourite music selection you choose something upbeat and positive that suggests success. The feeling of excitement grows as you switch on the music. Your mind fills with images of your new villa with its breathtaking view over the sea from the hot tub. Designed to your specific requirements it is literally perfect. As you continue to enjoy you day more and more, you notice the office workers hurrying back from lunch. Not for you ever again; you are a successful entrepreneur, you are free. Your mind wanders as you take in the expected luxuries and total freedom of the week ahead.

Feeling like a million pounds, you hope secretly to pass by certain people you know, those who said you would never do it, who never gave you support when asked. You call a few close family members and friends, and invite them around for the house warming. You order chilled champagne and lie back in the pool with a big SMILE on your face. You toy over all the things you are going to indulge in over the next couple of weeks, months, years. An occasional thought wanders back to those you have left on the 7:32 to Waterloo that morning.

The most pleasant feeling though, is that of success, coupled with the rise in self-esteem and pride. It has not been easy, but you have made it. You think back to your moments of doubt and hesitation, thankful that you did not give up or chicken out. You think back over the obstacles you overcame and feel very proud of your success. You also think of those you love the most and what you are now able to do for them.

Americans call the above 'dreambuilding'. Write down what you would want when you have achieved success, then go out and taste it now. By doing this your mind sets up the future you are working towards. Involve all your senses in a real taster. Go out and visit your dream house, test drive your dream car, look at brochures for your holiday of a lifetime. The taster gives firm images of what motivates you, making them real: a sort of future memory. Research has found that this simple idea is not only pleasant, it does increase motivation and focus and keeps you on track to achieve the future you desire.

Progress now

Write down what you would do on becoming financially free in your own business.

You will never have to work again, although you probably will want to, as you love your work. What you have worked for has turned from a dream to reality. For the next week at least you are going to soak up the reality on the beach, in the finest restaurants, with someone special to you. You are going to spend and spend: fashionable designer clothes, made to measure, parties, sports. You ponder a while on what you want to buy, knowing that money is no object now. Those months of focusing your money on investments ensure that your 'pot of gold' is constantly refilled and you can now afford to indulge yourself and still grow your wealth.

Back to the present. If the above appeals buy, read, re-read, live and breathe the book that is currently in your hands. Work, study, do the exercises, make the commitments and decisions. It is the answer, the guide book, you have been looking for. Get this thing called entrepreneurship done. Stop thinking, procrastinating, and go for it. This book is the route map that will guide you through. Everyone reading this book can become a successful entrepreneur. The only thing that can stop you is if you give up along the way.

What is an entrepreneur?

People have different understandings of the term 'entrepreneur'. The motives of an entrepreneur are numerous: some are purely focused on making money; some are totally focused on developing their innovations, and money is just the mechanism that allows it to happen, or even a side effect of success. Most entrepreneurs are after both. So when is an entrepreneur successful? Does making more money make an entrepreneur more successful? What do you think? Part of being an entrepreneur is doing your own thinking, making your own decisions!

There are two distinct aspects of an entrepreneur.

1 Someone, who through creativity, innovation, foresight and discovery, can identify commercial opportunities around him or her.
2 Someone practical who sees and exploits opportunities for making money successfully.

This includes the self-employed, small business owners, those embarking on setting up their own business, investors, artists, software writers, inventors, authors and songwriters.

In many successful enterprises these two elements are often found in two people. This is not surprising as practicality and creativity can, but certainly not necessarily, be opposites. In both cases, practicality and creativity are skills you can acquire from these pages. I will show you how to set yourself up to recognize opportunities that you are currently missing. Then comes the practical steps you must go through to turn these ideas into profit.

You have an entrepreneurial dream and wish to progress to the next level. You may not have even started in sales terms, but the idea is there or perhaps just the determination or desire. This means you have the spirit of an entrepreneur and that flame of enterprise needs to be nurtured and grown to a glowing furnace of fun and success.

Who wants to be an entrepreneur?

Back in the 1990s, working in my own recruitment business, I was requested by my staff to produce a list of questions to ask new candidates. One of them gave us an interesting and unexpected result.

The question was:
'If we could get you any job in the world, and put on your CV any necessary qualifications, skills and experience, as if by magic, what job would you want?'

The interesting and unexpected result was:
Out of the first 1,000 people we asked, 912 of them said that their dream job was to run their own business.

Hence the reason and target for this book. Many people want to be entrepreneurs, the economy wants more entrepreneurs to secure the future, and yet most people who want to do it never do. So my question is, and the answers in this book focus on the question: 'How can you become a successful entrepreneur?'

Explore this book and follow its treasure trail of tips: they have worked before and can help you achieve your dreams. Find answers to questions like:

- How do successful entrepreneurs think about money?
- How do successful entrepreneurs make decisions?
- How do successful entrepreneurs motivate themselves?
- How do successful entrepreneurs recover from setbacks?
- What is it that they do, and you can do too, that gives them their success?

Who will benefit from this book?

This book is aimed at those that want to start or have started their own enterprise and wish to create personal wealth from it. It covers entry routes, finance, venture capital, marketing, personnel, training, exit routes, etc. I will cover these aspects from a practical 'how to' and a 'what you should do now' perspective of techniques which have been proven to work. We will take lessons from both some of the most famous entrepreneurs and many who I know personally.

- Is this you?
- Want to escape the rat race?
- Want to be independent and financially free?
- Have a great idea you are sure would work?
- Spotted a gap in the market?
- Want to start your own business, but don't know what?
- Running a business but don't know how to get it to the next stage?
- Have an idea but don't know how to turn it into a business?
- You want to be rich?
- Have an overpowering desire to work for yourself?
- Tired of working to build up somebody else's business?
- Realize that while you are paid just for your time you will never make any real money?
- Want to do something on your own but are scared of the risks?

This book will provide you with all that you need to teach yourself.

Read and grow rich

This book can be your transition from dream to reality. This book is the spur that moves you forward with confidence.

Progress now

The book is full of 'hows' in addition to the 'whats'. So often with our goals, like a diet for example, we know what to do (e.g. eat less, exercise more), but how to achieve them can be more elusive.

If you do all the exercises in this book you will not only be on the road to your personal entrepreneurial success, you will be thinking success as you sleep. Yes, even while you sleep your unconscious mind will be reviewing and improving your habits and behaviour, to be more in line with your goals. By doing the exercises all your senses will be involved, and you will be conditioning yourself for success in the same way an athlete works out in a gym to programme his or her body to peak performance.

Right from the start I want you to read this book with a clear purpose. So now think what your dream is. I know you have one because you are reading this book! If you are browsing these words in the bookshop, make a decision now and take it to the cash till. What exactly does the word entrepreneur mean to you? How successful do you want to be? Think of your dream now. The following list of goals will help you formulate your dream:

- financial freedom (not having to work for a living)
- independence/being your own boss
- creative outlet
- fame
- chance to make serious wealth.

Ask yourself, what would happen if buying this book helped to realize your dreams of being an entrepreneur. If it released all of your skills, ideas and ambitions focused towards your goals.

Reading this book repeatedly will bring about the desired results. This is done through a variety of advanced linguistic techniques. The main messages of the book are directed at your unconscious, where the habits that determine your destiny lie. Knowledge about what to do, even how to do it, is not enough to achieve success. Your behaviour has to be changed to react automatically, taking you towards your goal. You cannot achieve your goal if you have to take conscious control all the time, you will just talk positive but behave in your old way.

Suggestions are therefore made at various levels, directly, indirectly, through metaphor and a large variety of linguistic instruments. They have been constructed with considerable care and checked meticulously by a panel of experts. However, you need not concern yourself with that. They are all in an easy-to-read plain English style, that has been designed for simplicity, practicality and fun. Above all, follow the advice; it works and will work for you.

There are practical exercises that you can try throughout the book. These, as you will have noticed already, are shown in **Progress now** boxes making reference back to them easy. At the end of each chapter I give three tips and two tasks for you to carry out. Make your own notes and keep them with this book.

While you are pursuing your personal entrepreneurial goals you can also revisit this book, reading a chapter or even a paragraph to recharge your energy, positive thought and attitude. It is like going into a service station for more petrol: there's nothing wrong with the car, but we all need a boost of energy now and again.

You know you will have to make some changes or give up old habits and attitudes. Not making changes is usually the most comfortable option in the short run. We like to remain with the familiar; it gives us the feeling of security. This safe feeling can be our greatest enemy or our greatest ally. The vast majority of people go through their careers on a conveyor belt until they receive their pension. They work for money, not being particularly greedy, just wanting to be financially safe and secure. They have what I call a 55-year plan to be financially and professionally free. This book is not targeted at those people. They will probably be watching television or working out how long it is until they collect their pension.

If, on the other hand, you hold the view like me, that life is a precious gift and you want to make a real difference, excel, create, achieve, grow, learn, develop, produce, win and accumulate wealth, then read on. This book will save you making a lot of mistakes. Learning from mine and other people's is a far better and faster way than learning by experience.

If you truly want to succeed passionately at something in your career, all you have to do is make the decision to achieve it. None of this trying your best stuff; commit to doing it and cut off all other directions. Burn your bridges and make success the only option, otherwise you will always wonder what you could have become, could have achieved. The rest is detail and technique, of which you will find all that you need in this series. Every day is unique, so don't waste it, you can never get it back. Make sure that you are planting seeds that grow to make your future days happier.

Read this book, do the exercises and together we'll transform the quality of your enterprises immediately and forever. This book is a collection of small interactive modules for growth. Each chapter stands alone, and yet still there is a real synergy in reading the whole. To gain real benefit, you should read the book three times. Each time it will appear to be a quite different book. Thoughts will be triggered and inspirations gained on each new read. Many language techniques are used, designed to aid and accelerate your learning. Single words can change lives, so be assured that I have used them with care. Things you have learnt will be turned from knowledge of something good to good habits, things that you do without having to pay conscious attention to them.

Remember, you can email any comments, questions and challenges to me on alex@clubentrepreneur.co.uk. There is also a selection of useful websites at the back of this book.

Sources of success secrets

The Billionaires Club

Imagine that you had direct access on videophone link to ten people who were self-made billionaires from a variety of industries and locations. Whenever you were at a moment of decision or seeking coaching or advice, you could ask not one but all ten of them what they would do if they were you. Imagine what it would cost to keep such people on the payroll only for when you needed their counsel? You cannot make a billion and remain anonymous and unnoticed; you will have left a trail of evidence. A good tracker can figure out how you achieved your goal and your method can be used again. Valuable practical principles can be learnt from the real world of success.

I have analysed the evidence of entrepreneurs who have made it to the highest level. These include Sir Richard Branson, Sir Alan Sugar, Bill Gates, Pierre Omidyar, Jeff Bezos, and also people of yesteryear, such as Aristotle Onassis, Ray Kroc, John D Rockefeller, Paul Getty, Henry Ford and Walt Disney. This research was done by looking principally at biographies to establish the subject's values, beliefs, passions, drives and motivations. I also met two people personally in the billionaires category. I looked for the language they used as this always carries with it, behind the content, the blueprint of their success.

Progress now

Read the biography of someone who is a self-made billionaire. There is a suggested list in the bibliography at the end of this book. Your goals may not be that big but it will still teach you what works well in business, principles that hold true no matter the size or industry.

Develop the habit of constantly reading such biographies. Success leaves an audit trail. When you have challenges in your enterprise ask yourself what these people would have done.

The self-made millionaires

I interviewed several self-made millionaires. Interestingly, while I identified many of the same traits and behaviours as in the billionaires group, there are some clear differences. There are things members of this group do *en masse* the same as the above group, yet there are also clear behaviours quite different from the Billionaires Club members.

Progress now

Find someone local to you who is a self-made millionaire. (There are more than 185,000 of them, at the time of writing, in the UK alone.) It may be someone you worked for, someone you met, someone related, or maybe someone with a lot of media coverage. It may be the proprietor of a business that has prospered. Whatever it takes, track one down. Then study this person in every way you can. Get their business report and accounts, invite them to lunch, talk to people who work for them. Learn as much as you can about their business philosophy.

Expected millionaires

This group consists of people who have started their own business, which is running profitably and is growing fast, and intend to make it to the Millionaires Club. Have they got the traits of those that made it? How hard did they find it to start up? What obstacles did they overcome?

Progress now

What makes you think you have got what it takes to be a self-made millionaire or billionaire?

What makes you think you might not become a self-made millionaire or billionaire?

Small is beautiful

These people have set up their own business to do their own thing, are profitable and financially free but wish to remain small.

> ## Progress now
> What exactly is your business motive?

Other experts in the know

This section covers a variety of experts in the field and also many written pieces of work, which are listed in the bibliography at the back of this book. These experts include people who deal with entrepreneurs on a daily basis: venture capitalists, business angels, consultants, advisers, etc.

How to see the world differently

An entrepreneur sees things that others miss. They can see resources or potential resources that can be used or utilized in a more beneficial, more profitable, way than they are being used now. It is the cornerstone on which capitalistic society is based.

I asked the 912 people I mentioned earlier some further questions, and I have listed their answers in order of popularity. These were corporate executives seeking a new corporate executive position.

How do you see a corporate executive position?
1 Security
2 Comfort
3 High status
4 Professional experience
5 Maintain high mortgage on home
6 Good pension
7 Training
8 Interesting work

How do you see self-employment/entrepreneurship?
1 Insecure, home at risk
2 Danger and vulnerability
3 No regular salary
4 Most fail
5 Independence
6 Freedom
7 Unlimited potential income and capital gain
8 Early retirement if you want it

I asked the same questions to a number of self-employed people/
entrepreneurs:

How do you see a corporate executive position?

1 In prison, told what to do
2 Regular salary and benefits
3 A boss to report to
4 Office politics necessary to succeed and survive
5 Limited potential to grow. Not paid what worth
6 Insecure future
7 Not able to express own ideas
8 High risk, all eggs in one basket

How do you see self-employment/entrepreneurship?

1 Security
2 Financial freedom
3 Outlet for creativity
4 Independence
5 Own boss
6 Potentially unlimited income
7 Potentially unlimited capital gain
8 Paid what I am worth

In the following chapters you will find all the resources you need
to become a successful entrepreneur. Expertise in the realm of, say,
accounting, tax, IT and marketing can be bought in; you cannot
do everything yourself. To this end I have included a reference list
of further sources of information at the back of this book.

I started out as an entrepreneur in partnership. Self-employment
for the first time I remember as a nerve-racking experience. By
definition it meant jumping into a realm of which I had no prior
experience or familiarity. We all tend to be afraid of what we
don't know. Yet I was determined to run my own business, and
I had to make a start somewhere. It seemed to me that joining a
partnership seemed a good way of reducing the risks, not being
alone was comforting. The recruitment business partnership
was so successful that we won an award from *Certified
Accountant* magazine in our first year of trading. Looking back
I learnt many hard lessons.

In the recession of 1990 I owned a recruitment business near
London Gatwick Airport. Suddenly companies that had been
actively recruiting, now had redundancy programmes.

Candidates were literally queuing along the street outside of our offices to register. We cut all advertising and still they came.

Then one of the largest employers and my biggest client in the area, Air Europe, went into liquidation. That in turn affected all the suppliers that they previously used. Those suppliers cut orders to their suppliers and so continued the vicious spiral of recession. Newspapers' recruitment sections were emptying. The few people who were left recruiting in the area found the notion of paying a recruitment fee a joke when so many potential employees were ringing them up directly every day. The market that had taken years to build up had gone, and gone in a period of three to six months.

Those who used to be our clients were registering with us as unemployed candidates. I changed focus and offered a range of services from CV writing and career coaching to interview training. However it was not enough; we were tied into a 25-year office lease, which had taken a long time to acquire, but had turned from an asset into a liability. The rent was fixed at pre-recession rates. I had to declare myself bankrupt. I lost more than £100,000 of invested money and my business, my life passion. My house was repossessed and I too was unemployed. This is undoubtedly the scenario that stops most entrepreneurs from starting or from taking risks to get to the next stage. That is why entrepreneurship is not for the faint hearted.

There are no redundancy cheques for entrepreneurs that fail. Yet I shed no tears nor spent a single minute on a negative thought. I saw it as a step on the path to my goal. Looking back from now, I realize that despite having two business degrees, I learnt more about business in those six months than during six years at business school. In fact, I would say that what I learnt at business school hampered me, by not providing practically focused skills. (Although I would add that today this has been addressed on programmes of study.)

Now, you may look back at my story and consider what you would have done in the same situation. Thinking about what I learnt through the experience, and what I have learnt from studying many entrepreneurs, if I could go back in time I would not have failed in the above situation. On the contrary, I would have succeeded. I now know the secrets. You can completely avoid those negative experiences and ten years of learning just from following the advice in this book. Take a quantum leap and get a serious advantage in the entrepreneur game.

This may appear to be a less than positive experience. Winners in the entrepreneurial world are determined by how they react to whatever the world throws at them. Here is the secret, it really is simple to do this. Feelings are created according to how you make up your internal focus based upon what is happening in real life, the emphasis being on 'make up'. If it is all made up anyway why not make your internal experiences and feelings as pleasant, positive and created in a way that supports you? I chose positive internal experiences and thus I learnt, gained inspirations and enterprising ideas about how to propel myself forward. Most people allow their mind to drift when they need to harness its power.

People I knew came up to me and said how sorry they felt for my plight. What they were really saying was they were glad that what had happened to me had not happened to them. That fear, like any fear, has stopped them becoming an incredible success, from realizing their full potential and feeling completely free. I was happy because I knew that I was free and had no constraints of fear and worry. Besides, as an entrepreneur your next good idea can easily replace all that you have lost, and a great deal more.

Progress now

Close your eyes and notice what images and sounds are in your mind while you think about what you have read on the previous few pages. Take note of how you feel about them.

Now change things around a bit and notice how this changes how you feel and how you think. Move images nearer or further away. Change colours to black and white or vice versa.

Entrepreneurship is about deferred gratification. You invest now for a return in the years to come. It is about making money while you sleep. It is about developing assets that make you money without the need for your presence. It is about making a capital gain from the value you have added to a business. Employeeship is about adding value to the assets of entrepreneurs in return for the illusion of security. A regular job is instant gratification. People see it as the secure option but it can take no more than 30 seconds for the employment of a senior manager of ten years loyalty to be terminated. That is not a long-term investment. I think having ten clients is more secure than having one. I have never understood why a bank will lend money to a person with only one source of income over which they have no control.

This book is a system that will transport you to your full potential. I will identify and remove the brakes that are currently working against you and then show you how to press the accelerator pedal to success.

How easily can you be a successful entrepreneur?

Everyone can be a successful entrepreneur. Every entrepreneur can be a better one.

Everything you can see around you, the company you work for, every company you have ever bought something from, was created by an entrepreneur with a dream, a vision.

When I was in my early teens I wanted to start my own business. I don't know where the desire came from. My father was an officer in the Royal Air Force, so there was no commercial influence from him. In business I identified two types of people: entrepreneurs and employees of entrepreneurs. I was born into a capitalistic society, so what was the point of having a career as an employee? I made a decision that, whatever it took, I wanted to be creative and independent, and this meant the entrepreneur route. (Dad, of course, wanted me to be a fighter pilot. Strangely, to him, I saw that as more risky than entrepreneurship.)

This was perhaps a youthful perspective, but it shows clearly that being an entrepreneur is no more than a decision. To be a rock star, dancer, architect, actor, advertising executive, coach or pilot took talent and training, but to be an entrepreneur is merely a decision. Your criteria for success or even more success are totally yours as an entrepreneur. Everybody else in their career has other people to determine when they are successful and in what way. It is often unnerving at first but you can be professionally and financially free. This is the surest way to eliminate all fears. As one of the entrepreneurs interviewed for this book said to me, 'I am not motivated by cash, I am motivated by having more choices and I figured that you have more choices with cash than without it!'

What stops you being an entrepreneur?

- What stops you escaping the rat race?
- What stops you starting?
- What stops you thinking of an idea?
- What stops you knowing which business to run?
- What stops you growing from a small to a large company?
- What stops you being an even better entrepreneur?

Your particular 'what is stopping you ...' question depends on where your entrepreneurial dream is right now. You need to know what stage you are at. If you are still at the dreamer stage or on the road to getting going, the question might be one of the first two in the list above.

The focus of the question is interesting in as much as it assumes that you have control, or at least can take control. This is one of the fundamental rules for successful entrepreneurship. You have to control the world around you and not let it control you. This requires strength of character. Entrepreneurship is far more about guts than brains. The beauty of this is that most really brainy people will never have the guts to launch or grow a business, so your competition is seriously reduced. That is why there are considerable opportunities for entrepreneurs. You just have to keep focusing on the goal, rather than asking 'What if it goes wrong?'

It is interesting to note how many successful enterprises were founded by people with poor academic records. In fact, when I have seen failure, it is usually because of complexity instead of the simple and practical. Everyone can be a successful entrepreneur and this chapter prepares you for the journey of transition from where you are now to what you could and will become.

Fear – the dream thief

I believe there are a thousand ideas with the potential of eBay, Google or Virgin that are not businesses today because the entrepreneurs were too scared to get them off the ground. One of my goals with this book is to release some of the incredible potential that is in danger of remaining bottled up.

So 912 out of 1,000 people would sooner be running their own business than being an employee. I dedicate this book to those 912. Those who have entrepreneurial talent, ideas, drives, may even be operating a business full time and need to grow to the next level on the road to being financially free through entrepreneurship. This book will unleash you from what has been holding you back. Additionally, this book refers to many resources that will help you. You may be in business for yourself but you won't have to be by yourself.

> **Progress now**
>
> Does fear hold you back? If so, which fears and in what way? How can you eliminate that fear now?

A practical approach

This book is practical. I have two business degrees and I have learnt a lot of theory. There is little of my degree studies in this work; it is designed to enable you to teach yourself. Such theoretical material is, first, extremely well covered and, second, of little practical use to entrepreneurs. The interesting thing I have learnt is that on studying actual successful entrepreneurs only three of them had knowledge of the theory and none of them practised what the theory preached.

For example, a first-term student of Economics will learn the relationship graph of price to volume of sales and that it varies depending on industry. Even this basic assumption does not reflect the actual experience of marketing directors. Economics assumes that people are intelligent and logical. They are not. Put the price up and people often buy more, put the price down and often they buy less. Entrepreneurs have to deal with the real world, and the real world is unfair, prejudiced, irrational, unpredictable, vindictive, decisive. Experience often hurts, it is a hard way to learn the lessons. This book will save you from that long-winded learning style.

If you want to learn the latest management buzzwords and jargon, look elsewhere. This book is unashamedly for people who want to make money by being entrepreneurs.

The results you get from this book will be determined by you. The more you work at it, the more personalized it becomes. It will be your personal success controller, keeping you on track to entrepreneurial success. I want you to be inspired, involved, committed, fired up, to do the exercises, fill in the blanks and above all be a tremendous success. This book will be your personal blueprint for success.

This is a personal book; tell your friends to buy their own copy. You will need to refer to it constantly, and to your own notes. In moments of challenge it will be a vital and trustworthy friend.

What is the aim of this book?

I can answer that in three words: your entrepreneurial success. Success now, success in the future, success despite any obstacle. Discover and believe in the person you could be. Uncover the hidden opportunities ... Recover from obstacles, or fear of imagined obstacles and grow.

What value is there in reading this book?

This book is designed to be of value at three levels. First, by reading particular chapters you will gain ideas and inspiration in the part of your career that is challenging you. Second, using it as a coach, you can keep coming back and reminding yourself of what has to be done. The third value is more complex and designed to appeal directly to your unconscious mind. Hypnotic and other neuro-linguistic language patterns are employed to make suggestions at an unconscious level to make changes for the better. They are used subtly and with care. So in reading the book it will not be just the conscious decisions you make that will help your career but the unconscious positive suggestions.

All of the techniques in this book have been used and brought success to entrepreneurs. Working in the recruitment business for most of my life I have looked for the 'person who outperforms'. I have also directly asked 'the successful' for tips and techniques. Luck has played a part, but there is clearly a lot we can do to determine our own destiny and greatly increase the chances of receiving good fortune in our favour. Reading this book is one example, well done. You now have a significant advantage over your competitors.

As a personal career coach I have first-hand knowledge of the more common questions people ask and obstacles they struggle with. So this book focuses on practical approaches to common challenges.

You may like to mark words, phrases or sections of this book that are pertinent to you with a highlight pen. I have included exercises and suggestions to increase the interactivity between you and the ideas I have taken from successful entrepreneurs.

How to make a million

I used to run something called the £100K Club. At some of the meetings I asked members of the audience the following question: 'What is the easiest way to make a million pounds?' I then asked them to list three ways in priority order. The top answer was winning the lottery, the second by inheritance and the third by being an entrepreneur.

Neither of the first two answers provides me with lasting satisfaction. I don't do the lottery: none of the prizes appeal and there is no stimulation or competitive fun for me in picking random numbers. Those who win the lottery often become unhappy as it robs them of what they might have become or achieved as a person. And I don't like the idea of receiving money from the demise of someone I love.

Money is often the measure of success but I see entrepreneurial success in terms of adding value, giving more than you take, creativity, innovation and fun. These are the things that give me satisfaction and make me feel good at all levels. I have owned luxury cars, taken exotic holidays, etc., but these are just things. So I want readers of this book to move answer number three to number one. You have much more control over number three.

It really is a lot easier to be a successful entrepreneur than you think. Thinking success is hard, or thinking that you won't make it can be a larger stopper of success than anything out there in the economy. The good news is that these issues are all dealt with amply in this book; if that is your concern let it be my responsibility. All experience can be learning that allows you to increase your progress rate towards your goals. In all events you can focus on the positive or the negative side. Decide which now, ahead of time, and everything that happens to you will turn to advantage. That is one of the principal secrets of entrepreneurs, what they do differently. All it requires from you is a decision. We will explore this idea at length later in the book.

Progress now

Which of the following do you think could make you a million fastest?

- Inventing a pill that increases your metabolic rate and reduces weight.
- A piece of software that will motivate you when necessary.
- A new audio programme series on practical steps to increase wealth.
- A property business offering shared ownership to renters, thus making them long term and caring of the property, reducing the deposit level they have to find.
- An international club connecting business people around the world.

On being a happy entrepreneur

I have found, from interviewing entrepreneurs, that being happy and being an entrepreneur go together.

A warning: this book will share with you the secrets of success learnt from successful entrepreneurs. However, there is perhaps a price to pay. The success formula involves adapting values, beliefs and attitudes, which inevitably means making changes. Certainly many of the successful entrepreneurs, whilst successful with money, were unsuccessful with other aspects of their life. So I have gone a step further and provided a whole chapter on how to make changes and be a better entrepreneur without paying an unacceptable price. In other words how to have the cake, eat it and still make money from selling it.

Progress now

What decision can you make right now to help you become a millionaire through your own enterprise and enjoy the journey?

What three things have changed in you in some way from reading this chapter?

Three tips

1 Knowledge reduces risk.
2 Knowing what you want with absolute clarity is nine parts of success.
3 Only action produces results.

Two tasks

1 Write down the three reasons why you bought or borrowed this book.
2 If you had three wishes right now, what would you truly wish for?

02

what type of entrepreneur are you?

In this chapter you will learn:
- some important considerations before starting
- the profile of the successful
- what an entrepreneur has to do
- the different types of entrepreneur
- how you can SMILE

'If you hear a voice within you saying, "You are not a painter," then by all means paint … and that voice will be silenced.'

Vincent Van Gogh

'There is not a person anywhere, that is not capable of doing more than he thinks he can.'

Henry Ford

How do you get started?

Over the years after talking to many budding and existing entrepreneurs I have come to realize that the word 'entrepreneur' is just too general. Stop ten people in the street, ask them what the word means for them and you will get ten different answers.

The danger is that when someone 'escapes corporate world' they tend to think of the 'start up' business (see Chapter 3) as their only option. I have identified five classifications of choice (not including corporate and social entrepreneurs) and the start up business is usually the worst one for them to cut their teeth on. Read on to find out why …

There are five main types of entrepreneur although some are elements of more than one. Understanding these is an essential first step before embarking on any venture.

How you start depends on your motivation. The most common career goal I hear from aspiring entrepreneurs is the ability to control their own destiny. This held true for each of the five categories below. Each category can be started on a part-time or sole trader basis. I emphasize this as many successful, now large enterprises started this way. Those that wanted to get bigger did so in reaction to their market demand, and thus there is an inbuilt safety element and the capital costs are kept to a minimum.

Many entrepreneurs start by working part time while maintaining their main income. Often this can provide a second vocation that could be expanded should redundancy strike, or when a major growth opportunity presents itself. When practical, this choice can provide a safe bridge towards becoming fully independent. Others go for it, putting in all their personal resources. Some raise venture capital. Later in the book I will share with you some alternative sources of raising capital with minimal risk or cost. In this chapter we shall first look at what being an entrepreneur means, followed by a discussion about the five categories. By the end you will be in a position to consider what type of entrepreneur you would like to be.

> ## Progress now
>
> If you have not started or are currently running a business, circle the category below which applies most to you.
>
> - Go it alone, doing what you do now (i.e. self-employed usually though not necessarily in your current trade or profession).
> - Want or have your own business yet wish to remain small and independent after having achieved financial and vocational freedom.
> - Have creative ideas or have access to creative ideas and have a long-term vision to build a substantial enterprise.
> - Build own business as part of a larger group, for example through franchising or network marketing.
> - Buy a business.
> - Inventor, artist or other originator of new things.

You can start on your own even part time for most types of enterprise, whatever are your ultimate goals. My research shows that, if practical, this path tends to yield more success than the others, followed by buying a franchise in an established operation. Buying a business is also a safe route, as the business should be profitable already. Starting small is the ideal way to test the market and get lots of live feedback without any major commitment.

You can then risk putting more resources behind your ideas from a situation of growing confidence. I have met many people who have, say, been made redundant or come back from abroad with a capital sum wondering what to do. That dream to run a business though suddenly seems a lot different from the other side of the counter.

What are the key qualities of an entrepreneur?

Someone who can make things happen. Innovation, creativity, risk taking, independence and a strong character are at the heart of entrepreneurship. A person who has decided to take control of their future and become self-employed, usually but not necessarily by creating their own business, product or service. Entrepreneurs thus add value to society by providing what the consumer requires, especially when they change their wants and needs.

Entrepreneurs compete with themselves, always wanting to improve their own performance. They never believe they have reached their potential and know that success or failure lies within their personal control or influence. You will need strength of character without a doubt. I think that it is no coincidence that many of the successful entrepreneurs on both sides of the Atlantic have or had a strong character and maintained a high standard of honesty, integrity and ethics.

John D Rockefeller for example was clearly strongly influenced through his life by his Christian values. This, or 'faith' generally, I believe, was and often is the strength and stability that helps the successful through their challenges and maintains their sense of meaningful purpose. It also encourages people to do business with them, where 'my word is my bond', and deals were often done on no more than a handshake. If you don't trust somebody's word and a handshake, their 'attractive terms' are unlikely to be accepted!

What does it take to become a successful entrepreneur?

What images does the word entrepreneur conjure up in your mind? For most they are attractive ones of adventure, freedom, independence, fast cars, luxury houses, holidays, success, wealth, etc. These are certainly real rewards of success. Like everything worth having though, there are some challenges to overcome along the way.

Hard work, for example, is certainly a common habit of successful entrepreneurs. Yet hard work to be effective has to be the right work. In the early stages of the business you are the most valuable resource. Therefore how you spend your time can be your most important decision. Take a moment and ask yourself this question: 'What is the most valuable work I should be doing this week?'

You need to start thinking like a great entrepreneur. People make the mistake of behaving and even spending like they are already wealthy. This is how they see a successful entrepreneur behaving. However, how the great achievers behaved at the stage you are at now is the key area to model. Here, and usually later, they are extremely thrifty, wanting every penny to work in their business. The secret of real success is not in the eyes of others. Is status important to you? It is important to most people; it is not about the outward image but the internal thinking. Entrepreneurs are not as motivated by external measures such as status and material possessions but more by internal satisfactions. They can become famous from achieving wealth and high living standards but quite often this is a side effect of their motivations.

An entrepreneur:

- has to think of new ideas, match and deliver them to a market at a profit.
- has to lead their team against established competition with minimal resources.
- has to raise finance without a track record, collateral or internal experts.
- has to constantly stake their personal reputation and give guarantees.
- has to pay their staff and only pay themselves when prudent to do so.
- has to be prepared to lose everything if things go wrong.
- is personally threatened when the bank or a creditor puts on pressure.
- has to be harder, more flexible, streetwise than in their previous corporate life. Their survival is dependent on managing company politics and policies; yours is surviving the jungle of the fittest where nobody seems to be on your side
- has to be good at multi-tasking, as initially they will have to do everything themselves.
- Has to take full responsibility for whatever happens.

Progress now

Who is more successful, a millionaire or a billionaire?

My answer to the question above would be that it depends. For me I would have to know what their objectives were and if they were happy. This means that the answer might be neither of the above.

Being a successful entrepreneur is about improving society, adding things that were not there before. This includes personal wealth accumulation, but if that is your only target you are nothing more than a miser. The wealth of money is nothing compared to the wealth of being totally free to think, create, innovate at will, and the knowledge that you have added value to society. An entrepreneur is an innovator, inspirer, leader, creator who adds to the lives of customers, staff, shareholders and themselves. Their life is full of excitement, energy, fun and friends. From my experience in the recruitment industry it offers more job satisfaction than any other.

The potential rewards though are very high indeed; your potential income and wealth are unlimited. The timescale can also be a great deal shorter to success. It is not an easy path, but with this book it is a much easier one, learning from those who have trodden the path before you, passing back their advice. Once you have started along this path there are only two things that can stop you reaching the end, in my opinion. One is giving up and the second is not learning as you go.

Let us now move on to look at the different types of entrepreneur.

SMILE your way to success

SMILE is my acronym for the five types of entrepreneur. You may be a hybrid of more than one. Knowing your profile is important to maximize your chance of success and happiness.

- **S** is for System, someone who is happy to buy into a proven formula and work it.
- **M** is for Money, for those whose only measure of success is money in the bank (not what you buy with the money).
- **I** is for Innovator, the creative among you who enjoy developing new ideas.
- **L** is for Lifestyle, for those who want to work their hobby.
- **E** is for Empire builders who want power and influence and to see their brand everywhere.

It is important which type you naturally are and which type you want to be, as there may be a difference. Each type has different strengths and weaknesses, each a different path to success (covered in the next chapter) based on a foundation of common principles. In practice you may be a composite of more than one. You smile as an entrepreneur when you know which one you are and focus upon it.

System entrepreneurs

Business is systemic. It is about the working in harmony of a variety of resources, people of different disciplines, level, and locations, equipment, offices, computers, marketing, accounting, etc. They all have to work together and are dependent on each other. Thus when the system is well designed it caters for all needs and is reduced to the simplest formula possible. That way everyone understands what is expected of them. Growth is made easy because the system is just being duplicated, a proven formula grows another tentacle.

The great success of McDonald's is an extremely efficient business model. It operates all of its '30,000 plus' restaurants around the world to the same basic formula. Every process is in the manual. Every situation that might and has arisen is dealt with in exactly the same way everywhere.

So once the original creativity has been innovated and then tweaked for efficiency a business can grow by taking in partners. In the case of McDonald's this is through franchising. One must not tinker with the proven system, nor wish to, as that road leads to failure.

Another example is in network marketing, often called multi-level marketing or referral marketing. A distributor network is established based upon a system that works. So are you prepared, happy even, to work the system that someone else has designed in which you have no say? If you are, then working the system can make you wealthy, there is no doubt of that, as long as you choose a good franchise, network marketing or system to join and that you work it in the way it was designed to be worked. Risk is greatly reduced, there should already be a proven market. Clearly there is no need for creativity, so if this is not one of your skill sets, being a system entrepreneur should appeal.

Money entrepreneurs

Money entrepreneurs are focused on storing as much financial wealth as possible. Their goal is money itself and not the things they will buy with the money. Their goal is high wealth not income level. In the extreme, these people will have no concept that there could be any other objective in running their own business. They tend not to enjoy their work as they will always focus their energies on where most money is, rather than their own passion. They have the advantage of being naturally in touch with the market and they will offer only things that they know will sell well. When they are successful they use their money to make more money taking full advantage of compound interest and leverage principles. They want to become as wealthy as they possibly can.

In less extreme cases they realize that the first goal of any business is to make a profit consistently, otherwise there is no business. They are also prudent enough to store money through a good period as an insurance against a lean period. To some extent we all need to be money entrepreneurs; it is, after all, what makes the world go around. The other advantage in setting your goal as money is very easy to measure. Sales and profit targets are either reached or not. It is thus simple, measurable and must be a prime focus of any enterprise, whatever are the other or driving passions.

Innovative entrepreneurs

To many the word 'entrepreneurs' is virtually synonymous to the word 'creative'. After all, a new enterprise does things differently from what has gone before it. A company can even be seen as an art form. Amazon changed the way we bought books. McDonald's changed the way we ate, eBay® changed the way we bought things. Tim Berners Lee, creator of the world wide web, changed the way people all over the world talked to each other.

The joy and challenge of creation becomes entrepreneurial when it meets commercial goals. Art might be beautiful but is there a market for it? When you focus your attention on the needs of people that are not currently being met as well as they could, you have the potential to create something better. Creation gives what business people call a USP – unique selling point. It becomes special, giving an edge over competitors.

Creative people, therefore, become innovative entrepreneurs when they start their focus on potential customers. They create better things, ways of doing things. Does this sound like you?

Lifestyle entrepreneurs

How great would it be for your hobby and passion and your business to be one and the same? When you love every minute of what you do, profit is a bonus, not the point of the enterprise. After all, if you had riches you would just spend all your time on your hobby anyway, so why not short-cut the process? A lifestyle entrepreneur is one whose primary motive is working their hobby.

When you plan to remain small you can cover for each other, work as a close-knit team, and management is relatively straightforward. Once you have a secure client base, profits can be high and the lifestyle can be thoroughly satisfying. You also have a capital asset that you can sell, should you wish to.

Employing staff immediately allows greater efficiencies in terms of delegating specialist tasks. It also means greater responsibilities and staff need managing. You need to make sure that your productivity, while training, managing and motivating, is not compromised. They are not capitalists, they are just selling their labour, and for a monthly bill you have to keep paying. For most, loyalty will be dependent on you paying them, although I have personal experience of members of staff offering to forgo salary when the pressure was on. These are rare, special individuals. Your challenge as an entrepreneur is to ensure that the value they add to the enterprise is more than you are paying them. You have a very strong direct effect on their productivity. You can choose them, train, lead and motivate them to give their best. You have a moral responsibility also for their career. The human race does not exist to be exploited for profit. They are stakeholders in your business, dedicating a large chunk of their life to making it work.

Empire entrepreneurs

Empire entrepreneurs want their brand, their name to be everywhere. Whatever stage they are at they want to be bigger, with a bigger reach, more power and influence. They have no end position, they always want more. Just achieving financial freedom is not enough for them. They love growing and will continue for ever.

Are you the next Bill Gates? Do you want to be? If you had his financial wealth what would you do with it? Your answers will give an insight to your values and motivations. The British army unit the Special Air Service has a motto, 'Who Dares Wins'. This enterprising group achieves things even if they seem impossible. This is the attitude you need to adopt to build a major multinational group (but only use the door when you enter the office!). First, think big, believe that you can, research your plans thoroughly and perfect your formula for making money and how you intend to grow it. How, for example, will you finance such massive growth and in what timescale? There are always options: franchising, venture capital, partnering with a major company. These all need to be worked through to find the most appropriate choice.

You need a vision of the future and to think long term. Rockefeller clearly rose above his competitors by seeing the importance of economies of scale and how they could operate in his industry. Like many great entrepreneurs he was obsessed with efficiency and control of costs. Aspiring entrepreneurs who come to me for advice are focused on sales and marketing. I thus find it interesting that the great successes in business had their focus on the other side of the profit equation.

You can start small and grow in reaction to your market. Michael Marks, for example, started retailing his goods by knocking on doors and standing on street corners. This led to market trading, then a shop, then another shop. You may have been in one of them, they are called Marks & Spencer. His famous phrase 'Don't ask the price, it is a penny', did not come from marketing genius but because he could not speak English when he started. A simple sign on his stall solved any problems, and made life easier for potential customers. Yet this simplicity of pricing existed for a long time in the company, showing how much easier it is to run a business that has simple principles and focus.

The profile test

To an entrepreneur achievement can mean wealth beyond their wildest dreams. Entrepreneurs, certainly in America which is a relatively young nation and in Europe, form the largest grouping of millionaires. That is why entrepreneurs are prepared to take the risks and, even in their darkest hour, few would want to be an employee again.

When pure 'money entrepreneurs' are successful, they use their money to make more money, taking full advantage of compound interest and leverage principles. That is why people who win the lottery invariably are not happy. Entrepreneurship can give you satisfaction on a whole range of levels.

For this book one of my research avenues was profiles of famous entrepreneurs. There are many works on each person as well as many people to choose from. I strongly recommend you read business biographies. Make them your role models and personal coaches. Their ideas, beliefs, values, strategies, techniques, passions, drives and motivations are all clear through reading, often between the lines. I looked for things that they had in common. These common principles are in every chapter. I want to help you go beyond your expectations as an entrepreneur, and thus have focused on the practical. I have included, at the back of this book, a bibliography of biographies of famous entrepreneurs.

Look at the five types of entrepreneur (SMILE). How much does each type appeal to you? Mark them out of ten, where 10 = appeals most and 1 = appeals least. Finally, list them in order of priority.

My results are as follows:

- Innovator 10
- Money 4
- Lifestyle 3
- Empire 2
- System 1

Now for me, System is the lowest scoring category and Innovator is the highest. This means I need to be creative, working a proven formula would drive me crazy. I would be always wanting to make improvements and change things, adding my own style. That just does not work with a franchise or network marketing business. So, I choose start up (see Chapter 3) as it allows me full scope to let my creative juices flow freely.

Now, what about risk? Well for me, I have been there and done it before, so the risk associated with start up is very much less than for a novice. I also have a strong sales background which helps for this type of enterprise.

If, like me, Innovator is highest or high you will be happier in situations where you can apply your own ideas. Start ups are an obvious choice, whereas franchises and network marketing opportunities should be avoided.

If Money is your top choice you could well be the opposite of the above as risk is greatly reduced and you are working a proven formula designed to build wealth.

Lifestyle at or near the top might mean you want to work your hobby or be a self-employed consultant. Limited potential for profits but if you can make ends meet and do what you love, you have a formula for happiness.

Empire builders should go for start ups, network marketing or buy an existing business with a brand that gives it the potential for growth. The latter two are far less risky but the first offers a complete blank sheet to express ideas.

At the next level, analysis depends more on specific circumstances, for example if you are interested in health and beauty products, tired of being short of cash, wanting the good life and four more or less equal top for you are Money, System, Lifestyle and Empire. Then an established network marketing business distributing health products could be ideal for you.

When you know your profile you need to assess the profile of each opportunity and see quite simply if it matches yours.

In the next chapter we will look at the entrepreneur opportunities that are available.

Three tips

1 Know your type.
2 Make a plan based upon your type.
3 Keep to the plan.

Two tasks

1 In three sentences, in light of the above, define your dream exactly.
2 Think of two famous entrepreneurs, figure out what type they are and thus what motivates them and keeps them going.

03

entry routes

In this chapter you will learn:

- street SMARTS to ensure you go for the right opportunity
- the positives and negatives of each opportunity
- why a start up might be your last choice
- how to do it with a partner
- why you should consider the end goal now

> 'We can't solve problems by using the same kind of thinking we used when we created them.'
>
> Albert Einstein
>
> 'Risk comes from not knowing what you're doing.'
>
> Warren Buffett

Street SMARTS

Once you know your entrepreneur profile type you are in a position to recognize what type of opportunity will be the best and most appropriate one for you.

In this chapter we look at how to give you your Street SMARTS which is my acronym for the six main groupings of opportunity.

- **S** is for Self-employment
- **M** is for Multi-level marketing
- **A** is for Acquire a business
- **R** is for Royalty
- **T** is for Turnkey operations
- **S** is for Start up

Let us look at them each in turn.

Self-employment

Your career and perhaps your out-of-work activities have made you an expert in something. You hear about people with whom you identify, with how much they bill per day, and you think: 'That could be me'. There are no real set-up costs and already you have an address book full of contacts.

So you make the move. You are self-employed, independent, your own boss doing what you want. You are free to follow your dream. The sky is now the limit.

Well, perhaps. The dream can turn to a nightmare if you do not follow some basic principles of business. Profit must be your first motive, not doing what you want to do or even helping others. If you do not consistently make a profit you won't survive.

> The biggest mistake self-employed consultants make is to focus on what they want to do and not on what somebody wants to buy. This holds back their profit potential. Their focus in not tuned in to the market, which means they continually miss opportunities.

You eagerly prepare what you want to offer (materials, website, business cards, newsletter, etc.) until you are proud of all of them. Then when everything is ready you go into selling mode: network, advertise, canvass, call prospective clients, attend events, etc.

If you want to make money this is not the best approach. Do it the other way around. Forget the website, well-designed business card, newsletter, at least for now. Invest nothing apart from your time. Instead talk to people generally about what you can offer and ask lots of questions, and listen to the answers. Do it with an open mind, assume nothing, and don't filter out what you don't want to hear. When six out of ten people tell you about something that is a problem for them then you have a market need. When one person tells you they have something bothering them now, you have a sale. If you can package something together that will solve their problem then you have a long-term profitable business. A business that won't need a lot of selling, because it relies on listening. When you have done this, design a website and business cards focusing on how you solved this specific problem. Design it for your potential market to be impressed and served.

> People pay money to get someone to do something for them. They don't pay you money so that you can do what you want to do. You need to be a business person first with a close ear to the market and a practitioner of what you do second.

You are ready to start a business when you have the answer to the following question: 'Who currently desires something that is currently unfulfilled in the general area that I offer skills?'

And when you have the answer, ask: 'How can I serve more people for less work at a better price?'

The next mistake often made by the self-employed is not really knowing their own skill set, and thus not selling in the area that gives them greatest potential. I meet all the time:

- NLP practitioners who suffer phobias
- sales trainers who have not got a strong portfolio of clients
- telesales course providers who mailshot their courses
- financial advisers who are broke
- relationship experts who are desperately lonely and single.

What qualifies you to be a consultant to others? What are your credentials? What are your successes and talents? These questions are different from; What are you most interested in doing? If I buy services from someone, I want them to be successful in this area not just knowledgeable and certainly not experienced through failure alone. UNLESS they have overcome it.

The next huge mistake is thinking that you have your own business because you are a freelance independent consultant. From a financial/business point of view you are actually in no better a situation that your employed counterparts. You are also now personally responsible for everything.

Your financial formula is simple and much the same as an employee. What it boils down to is selling yourself for an hourly rate. You can increase that hourly rate or the number of hours you work in the week, but both have limited scope. No leverage. No money when you sleep. No passive or residual income.

In fact the self-employed consultant is worse off because they have what I call negative leverage. Their employed counterpart has all sorts of support available to them: secretaries to open and deal with the post, IT experts, a sales and marketing department, bookkeeping, web design; all sorted. The self-employed consultant thinks they can fee earn 20 days a month. They soon realize that marketing, attending courses, having the flu, administration, preparation, etc., are all unpaid activities that burn up a lot of time.

You need to think differently and stop being like a little mouse going around and around on a treadmill in your cage.

If your target is to be the leading expert in your niche, do the following: produce materials that can be sold with no extra input from yourself. Then employ someone to do all support tasks previously mentioned. If you can bill anywhere between £100 and £2,500 per day for your services then employing someone part or full time will make you more profitable. Analyse everything you do in the week by the hour and put a value on it. Bookkeeping can be done for £x per hour, admin for …, etc. If you are not at your top rate, farm it out. Experts like accountants, and website designers are also cheaper. Because they take a fifth of the time you would, to do the tasks and get it right a lot more often. Don't be shy to increase costs to buy yourself more time. Get going first and use that initial money to jump to the next step.

If you want to get rich this way there are two choices: you need a formidable day rate, most of which you then invest wisely against a rainy day. Or you need materials that have got a clear market AND you have found a means to tap into that market. Produce, for example, an audio clip for internet download, DVD, video, CD-ROM, book, board game on how you do what you do. But make sure you have a route to your market first. The best ways are the ones that are free. There are so many of those that I would not look further. Anyone with a website dealing in your area is a prospect so ask to put clear adverts on their site for a sales commission. Amazon will put your book or audio CD on their site. So will thousands of other web masters. This is all potential passive income and all free advertising which does not continually drain your resources.

In summary, there are six ways you can make a good financial return as a self-employed consultant:

1 Consistently secure very high billings and invest the bulk of it.
2 Produce products, sold through others, that can give you a long-term passive income.
3 Build a business, not dependent on you, that can be sold.
4 Market a patented system for other self-employed people in your field to follow.
5 A mixture of the above.
6 Inherit a fortune or win the lottery while you are working!

Loneliness is another potential pitfall. You have no one to bounce ideas off. Being your own boss for many people makes them realize just how much they were dependent on their boss for motivation, stick or carrot. No one is watching over you.

The self-employed are often fearful of selling. There is no boss now to make them do it. If you have something good, believe in what you offer. Then all you have to do is go around asking how you can help people. Focus on solving their problems. If you focus on helping others instead of yourself you will find deals come to you. It will also take your mind naturally into a healthy market research mode. You will come across as genuine and professional.

Self-employment, or starting something while you are still in full-time employment, can be a good first step as an entrepreneur. We will be covering some such options later. You have broken the corporate chains and you are your own boss. You are still at this stage though dependent on earned income from your own labour. To become rich and secure you really need to earn from things other than your labour. If you are ill for two weeks or take a holiday the business is closed. You are limited by the highest rate you can charge and the maximum number of hours you can work.

This, however, might be the lifestyle you want. You are your own boss, you do not have the responsibility of others, and you can be creative in your own way.

At this level greater efficiency can be made by delegating as much as possible. For example, employ a part-time bookkeeper on an hourly rate to do your accounting. The cost should be a lot less than your charge-out rate. Everything you do you must cost by the hour. Anything that is less than your charge-out rate is a contender for subcontracting.

If you wish to progress as a business you need to do at least one of two things:

1 Make products relative to your expertise for sale.
2 Expand, which usually means taking on staff. The advantage is that you can wait until you are overwhelmed with work then grow from a position of strength and security.

Multi-level marketing

Multi-level marketing, sometimes known as network or referral marketing, is a potentially great way to run your own business with many substantial benefits. The idea is that you sign up for a distributorship with a network marketing company. Then you have the right to buy their products as a wholesaler and the right to sell them on without having to fund the cost. Therefore, you can consume and you can sell and receive the commissions. You can sell on two bases: retail, which is straightforward, or you can introduce somebody to the business so that they become a distributor. Bear in mind that, as there are no retail outlets and many of the costs associated with a traditional business, the distributors share the higher profit margins.

As you introduce more people and the people you bring in do the same, over time you should have a self-developing network. Say, for example, you introduce three people. Then those people introduce three people each. Then those nine people introduce three people each. Then those 27 people introduce three people each. Then those 81 people introduce three people each. Your income is a percentage of the total sales coming from your group. This rate gets higher as your network grows bigger. Therefore you can grow your network only by helping those in your network to grow theirs. Those who introduced you have a responsibility and an interest in supporting you in every way. As everyone's income is determined by what they initiated, everyone joins on the same level.

Some people who don't understand it accuse it of being pyramid selling, which is something quite different. When you join a network marketing company, whether there is one person above you in the network or a thousand has no bearing on what you earn. In pyramid selling the more people above you the less the cut you take.

Good organizations don't commit you to a minimum purchase level and have regular training support from leaders. The advantages are that you need no real capital to start off and you can start while still in full-time work. You are operating a proven system that works. When you have a network you have a passive income, even if you take a holiday. The success of network marketing is staggering and has created a large number of self-employed millionaires.

Often people work as a couple, sharing the duties where they are best suited. It really is a system where you get out in direct proportion to what you put in, and couples can push, encourage and support each other. It does not happen over night; it is certainly not for someone looking to 'get rich quick'. Initially, like any entrepreneurial opportunity, it means investing long hours upfront for financial freedom in the future. The rewards do not come short term, like in an employee opportunity.

Those who do not stay the distance and drop out tend to bad mouth the company. Understandably who is going to say it was them rather than the system that failed? You have to be prepared to take rejection as most people to whom you offer the business opportunity will not join, or worse join half heartedly then drop out when they realize it is a long haul. People sometimes get over keen on persuading others to join their network, which becomes irritating. Most successful people in this category who I have met clearly have high standards of honesty, integrity and leadership. There is no disputing, though, the thousands of people who have become millionaires through network marketing. In the USA, which produces a lot of statistics, each year's new crop of millionaires include more than one in five who achieved it through network marketing. It is worth considering as it involves only a token investment and can be started part time from home.

As someone who has been employed in sales, I know that companies for which I worked 20 years ago are still milking clients who I brought to them. In network marketing you earn permanently on anything that you develop.

To succeed at it you have to be more focused on helping other people succeed, to succeed yourself. It is not about creativity, it is about duplicating a proven system. If you want to be independent and become financially free but do not have a creative idea or capital to invest, it is certainly worth looking at. Apart from your time there is also no risk of capital loss. There are many companies to choose from and their names appear in many business listings. Later in this book I have included a case study of someone who has made and is still making a success of this route. As most people join on a personal introduction (they prefer to give their advertising budget to distributors), one can wait a long time before someone prospects you. Try surfing the net and pick a product/service that interests you, that you believe in and that you therefore wish to promote.

Acquire a business

You could buy and then improve an existing business. This can be done through a management buy out (MBO) from inside, or buy in (MBI) from outside. Or you can just buy a business from the market. Let us look at MBO/MBIs first.

For an MBO/MBI an entrepreneur needs the backing of a financial institution to put them and their team in charge. They see the main asset of any company to be the team who manages it. Even in this technological age it is still people who make the changes. A new team is often successful in a failing business. Often the management has, by definition, bought into the old ways of doing things, which is where their knowledge and expertise lies.

A new team has not bought in to the old ways and sees things from a totally fresh perspective. This seeing things in a different way is right at the heart of entrepreneurial skills. Turnarounds are all about using resources in more opportunistic ways. Often entrepreneurs go in with advantages over the old management. If they are buying in through a financial institution, a strong backer will give them all sorts of advantages. That backing alone will give the team the ability to negotiate far better terms with suppliers. Debts on the company are now far more secure and, with backing, growth is a real possibility. Therefore, both price, in the anticipation of bigger orders in the future, and terms of credit can be made on more favourable terms. There are plenty of examples of companies being turned around by doing just that.

A close friend of mine, Alan Lowden, on the back of some outstanding early successes developed a reputation for being able to turn around established businesses in a very short period of time. This reputation led to him being put into several enterprises by venture capitalists. He received an equity deal without any personal investment. Ask yourself if someone gave you serious financial backing what you could start up or substantially improve. If you have convincing skills on your CV, there will be people who will back you. You are a formula for making money, just waiting for the right opportunity. All you need is expertise and a track record of success usually in a specific sector, with a determination to get a backer.

At one point I was brought in as MD to a recruitment company with seven branches. My task was to take it from a significant loss-making situation into profit within one year. I achieved this and then proposed an MBO to the owners. I had a backer and a team in place. If this sort of proposal might appeal to you the British Venture Capital Association (BVCA) will supply you with a handbook of members who list their specialism in this type of deal. A going concern with a proven and committed management team in place will be attractive. The extra ingredient they will be looking for is to be convinced that you can substantially grow the enterprise. Incidentally you can buy a company by factoring the company's outstanding invoices – a simple way to raise all the money you need.

If you have expertise in an industry and a loyal team, then an MBI could be a viable option for you. Simply you find a financial backer to buy a company and put your team in to manage it. Often venture capitalists will already have stakes in companies that are not going to plan and putting a fresh management team in is very attractive to them. You have to convince them that you can make substantial improvement where the current team is failing. You may even spot one or more companies in your industry that you can form into a group under your management.

If you have a pedigree in an industry and a convincing strategy, you have an opportunity to avoid the high risks of a start up and concentrate on an organization that is already up and running. Many businesses have had dramatic turnarounds when a new management was put in place. Individuals like Lee Iacoca (Chrysler) and John Harvey Jones (ICI) have both made dramatic changes to the companies they led when they were given the helm. This reinforces my view and certainly the one taken by venture capitalists that any company's greatest asset is its management team.

Alternatively, you can just buy a small company from the market. There are business brokers such as the Avondale Group that are brokers for businesses and will offer a range of sectors and prices, and advise you every step of the way. Buying a business has many advantages. First, it is far easier to raise finance because there is a track record and profits to offer. Second, it can be bought with the help of owner financing or by factoring the company's own invoices. Often you can pick a business where you immediately add value through your contacts, expertise or other assets. Getting a company to increase profits is a hundred times easier than getting a start up to break even. As valuations of small businesses are based on a multiple of profits, you can literally increase market value every day. Risks are clearly far less when acquiring an already profitable business.

Royalty

In this category of entrepreneur I include people who are not necessarily running companies at all. They are included because of their personal enterprise in creating something new that has a commercial potential. They have the potential to make a substantial passive income source. In fact, many inventors go on to run companies, but this is not essential.

This category obviously includes me as the author of this book. I also produce audio books. All of these products are produced, marketed and sold for me by someone else. My risks and investment are minimal, apart from my time, and the potential income from royalties and spin-offs such as talks, training and consultancy can be substantial. You can do the same for whatever you do and produce any number of information products on your expertise.

Alternatively, you may be a potential inventor, working on an item that will do something really special and be in demand. James Dyson developed a wheelbarrow with a ball instead of a wheel. He then went on to develop a new system for a vacuum cleaner. His challenging of the existing ways of doing things is an inspiration to us all. If this is the sort of entrepreneur who inspires and motivates you, the thing you need to know most about are patents. However, in a global world don't rely wholly on this protection. Suing someone who breaks your patent, or gets near to it can be very costly in time and money: two resources of which you will have a very limited supply. Besides, until you have a large established market no one will probably notice or be interested.

Consider not just who your invention would benefit but who it would threaten. Does it render an existing product obsolete? If so, the current manufacturers are most definitely threatened. They will have a lot of power to protect their interests. Having the law on your side may not prove to be that beneficial if you have to finance a long drawn out legal battle conducted in several countries.

One option, of course, is to take your invention to that big company in exchange for a royalty deal. If you cannot beat them join them. They have resources for finance, marketing, development, testing, etc.

Turnkey operations

A turnkey operation is where you buy a business system from somebody which is prepared, tried, tested and proven, and ready to go. You just have to turn the key to get it going. The most common type is a franchise that means buying an operating unit from a company and paying an ongoing management fee. The advantages are that you are buying something that is proven, tested, has a workable system for every process and, of course, you are not alone.

The modern day form of franchising, called the 'business format franchise', was really started by Ray Kroc when he decided that this was the best way to develop his McDonald's restaurant. Six thousand units later, when he became the world's largest restaurant business, nobody could doubt the success of the franchising formula. There are now well over five times that number of units. As each franchisee finances their own business it allows the growth of a substantial number of outlets. There are now many franchises available, from high street shops to management consultancies.

If you have a capital sum to invest, a franchise greatly reduces your risk and bypasses many of the problems start up entrepreneurs have in more traditional businesses. Every problem has already been looked at/occurred in a franchise and there are full support services available. Typically, franchisors make their money by charging a percentage of sales for their support, branding, marketing, etc., and when there are products involved they also can control and supply the product. The strength of a franchise is its proven system. It is, put simply, a formula for making money where all you have to do is turn the key and run the operation.

Any business is a risk, although increasingly people find their jobs to be insecure and are thus more likely to make the leap, as the risk perception divide narrows. In a job, however well paid, you have no leverage. You will always be limited to what boils down to your own labour.

The business format franchise really started in the UK with pubs, then car dealerships. Then came a plethora of fast food chains starting with the most famous McDonald's. Ever envied the daily cash receipts of your local McDonald's? Don't be naïve though; even with McDonald's you cannot sit back and just expect it all to happen. This is often the failing of franchisees who expect to sit back, employ someone and just receive the profits. All businesses have to be worked and grown. Even McDonald's a few years ago put in its first loss in history. Many franchisors have told me that their biggest headache is that people may have the cash and interest, but this does not mean that they have the skills or even the motivation necessary to make it work. Like all entrepreneurs they have to take responsibility to make their success.

A turnkey operation is clearly for the System entrepreneur types who have some money to invest. For further information on franchising, see the companion volume in this series, *Teach Yourself Franchising*.

Start up

Start ups are the hardest form of entrepreneurship. Obvious if you think about it. The business products/services are new, there are no established customers, there is no proof that anyone will buy, the business model is unproven, the management team or person is inexperienced. There are no repeat orders or loyal customers. Even with first sales reaching breakeven can take a number of years. The entrepreneurs have to somehow finance their own living and try to avoid draining precious resources from the business. All of this means that the pressure while doing this is immense and growing. People around you will cast doubt, and you will cast doubt on yourself. If capital gain is your main goal then buying a business is far quicker and far safer, with a far more certain, far easier to finance, end result.

However, the world's richest people are those who followed the start up route. Their names and companies are all around us. The two people who started eBay® became billionaires before ten years had elapsed. The Google™ entrepreneurs achieved billionaire status in nearer five years. Bill Gates, of course, is the richest man in the world. All of these people individually have more wealth than the combined England football squad and the top ten selling rock stars!

So we are talking of very high risk with the highest possible pay off. In addition to this the entrepreneur has complete freedom to be creative. So start up is the option if your profile is strongly **I** and **M**, less of **L** (SMILE!) and perhaps some **E**.

Tea for two or three

Whatever business opportunity you go for you may consider doing it with a partner(s).

There are many advantages to partnership, not being alone being a major one. There are, however, some ground rules. I have found that when partners are not equal, even for good reason, sooner or later this will lead to conflict. Issues around unequal contributions should be balanced in some other way, keeping share holdings equal. Perhaps on first drawings from profits, or a debt to the company from the less contributing partner. This money value can then be equalized by one of the partners drawing less for a while, for example. There are many easy and practical formulas; this is one of the advantages. Another is that your reports and accounts are private and can remain confidential to the partners. A disadvantage is that you are liable personally for any debts of the enterprise and liable for any actions any partner makes.

Everyone will want their ideas put forward. The strength of the partnership should be in all the partners having ideas. If one of the partners considers their ideas as leading and better than the others conflict will again arise. The partners have to have the same objective for the business. If one, for example, is motivated purely by profit and another by achieving excellence and leadership in a product line, then at some point the objectives will be divergent not convergent. Again conflict arises.

If you want a lifestyle business then you want to keep the whole equity. If profit is your main motive then your interest will be maximizing the value of your shareholdings in the future. The partnership formula in itself does not suggest you even maintain a majority.

Would you prefer to keep 100% of all your researched ideas? Or 30% with an experienced partner and £500,000 of venture capital in the bank. The point being with the financial head start that 30% is likely to be worth more in five years than the 100%.

Exit routes

By this point you should know the type of entrepreneur you are and what entrepreneurial opportunity classification is most suitable for you. Give some thought now to where you want to end up. We will revisit it in the last chapter, but planning ahead is essential.

If you have a lifestyle business you will probably want to do that for ever. If money is your main goal then your best bet is probably to sell for capital gain. Current UK tax laws favour this route and it gives you a chance to not have your eggs in one basket. You can re-invest three quarters of sales proceeds and start a new business with the remaining quarter. If you are an E in SMILE, buying other businesses will probably be the faster, most attractive route for you. Franchises often grow by buying more franchises in the system in which they have already proven their success.

If you have invested in multi-level marketing then you can stop at any time and enjoy the ongoing passive income. You now have time freedom which can be invested in other activities, business or personal.

I will discuss exit routes in detail later in the book. For now, the important thing is to set the end goal so as to accurately determine the detailed steps on the path towards it.

Entrepreneur interview: Austin Reynolds

Austin exceeded his £1million cash in the bank target soon after starting in business. He has since multiplied his net worth several times. He lives near Weybridge, Surrey, with his partner and two children, and spends his free time at Motor Cross events or doing local charity work for the Catholic Church.

Alex: What is your career background?

Austin: While at school, I noticed that 70% of the properties around where I lived needed preserving with creosote. It was obvious who was a good prospect. I started by knocking my neighbours' doors and soon had a thriving business. I went back to school after the summer and left with one O-level. I wanted to work in sales and I got a job as a trainee in a shipping office. I was fired after eight weeks. This greatly affected me and I decided that my future would not be working for someone else.

At 19 years I was offered a job in sales with Morgan Crucible in Leeds. At 20 I was made sales trainer on the back of my success. At 21 years I was made Regional Sales Manager with six staff. At 23 years I was headhunted by a small signage company.

By 25 I knew enough to work for myself. I set up in business from my back bedroom with a telephone, a fax machine and cash to last two months. I took orders from clients with a need for signs and procured suppliers, making sure everything went smoothly, as the middleman. I had no printed stationery or even a vehicle. I moved around by borrowing my dad's, mum's or girlfriend's car. Everyone who visited me, I gave something to deliver on their way home. I set daily targets on a wall chart, and only focused on profit; sales figures do not interest me. When I could consistently reach a target I would increase it. I always had to achieve what I set for myself, at all costs. I believe that in business you have to be patient and I never waste time on small enquiries.

My philosophy was, don't borrow, buy what you want, when you can afford it. I always expect and deliver an excellent customer service. Honesty, integrity, trust are the most important ingredients to build quality long-term relationships and reputation. I have never had a cash flow problem to this day. I have never had to concern myself with interest rates or bank managers. My sole objective and focus was to put £1million cash in the bank as soon as possible. I can sleep soundly at night. For three years it was just me, and in my final year I turned over £780,000 and personally earnt £280,000. I bought a very large house and expanded from this base.

Sales and profits continued to rise year on year and I had soon over £1million in the bank without any debts, other assets and plus, of course, a valuable company. Material things never interested me and I have no need to impress anyone, so the business has continued to grow from there.

When I look at a supplier I look for excellence in price, product, delivery and paperwork. I monitor their performance constantly. Good personal relationships are key with both customers and suppliers. I always pay them promptly, not waiting for payment from my client.

In my business there is nothing unique, compared to competitors, apart for us as individuals. I own the whole firm and believe in having one boss. I also believe that whereas it is wise to pay too much, it is worse to pay too little and risk quality and value.

I was wondering what to do with the cash mountains that have been rising. So I have set up Austin Reynolds Special Projects and have made some investments developing substantial properties; there have been four such projects in the last three years. I wish I had done this earlier as the early 1990s was a very good time to invest in properties. I have also set up a credit company.

Alex: How do you define success?

Austin: To be able to sleep at night. To know when you have finished, i.e. reached your goals.

Alex: What advice would you give somebody starting out?

Austin: 1 Don't borrow money.

2 Start small, have a big idea, and break it down into manageable chunks.

3 Flash means crash. (Referring to buying flashy cars or whatever following initial success.)

4 Know your ultimate goal and keep going.

5 Agree hours of work and play and stick to them.

6 Work smart and hard.

Alex: How do you spot an opportunity?

Austin: Think then follow it through. While driving if I notice a new large construction site I will stop, reverse, and do something about it.

Alex: What would you have done differently if you could go back in time?

Austin: Invested my surplus cash in property in the early 1990s.

Alex: How do you motivate yourself when things don't go to plan?

Austin: Self-belief. Nobody is as good as I am.

Three tips

1 Avoid bank loans and overdrafts, they are not the answer.
2 Know your goals and don't let anyone talk you out of them.
3 If you follow your passion you will have an abundance of motivational energy.

Two tasks

1 Ask yourself: 'What is the best and most appropriate opportunity open to me right now?'
2 Decide what type of opportunity you would be most happy with.

04

seeing opportunities

In this chapter you will learn:
- that there is an abundance of opportunities
- that s/he who pays the piper calls the tune
- the six magic questions to ask each day
- the 'mindset' you must adopt
- how to have a 'lucky day'

'Entrepreneurs are simply those who understand that there is little difference between obstacle and opportunity and are able to turn both to their advantage.'

Victor Kiam

'The entrepreneur in us sees opportunities everywhere we look, but many people see only problems everywhere they look. The entrepreneur in us is more concerned with discriminating between opportunities than he or she is with failing to see the opportunities.'

Michael Gerber

What shall I do?

The question 'What do I want to do?', must be adapted to 'What do people want to buy?' I see businesses on and off line opening all the time which clearly have no market. You may live in Oxford and dream of owning your own yachting supplies shop, but do you have a local market? Work is ultimately about doing something for somebody else. The real trick is to marry what people need to what you have a passion in and capability of supplying. Remember that if you start by finding a market, then selling will be relatively easy.

You can become self-employed, take on a franchise, buy a business, join a network marketing company, become a corporate entrepreneur, invent a new device or launch something new with the intention of making it a major multinational. Opportunity spotting is not just about getting an initial idea, it is a way of life. It covers every aspect and process of your business, all the time. Even after you have just improved a process, you should immediately start looking for opportunities to improve it further, never being satisfied with performance. We will now explore some of these options so you can decide which one is for you.

Here are a few examples of where you may look for opportunities:

- a new product or service
- enhance an existing product
- a new market for an existing product

- a new application for an existing product
- a source of grants or awards
- better arrangements with suppliers
- better promotion, advertising
- improve efficiency and speed of ordering
- new contact sources
- new and better ways of doing anything
- ways to leverage your current resources.

Progress now

Which three areas of opportunity would be most valuable to you right now?

Which of the following do you think have the best chance of success (and why)? These are all ideas for businesses that have been put to me for my opinion.

1 A watch into which you can speak the name of a country and it will give you the time, news, weather and other information about that country.

2 An alarm for parents so that when one of their young children is more than 50 metres away they are warned and given a direction indication.

3 A water cooled pillow for people who are heat sensitive at night to help them sleep.

4 An open training seminar called 'How to overcome shyness'.

5 A vanity bathroom mirror with a slight angle on it to make people look thinner than they are.

6 A wool shop in a residential estate.

7 Chameleon clothing: one suit that can be changed into anything to suit the occasion.

8 Jewellery for pets.

My answer in all cases is 'it depends'. I then would want to ask: 'Who is going to buy this, in what quantity and at what price?'

From confusion to clarity

What other words come to your mind when you hear the word 'entrepreneur'?

Here is a list that was produced during a Club Entrepreneur meeting.

creative	endeavour	gamble
money	lending	negotiator
ideas	project	challenge
opportunity	risk taker	possibility
profit	venturer	niche
independence	ambitious	marketeer
competition	drive	promotion
arrogance	enthusiasm	wheeler-dealer
change agent	imagination	catalyst
millionaire	big picture	initiative
teleworker	dreamer	visionary
freedom	inventor	selling
inspiration	opportunity	innovator
adventurer	leader	fast track
motivator	investor	success

Progress now

Circle words in the list above which seriously interest you and with which you identify.

What key personal qualities do you think a successful entrepreneur has?

What are your personal qualities?

What do you think would be worth improving?

What action are you going to take to achieve that?

Acting on inspiration

Have you ever travelled abroad and had the following interesting experiences?

1 Noticing something in that country which you consider better than at home and you cannot imagine why it does not exist where you come from?

2 Noticing something that is worse in the country visited than at home and wondered why they do not do it your way?

3 Noticing something quite different and cannot figure out if it is better or worse than at home, but it has given you ideas?

That is the entrepreneur in you trying to come out.

To illustrate this, my wife recently came back from visiting an English friend who just moved out to Texas. My wife works in a school here in the UK and, with her friend's three children, went to the local school in Houston. She was impressed by how confident the children were in speaking at the age of four, and learnt that presentation and public speaking is taught at school. She would like to bring that idea home. She also noticed how developed US children were with arts and crafts. She came home and set up a business called Crafty Kids, which now produces regular profits.

At the end of the street, an American couple greeted them saying: 'Hello, good morning, how are you? What part of England do you come from?' They had not spoken, so how did they know they were from England? The answer was because they were riding bikes when Americans would have been in the car. Would bicycles or even pavements for walking be something of value to take from England to Texas? So you can see there is a fine line between spotting a gap in the market and something that is not there because there is no demand. Demand, incidentally, is something that you can influence, you can create it and increase it, but it is an easier journey to ride a crest of a natural wave.

This is how entrepreneurs think: they first observe, analyse and constantly ask themselves questions like the above. They keep asking 'Why?' questions. It is easy to get it wrong, but that gives you valuable information to help you get it right next time. In addition, when you get it right, the payoffs are truly exciting. Actually the process of being an entrepreneur is an exciting adventure in itself. Is your work at the moment an exciting adventure? It should be.

You need to maximize the use of resources, relating this all the time to potential sales and profit. Look around you: what is there that could be used in a different way to more effect? What resources can you see that are being underemployed? What needs are being frustrated? What technological, cultural, sociological or other changes are going to create new needs? This is why entrepreneurs start turning their garages into cheap and convenient offices.

The opportunist

Non-entrepreneurs think that we find an idea then run with it. In reality, you need to be constantly looking for new opportunities and constantly updating your original one. Ideas in themselves are ten a penny; the real game is to turn ideas into commercial reality and not just talk. Entrepreneurs are not in the business of saying, 'I told you somebody would invent a product that would do that.' You have to make things happen through your belief, conviction, determination, enthusiasm, commitment and a practical ability.

The five steps to spot opportunities:

1 Ask these magic questions:
   a What or whom has presented a potential opportunity to me today?
   b From the people who I met today, what need do they seem to have?
   c What have I kept hearing from people over the last week?
   d What is happening out there right now? What does this mean there is an increased need for?
   e What do you think people would buy in great numbers if it existed now?
   f What service or product would you buy today if it existed?

2 Read the magic questions at the start of the day, print out a copy and stick it on your wall.

3 Observe and listen as you go through the day.

4 Wait. The questions are in your unconscious working away. You have trained your mind to focus automatically on opportunities. Soon ideas will start flowing. Soon you will realize that commercial opportunities are presented in front of your nose on a daily basis. It is just that they have been invisible to you, and others, before.

5 Never stop looking for those opportunities.

The four steps to turn opportunities into profit:

1 Establish a market price and how to reach it.

2 Determine how much it would cost to produce an initial stock of the product or deliver the service.

3 Work out the finances.

4 Remember to think big but get some feedback first with limited risk. All results are valuable feedback, keep listening.

Your lucky day?

Opportunities come in many shapes and sizes, and they keep coming. They are like trains leaving a mainline station: if you miss one there will be another one leaving at some point. Who knows, it may even be missing a train that puts a once in a lifetime opportunity in front of you. While having an unplanned coffee, you may notice something interesting about the people in the café. Something that you realize would be really useful to them while waiting for a train. Alternatively, perhaps you get talking to someone at the same table and the conversation triggers an idea, or maybe both of you together can offer something that you could not offer alone. Many partnerships have been built this way. It makes me wonder what opportunity will come your way tomorrow. More importantly, will you recognize it and grasp it with both hands?

Ray Kroc on his rounds selling his restaurant equipment called one day on the McDonald brothers' little place. Now, if he was focused just on how much commission he could get selling to this one burger bar, where would he have been today? I wonder how many times you have been on a visit like that and missed the potential that you could have seen. He knew how to ask himself the right questions.

Aristotle Onassis while working in Buenos Aires noticed how popular Rudolph Valentino was with the ladies. He marketed a cigarette targeting this group.

When John D Rockefeller was in the oil business he saw the massive advantages that size brought in terms of negotiating railroad freight rates. Therefore, he focused on joining together many small operators to gain a monopolistic position.

What in your industry is outdated? What is happening that everybody takes for granted, but in fact it no longer has a use? Companies are very quick to make people redundant. They are less quick to make things, processes, or ways of doing things redundant, particularly if the management team's power base is their knowledge and experience of doing it in that old redundant way. That is the opportunity ground for entrepreneurs to enter and update things.

So many firms have resisted the onset of the internet and telecommunications revolution. Older managers are suddenly threatened by a redundant knowledge whilst twenty-somethings are becoming billionaires in their industry. Turning a large company around can be like turning a supertanker around in a harbour. The entrepreneur can move quicker and is not hampered by old outdated ways of doing things, or outdated people resisting change.

In a changing world, the consumer will be looking for new things all the time. Needs change, they are not constant, things go in and out of fashion.

How entrepreneurs make their own luck:

- They look and listen for opportunities constantly.
- They believe that in everything that happens there is opportunity somewhere.
- They think ahead and plan for every contingency.
- They get in tune with what people would pay money for. They then make this their focus.

Certainly there is something in being in the right place at the right time. There are still many parts of the world where being an entrepreneur is frowned upon or even illegal. However, it is human enterprise that creates everything around us. It is the entrepreneurial tradition that made and continues to maintain the USA as the richest country in the world with more than 25% of the planet's wealth and less than 5% of the population.

Failure and other opportunities

You need to have the ability to learn from failure, both your own failure and, more importantly, that of others. It is a lot less uncomfortable to learn from others' mistakes! I really recommend this route first. Information and opportunities are coming at us from all directions non-stop. The trick is to delete the vast majority of it that does not hold opportunity, so that we can see clearly what is left. As Richard Lowden of Eurodrive® Car Rental says, 'Every time I receive a setback, I immediately ask myself "How can I turn this to my advantage?" All others do is focus on solving the immediate problem.'

Often a failure can be the inspiration for a new launch. Sometimes that failure can be the rejection of an idea you have and your employer rejects. The idea fails before it is given a chance. I wonder how many ideas are rejected every day by companies that would have turned out to have been great successes. I am yet to meet a venture capitalist who does not tell me about ideas that they rejected which others took on board and which became a great success. I have yet to read a biography of an entrepreneur or an inventor whose ideas did not meet rejection and failure. Their real skill was in finding ways to make their ideas work commercially.

Entreployee

You must be prepared to get out of the 'salary mentality' and sacrifice the short term for a considerably better long term. Many new entrepreneurs compare how they are doing to their previous salary. Understandable, but it has no relevance, and takes your thinking away from a useful productive focus. You will need patience and belief in yourself to keep going.

Here is my impression of an employee over eight weeks.

work → salary → work → salary

Here it is again, a bit closer to reality.

bad month → salary → good month → same salary

A job is a business with one client, with no scope to expand, where any capital gain or goodwill you develop is for the profit of that client. If you do well in the year you could earn 20% more in year two and that would be an exceptional success. An entrepreneur looks for leverage of 200% in his first year. Therefore, you have to think bigger. Many prospective entrepreneurs just watch others succeed, fear and the lack of an idea stops them from starting.

Why do you want to be a very successful entrepreneur? People who have been employees for a long time have got used to being motivated by their need for status. Company cars, size of office, pile on carpet, salary grade, executive washrooms, car parking, are graded by status. Entrepreneurs on the other hand will lead a company and muck in with everybody. They roll up their sleeves. This is not just a common expression; entrepreneurs think of their business as their baby and take full pride in every aspect, they will do any task that needs doing. Michael Marks, for example, if he noticed a mess in one of the Marks & Spencer stores, would clear it up himself.

Employees are rewarded by being given material bonuses that are visible signs to others of their success. This trains their unconscious mind to search for more recognition. So they go out and buy expensive clothes or the latest electronic gadgets. Then they discover the marvellous world of plastic cards that will allow them to reward yourself as much as they think appropriate. So they no longer have to wait for the boss to recognize their worth and give them a rise, they can give one to themselves. Therefore, they go out and buy a nice car they cannot afford or need, a nice holiday, new clothes, a new kitchen. Then to keep really up with the Joneses they buy a large house on an equally large mortgage. Every night they worry about the breadwinner losing their job and how to keep meeting all the growing payments even with the job.

Advertisements on television for loans now use consolidating other debts for a better interest rate as their main benefit in taking out a loan with a particular lender. This tells me just how many tens of thousands of people are living beyond their means. If this is how you financially manage your personal life you first have to learn financial discipline. I have found though that behind these behaviour patterns is someone who is frustrated at work and seeking to escape through retail therapy. Addressing the frustration by making some changes is the answer. Make a decision to find out exactly what you want to do, and do it. Stop talking about it. Then tear up the credit cards. The threat and fear of going hungry will make you magically resourceful, you will be surprised.

The jump from employee to entrepreneur can be hard, but is a jump worth making. So many venture capitalists' and business angels' networks are inundated by would-be entrepreneurs. Their business plan seems to focus on them receiving a good secure salary. Investors want to invest in a business not pay you.

If you have been an employee for some time, you have got very used to receiving a salary at the end of each month for your labour. As an entrepreneur it does not work like that. Your thinking has got to change. You are now with the big boys. At some point you have got to come to terms with this. Entrepreneurs are not focused on their salary, they are focusing on wealth building. Entrepreneurs are arguably successful when the enterprise is no longer dependent on them. They have a business and not just self-employment.

Employee thinking	Entrepreneur thinking
I need a monthly salary	I need to make a profit
I need a good pension scheme	I need a capital gain to retire on
I want a promotion	If you want to get to the top, start there
Thank God it's Friday	God, it's Friday already
If I qualify I can get a good job	If I set up my own business I can employ well-qualified people
I want a better job	I have a dream!
What do you want me to do?	What needs doing?
I have a great idea	Here is my new product
I need a secure job	I want to be financially free
I look forward to retiring at 65	I never want to retire, but I will be able to soon
High status	Control own destiny
Keeping on the boss's good side	Independence
Keeping to my strength area	Creativity and variety
Frustration	Incredible job satisfaction
Fixed income	Unlimited income
A higher salary	Capital gain
I have done my best	Never give up

Progress now

Circle the statement from the table above which most closely describes you. Are you ready or do you have to make some changes?

Where do I start?

You start by asking questions and then more questions. Questions get answers, so make sure that yours are well chosen.

'Why' questions, like:

- Why does it happen like this?
- Why can I not get what I want?
- Why do people tolerate this?
- Why has nobody improved this?

'What' questions, like:

- What assumptions are applicable here?
- What was once useful but is now redundant?
- What has changed recently?
- What is redundant here?

'How' questions, like:

- How can I improve this?
- How could it be done better?
- How would I have done this?
- How can I profit from this right now?

'When' questions, like:

- When does this not work well?
- When is the market for this ideal?
- When was this process established?
- When will this idea be outdated?

There are many ways of taking a product and, by giving it a twist, turning it into a moneymaker.

Progress now

Write three of each of your own Why, What, How and When questions on separate pieces of paper. Shuffle the papers and turn them face down.

Now pick four questions randomly, and write them down on a clean piece of paper. You are ready to start the game. You can involve any number of players.

Think of any product or service that you have bought in the last month. Ask those questions of the product or service you thought of until you have at least three answers to each question.

At the end of this exercise ask the final question:
From this new knowledge and perspective what improvement, enhancement or new product or service comes to mind that has a market?

You now have the raw ingredient for a new business that already has a potential market.

Welcome to how entrepreneurs find those new ideas. It is all about the type of question you ask and in what order. The random selection allows you to look at it in a way you would not normally think of. That is how you can see what has always been there but that you never noticed before. The next point, that you might have already realized, is that there are infinite permutations of question sets and therefore an infinite number of potential ways to enhance, re-invent or create a new product or service. There is an abundance of opportunity available! There is no such thing as scarcity and market size.

The buck stops here

You are the boss. Everything is your responsibility, even if it is someone else's fault. Remember, winners take responsibility, losers take the blame. So pick your staff, suppliers, premises, marketing, etc. carefully. Take responsibility. This does not mean you have to be an expert on everything or indeed anything. You can employ experts. If you don't want to be the boss you can employ someone who has more experience at it than you. This depends on what type of entrepreneur you have decided to be. The creative entrepreneur often inspires leadership but when it comes to day-to-day management they would sooner delegate. They find it boring and mundane.

There are many different leadership styles that work. There is not one magic formula, although you are setting the culture for the organization that you are building. There are many books on leadership and management. This area is well covered. I am interested in specific challenges that occur more to entrepreneur-based companies and how to deal with them.

The entrepreneur typically is stretching the resources to meet the monthly payroll. Many of the entrepreneurs I have talked to, have had to maintain and motivate their staff when they could not pay them. That is leadership!

Pennies from heaven

Successful entrepreneurs, of any type, contrary to popular belief, live frugally wanting to invest every penny in their business. They now control their lives, they have made a decision to determine their own destiny. They don't need material, external consumer products to give them status or to make them feel good. They are already free and getting freer. Even when an entrepreneur has made significant wealth, statistics show that the wealthiest people in the country are not the highest spenders. Old habits die hard and wealthy entrepreneurs are surprisingly unlikely to run out to buy flash cars and houses, even now that they can pay cash. If they buy a big house it is probably to use a fair part of it as a cheap office. The house they do buy is also unlikely to be as big as the house they could have bought.

Entrepreneurs will have credit cards but they will use them quite differently. They don't focus on treats and rewards but use them as an easily accessible form of investment, usually for a short-term purpose due to the interest rate.

Therefore, if you have been in that routine for a while, the danger is that your natural entrepreneurial instincts have been eroded. Your natural instincts are to get things you want by making money to pay for them. That way reward and pressure is directly related to real success or failure. This system programs you to avoid failure and seek more reward, and to do this you make more money. So if you want to be an entrepreneur, harden up and give up your credit card lifestyle. If that means you go hungry, then go hungry; in practice you won't, that is the whole point. Your unconscious, always seeking to protect you, will focus on taking positive action. You need to get in the habit of short-term pressure, long-term gratification.

Transformations

Large companies have a whole load of specialist departments, big budgets and a range of resources. The entrepreneur has to source things without access to experts, dedicated staff and such resources. As an entrepreneur you have to make it happen yourself, often until you are big enough to enjoy those benefits yourself. If a start up entrepreneur wants to run a training programme for his six members of staff he probably won't have a training room, flip chart and budget. In addition, if he trains in the day the 'shop' is closed for business. These sorts of practical day-to-day challenges have to be met by thinking on your feet. An entrepreneur would typically network to find a trainer from whom he can pull in a favour, find someone who has a room that they are not using and ask around to borrow a flip chart.

A big company will hold a training course in a four-star hotel with a lavish meal. A typical training course will start at 10am and finish at 4pm. This sort of training might be useful in terms of the topic but is more than likely de-training the participants in entrepreneurial skills.

Progress now

Invent a new word. That's right, invent one. Did you know that there are thousands of words in hundreds of different languages that have no equivalent translation in English? In fact, if you are a native English speaker the syntax, order of words, spelling and grammar will set you up for a certain way of thinking, thus limiting you. Different languages also have different non-verbal languages. Watch people talking to each other in a swimming pool (i.e. no dress clues) and it is possible to tell their nationality from a distance. It is also possible to know what they are talking about. What I am trying to say here is that each variation represents a different way of looking at things, and thus a potential insight to lucrative commercial opportunities.

We can have and be heroes

To me, the greatest entrepreneur of all time has to be Walt Disney. (Typical choice of an I in SMILE, you rightly say; the Ms would have gone for Bill Gates!) Hidden behind this viewpoint, of course, is my definition of entrepreneur: creativity, adding value to society, fun, freedom for the mind to wander. Walt's drive did not come from the potential of making big money; that was a side effect that took a long time coming.

Other entrepreneurs were motivated by many different things. What they had in common is that they had a passion for what they wanted at an obsessional level. They mostly took some very big knocks along the way, even going bankrupt sometimes more than once before eventually being successful. Imagine, after going bust twice, having the confidence and belief for your third attempt! Entrepreneurs need a great reservoir of inner strength.

This, to me, explains why so many famous and not-so-famous entrepreneurs who I know have strong religious convictions. In their moment of challenge, their belief in 'God' picked them up again and bounced them back. It helped them to avoid the 'pity parties'. There are many biographies of people outside the entrepreneur model that are worth studying in this regard. For example, Abraham Lincoln had less than a year of formal schooling and lost 17 elections before becoming President of the USA. Many great and famous entrepreneurs have had role models or mentors, people they admired and learnt from in their early days.

I have asked the question to many people I have coached, 'Who are your three favourite entrepreneurs?' Their answers give away what type of entrepreneur they want to be.

Progress now

So who are your three favourite entrepreneurs?

Joining the club

Having run recruitment businesses, I have been approached by venture capitalists to help find board level executives for their ventures. This is a good source of entrepreneurial opportunity that many aspiring entrepreneurs do not think of. These opportunities usually have a big chunk of equity with them.

When someone can do something exceptionally well, it is usually easy for them. This tends to mean that they underestimate the value of that talent. The question, therefore, is to ask yourself and others: 'What is my outstanding talent?' Then ask: 'Who would have a use for that talent?' We need to work to our strengths. If you need other skills employ them, or contract them out. Too many books on entrepreneurship cover all the areas of accounting, marketing, personnel, etc. If you try to learn everything you need to know you will explode. Do what you are good at, recognize what you are not good at and what is needed, and bring it in or contract it out. Even when small, business is still a team sport.

Action stations

You must know where most of your revenue is coming from and focus your attention there. Once started you must build an organization that can exploit effectively the opportunity you spotted. You need the ability to see a market trend and act on it, to attract its money towards you.

Money magnet questions:

- Now what?
- Is my idea good?

- Is it original?
- Is it worth anything?
- Will it sell?
- What is nearest to money?
- What is most lucrative long term?
- What is most lucrative short term?
- What will people pay for?
- What do people not only want but need?
- What would my favourite entrepreneur do if he or she was me?

Progress now

Which of these statements are true for you?

'A traditional job would not provide me with the independence and financial opportunities that I seek.'

'I have always wanted to run my own business.'

'I had a great idea last year and somebody else did it this year.'

'I know what I want to do and how, but am fearful of meeting my monthly bills.'

'I see businesses around me and know I could make more profit from them.'

'I would like to retire before I am 50.'

'Nobody where I work wants to listen to my ideas.'

'I have a talent for noticing what others don't seem to notice.'

Progress now

What do you have a passion for?

What do you believe in?

What annoys you?

What do others say you have a talent for?

Who do you know with a problem?

Entrepreneurship is a practical action-taking endeavour. I think this is a reason why so many successful entrepreneurs had poor school and academic records. Their practical action nature would get too frustrated and not see the point. Opportunities have to be grasped quickly. The fast usually beat the clever in the entrepreneur game. Have both and you really have an edge. A competitive nature is also a common trait and sport seems to be something they would be more interested in.

Everything that you have done in your life so far has been a necessary path to the incredible destiny that awaits you. Soon you will realize this.

Decision time

Many entrepreneurs have a real talent in getting something created and off the ground. Often, however, this is the point where professional managers need to take over more and more. By recruiting people from quality big company backgrounds you will take on board the processes, procedures and organization that the company increasingly needs. Most entrepreneurs hate this sort of work and want to go on creating. Avoid people from your own industry though, as evidence shows that they will introduce you to the way your larger competitor does it, and to get ahead of it, from your smaller situation, you need to do things better.

So I advise it is important to know what type of entrepreneur you really want to be. As things progress, what role do you see for yourself? I am convinced that people must work where their passion and talent lies to really achieve great things. Don't be dragged into the role of MD if day-to-day management is not your interest. Don't be afraid of appointing somebody over you, who is more experienced in that role. If you are an inventor keep inventing, let somebody else work up the value of your shares.

Progress now

Of the three opportunities for which you can see a market right now, which one do you have an overwhelming belief in and passion for?

Three tips

1 Listen to the frustrations of people around you, and act on what you hear.
2 When in Rome do as the Greeks do. Be special, be different.
3 Go for one opportunity at a time, become an authority on it.

Two tasks

1 Change the wrist on which you wear your watch and notice how long it is before you stop looking at a bare wrist when someone asks you the time. Use this knowledge to change some other habitual aspect of what you do.
2 Think of three things that you believe people will want more of three years from now.

05

maintaining passion, persistence and personal power

In this chapter you will learn:
- why you need to feel fantastic consistently
- how to feel fantastic consistently
- to toughen up and take responsibility
- the role of negative thinking
- how to form the habits of success

'In desperation you can achieve anything.'

Vijay Dhir

'I have always been bored with just making money. I have wanted to do things; I wanted to build things.'

Walt Disney

Feeling fantastic

Success is an internal feeling of well being, it is not something external. Having things does not indicate success. One day we all have to answer for our lives according to whatever creed we follow. What is your god's definition of a successful life? I don't think he or she is going to be impressed by the amount of money you amassed. He or she will be more impressed by what you do for others. Entrepreneurship is all about finding out what people need and supplying it. It therefore gives us a great opportunity to raise our self-esteem and worth.

Like any determined pursuit, it is clear that the mark of a winner in the entrepreneur business is determined when things are going wrong. If there is a clear long-term vision and determination, anything in the short term will be seen as a temporary setback along the path to success. If your vision is more short term the pictures in your mind will appear overwhelming and dominate your focus and emotions.

Progress now

Think of your last setback. Close your eyes and see pictures appear as you recall the memory. Notice particularly how near or far away they are.

Now in your mind's eye push the pictures further away. Does that make any difference to how you feel about the experience? Which is most useful, near or far?

When the going gets tough, you have to get tougher

During a tough period you may be tempted to give up and take a regular job. Most of us, when we start our own business focus on it all going well. Those who focus on what will happen if it goes wrong tend to not start. In practice, I have not found a single entrepreneur who at some stage did not have to overcome a major setback. The biggest threat to your business is not your competitors or market, but you losing confidence and belief.

If the going gets tough, it is time to get creative and even more determined. This does not mean sticking rigidly to something that does not work. It means making it work whatever changes have to be made. Use your brain to get out of difficult situations. Your brain does not work that effectively if it gets itself into a negative state. Therefore, it is important to maintain your confidence.

Daily medicine

Play a personal development audio programme briefly each morning or read for just five minutes from a success related book. Not only will you learn, you will be constantly uplifted for the start of each day. Soak all these positive ideas into your unconscious, like a sponge, and you will find that you are developing the habits of those who you read about. That is why I constantly read biographies of winners.

Progress now

Make a firm decision to do the above.

The positive benefits of negative thinking

There is a myth that entrepreneurs are less concerned about security than their employee counterparts. This can be true, but often entrepreneurs just see it differently. They want their security to be under their own control, which suggests that they have a stronger need for security.

Entrepreneurs are more negative than positive. In fact, they spend more time considering what will happen if it all goes wrong, that one wonders why they don't choose an alternative lifestyle. The reason is because they focus on dealing with this negative thinking, and applying their positive energy to it. The world has a lot of negativity in it; mastering it is the secret, not avoiding it.

> ## Progress now
>
> Think of five things in your business, or planned business, that could go wrong in the next 12 months. Include anything that comes to mind: recession, offices flooded, law suit, competitors cutting prices, not raising enough finance, cash flow crisis, problem finding new suitable staff, etc.
>
> Relating to the above five things, I want you to think of actions you can take to prepare for such an event happening.
>
> Now, I want you to think of an action you can take for each of the above scenarios that would turn such an event happening into an opportunity for you?

Control your emotions

To anyone who has studied the stock markets or raised risk capital it is clear that investors, often well-informed investors, will react according to two emotions: fear and greed. Emotionally based decision making does not make for good business. To be greatly successful you must control both your positive and negative emotions. You must be as productive after a long run of bad experiences as you are after a run of good ones.

If you lose £1,000 and don't have control of your emotions you will lose another £5,000 while you are recovering from your negative state. What seemed to be a lot of money when you were an employee can be a fairly token amount in financing a business. You have to learn to think differently about money.

Most of the entrepreneurs I have studied have, at various stages, taken huge risks, even risking everything that they have. Many of them lose all and then start again! They were following a dream with passion and determination. Those who are focused just on accumulating money have a tendency to avoid risk as soon as they have something to lose, thus ironically limiting their potential. The risk takers love what they are doing passionately. The risk avoiders love money passionately and losing even a small amount makes them very unhappy. They typically like to keep their wealth in a variety of investments.

So if you are passionate about what you do, when the going gets tough, put your head down and work harder learning, changing as you go. Your work is the source of your results and, if you focus on where you are going, you cannot also dwell on problems that are day by day moving deeper into history.

From ambition to action

Be in a hurry, but walk before you run.

Ambition can be a dangerous energy. It can drive you forward at too fast a pace. Go as fast as possible but no faster.

Most average entrepreneurs have trained themselves to react quickly to anything that happens, maintain their emotional state and take action. The excellent entrepreneurs, however, have the advantage of anticipating things before they happen and taking preventive measures.

- If I was to have an absolutely wonderful idea right now, what would it be?
- If Sir Richard Branson was a director of your business, what changes do you think he would make?
- Is every part of me 100% totally behind and believing in this idea?

Carrot or stick?

There is an old expression that if you want to get a donkey to move then you have two choices: you can entice him forward with the temptation of a nice juicy carrot, or you can hit him with a stick. Generally, we don't like sticks, which is probably why they can get us to move more quickly than the temptation of the carrot. Incidentally, whereas I enjoy a good carrot, I can think of a lot more enticing temptations. What excites you the most? What would really get you moving?

So our motion is determined by the carrots and sticks operating on us. If you don't control the system, your unconscious and the environment will generate a system for you. I prefer to take control.

Sticks:

- the realization that if you are a failure you will have to live with it
- lose everything including your house
- unemployment
- letting your family down
- lack of financial security.

Carrots:

- job satisfaction

- realize your dreams
- incredible house, holidays, cars all paid in cash
- all the joys that success brings
- the rise in self-esteem and well being
- freedom to do whatever you want
- own boss, independence.

The very factors that make you pause before starting can help to motivate when you start. For most entrepreneurs, avoiding being hit by the sticks makes them take more action than the incentive of reward.

One of the obstacles to starting is the prospect of losing your current employment and all the benefits that it entails. So often entrepreneurs are created following redundancy when what you are giving up is so much less.

Personal power

When we feel low it may be because we are focusing on some bad news or what we perceive to be bad news. This leads to negative images and sounds internally which, in turn, leads to that low feeling.

Interestingly, we may feel low for no apparent reason. Then comes the really dangerous part. We search for things that are negative to justify our low feeling. We dwell on that and maintain our low feeling for even longer.

A low feeling can be caused by the physiological state of your body. What I call internal pollution. You need to cleanse it out, not add to it. Here are some suggested actions that will clear out this negative energy.

- Focus on the positive. Do this by writing down five things that are really positive in your life right now. Then write one page on each and re-read these notes every morning, updating them when appropriate. (I suggest you read a different book per month on business, personal development or biographies of those you admire.)
- Keep busy because taking action forces the mind to focus on the positive. In addition, action is what creates good news so get to it as quickly as possible. People who consistently work hard do not have time to feel low!
- Exercise because this flushes the system out and generates a positive flow of energy, so join a gym or health club. I also

suggest each month you buy or take out from the library a book on health, nutrition or exercise.

- Replace coffee, tea, fizzy soft drinks and certainly alcohol with plain water. You will be surprised how, quite literally, this washes away that low feeling and those negative thoughts.

- The best thing to do is to go on an organized weekend fast. I have been doing so through the Sivananda Yoga Vedanta Centre in London (they have centres throughout the world – visit www.sivananda.org) for more than 20 years and I believe that there is nothing you could possibly do that would give you more benefits in just two days. Coupled with meditation and yoga asanas the mind becomes exceedingly calmed and you will have access to parts of you that you never knew existed. An excellent starting point to creating new ideas.

Future positive

Think of today as the first day of the rest of your life. Imagine that you were born today and took over the body you now possess. You cannot change what happened in the past but you can choose to be helped or hindered from the experiences. If you choose the latter, and it is a choice, then you are also going to hinder your future. Put like that it is obvious which choice to take. The trick is knowing that you have a choice.

One of the techniques I use when I am brought in as a headhunter is to make a simple analysis of the verb tenses that somebody uses. I simply count every verb they say (or write) in three columns. I make sure that questions don't lead. I total up the past, present and future tenses that they use. This shows where their focus is. The successful entrepreneurs who I have interviewed all used the future tense then the present and then the past in that order. I wonder what would happen if you made a point of using the future tense. I wonder in how many ways this would improve your outlook, idea generation and confidence.

I am not suggesting that the past tense is negative, but it can be. We need to use our past to create a better future. People who use the past tense a lot tend to focus more on negative experiences than positive. It seems to teach them to believe in what they cannot do. Personally I think we all should challenge some of these assumptions. The word 'entrepreneur' suggests the future tense. It is about what is going to be. Other professionals, say financial auditors or archaeologists are focused on the past.

Progress now

Think of a famous entrepreneur who you admire. Search for a television or radio programme, perhaps an autobiography, in which they are interviewed or are appearing. Track their use of verb tenses. Simply take a piece of blank paper and write three column headings: Past, Present and Future. Each time they use a verb put a tick in the appropriate column. A pattern will soon emerge. Then draw your own conclusion and ask the question 'What else is significant that I have not noticed yet?'

My son, when he was young, walked up to me while I was writing, stuck out both of his fists and commanded me to choose one. I tapped his left hand; he opened it to reveal the white pawn. I reluctantly played chess with him and won. I beat him that month, then the next month, and the next month, then the next year. He kept coming back. Often he would walk away despondent, angry sometimes, but he kept coming back. Then one day he beat me, then he beat me again, then he beat me every month, then every year. He then played at national level and was defeated five games out of six. He left saying, 'I'll be back!'

Desire, aspire, retire

Many professional recruiters learn that the most placeable candidate, and hence the most likely fee, is the one with most desire to be placed. That is because desire is the energy that make things happen and leads to success, whatever comes in the way.

As a career coach I help to establish clients' desire. Often they have a degree of satisfaction in their job, but they are not fully satisfied. They still feel a degree of frustration. This frustration is part of their unconscious not having its needs addressed. It means that you are not working in the ideal position yet have a few of the elements present. Your destiny is to move on, but first you need to know where to go. On an individual basis it is quite easy to help someone find their true desire. It is quite warming for me to see their faces light up with passion as their true desire clicks into place and the energy builds. It is a powerful force.

Many of these people want to be entrepreneurs. I think they already are, and just need a little help to get to the next stage.

Desires to be a real entrepreneur are often in conflict with desires to avoid risk, and for instant gratification and security. These desires that hold you back are of two types. The first is under the heading of fears: fears about it going wrong, losing your house, not getting your job back, the unknown. Lack of self-confidence is in this category. The second category of desires, the enemy to the entrepreneur, is for short-term gratification. Increasingly society is being hypnotized by advertising saying, 'Consume now, and if you have not got the money we will give you credit so you can still consume now.' These short-term hungers are never satisfied, you just keep wanting more and more. You have to take control of your desires to grow to your potential as an entrepreneur.

Progress now

What desires do you have that are keeping you from your dreams?

What weaknesses do you have that are keeping you from your dreams?

From the above, decide what action you have to take. You need no advice from me here, you will know what has to be done.

Progress now

How to reprogram your habits so that they automatically achieve your goals for you:

1 Write down all the habits that you would like to change. Include those that you know are a waste of money, time or other resources, for example smoking, drinking, watching too much television, getting up late, spending to make yourself feel good, avoiding exercise, worry, talking yourself into a negative state.

2 Write down habits that you would like, for example: regular exercise, thrift, opportunity spotting, opportunity developing, being positive when you need to be.

Here is my formula to stop a bad habit:

- Do something different every time it comes up.
- Remind yourself of your goals and dreams.

Here is my formula for forming a habit:

- Think of something you love doing.
- Take those feelings and now think of the new habit, focusing on the long-term benefits.
- Bring those images that come to mind closer and closer.
- Do it consciously seven times in a row.
- Now do it seven more.
- It is now in your unconscious.

This is how young people learn to smoke cigarettes. The first few times they cough and feel sick; as they are determined to fit in with their peer group they persevere. Forming habits is really simple, I am just suggesting that we form good ones.

Entrepreneur interview: Christine Jones

Alex: What is your career background?

Christine: I started my career working as a statistician in a merchant bank in Fleet Street (London) at just 15. I grew up as a Catholic in the most loving family and was part of a strong community. I dreamed of going to university and becoming a barrister but my father had a very serious accident, so my dream of going to university, fighting for worthy cases in verbal battles was not to be. Instead, because I was good at Maths, I magically found myself working in a graduate training job 'thanks to the Catholic mafia' at the bank. I learnt about life fast, my colleagues were all graduates and were very good to me, but I was bored out of my head within three months! The structure was just not for me; I saw an unattractive future to avoid and was still lucky enough to be only 15.

This experience turned out to be a blessing; a pattern for my life began. From the adversity of negative situations a positive outcome will always emerge. In the 1960s you could leave a job on Friday and be in a new one on Monday. I became a serial job hopper! Each time I changed jobs I made new friends, learnt more skills and my salary went up. I became very good at interviews. I landed my dream job in January 1969 as the temps controller of a London recruitment agency. Commission was a big driver for me: low basic, high commission, performance related. Within four months I was promoted to branch manager. I had six staff (all older than me) while I was still 17. Life was great. I got engaged to my now husband. I loved my life, loved my man, and loved my job and all the people, staff and candidates. Our branch was so motivated, we thrived on beating targets and being the top performers.

We had to work on Christmas Eve so all the team decided to chip in and buy some wine as a 'thank you' to our temps. Unexpectedly the Area Manager visited and heavily criticized me with all the staff listening. I walked out, pawned my engagement ring and set up on my own.

In January 1970 I opened my first agency; I had just turned 18. I was greener than the grass. I made every mistake imaginable! I loved being in business, selling, improving people's lives and making money. My accountant gave me the most valuable business advice. He said, 'Christine, in business you need only three friends; your accountant, lawyer and bank manager.' This advice has proved priceless over the years. To this I have added my own: anyone I do business with I have to like, trust and earn money.

My time now is spent on 'Achievers Events', a motivation company, working with companies, helping their staff to achieve their full potential through unique and often profound training. I am also in the process of launching 'Attune', a fabulous lifestyle and well-being group, covering mind, body, spirit, wealth, career. We are working with a team of exceptional living masters including Dr Ali, the renowned pioneer of integrated health and international author. I am also working with Simon Treselyn, an ex-military intelligence specialist. Life is good.

Alex: How do you define success?

Christine: Loving life, my family and whatever I am doing, total self-belief and being independent of the good opinion of anyone else.

Alex: What advice would you give somebody starting out?

Christine:

1 Have a blueprint for success, a good business plan and an exit route
2 Be prepared to take the risk.
3 Make sure you are not under capitalized.
4 Have a plan B.
5 Be disciplined and work focused.
6 If it goes wrong don't beat yourself up, learn from your mistakes then stand up and do it again better.
7 Have mentors and heroes.

Alex: How do you spot an opportunity?

Christine: There is opportunity everywhere, so do what you want to do. Be passionate about what you do because it will take up every hour that God sends. Do your homework, take risks, be prepared to take the knocks. Even with this attitude it may take two or three times to get it right.

Alex: What would you have done differently if you could go back in time?

Christine: I would have sold businesses earlier at the right market opportunity. My ego made me not ever want to work for someone else and I missed opportunities. Having said that, I live by the wisdom of these words: 'What I can't change don't worry about, what I can – deal with, please God give me the wisdom to know the difference.'

Alex: How do you motivate yourself when things don't go to plan?

Christine: I have a little book called *Positive Thoughts for the Day* by Norman Vincent Peale that I dip into; it quickly re-energizes me. I am a totally positive thinker. I move on.

Alex: What would you advise the 'budding female entrepreneur' starting up?

Christine: Stop thinking like a woman and just be a businessperson. Don't give yourself an obstacle before you start, especially one that does not actually exist! Think of Nike, the goddess of courage and victory, and then be like the advertising slogan and 'JUST DO IT!'

Three tips

1 Eat lots of bananas. They are full of just about everything you need and have a natural packaging making them easy to carry around, ready to fill those energy gaps.

2 Allow only winners within your personal space and it will rub off.

3 Success is a decision that you make.

Two tasks

1 Ask yourself: 'What can I do right now to make a profit?'

2 Whatever level of exercise you do in a week, increase it by 10%.

06
the power of negative thinking

In this chapter you will learn:
- why you need to be more risk averse than a risk taker
- how to turn fear into your friend
- why you need to put your goals in order
- that 'positive thinking' can really let you down
- how to harness the power of negative thinking

'*We shall never surrender!*'

Winston Churchill

'*If you don't know how to have a good time with $10, a million won't help.*'

Dr Richard Bandler

Action speaks louder than words

Motivation works in two directions: helping us to get closer to what we want and further away from what we wish to avoid. A dream house motivates us to set up our own business to gain the wealth. The thought of losing our current home motivates us to not make the jump. So lies the dilemma. Thus is born the common belief that entrepreneurs are people who do not fear taking risks. We conclude that if we don't like taking risks we are not cut out for entrepreneurship. Wrong on both counts.

First, successful entrepreneurs typically are risk averse. Warren Buffett, the world's wealthiest investor, says there are two rules for business success: the first is never lose money and the second is never forget rule number one. Warren realizes, like all true entrepreneurs, that if he stays where he is, he is not going anywhere! So successful entrepreneurs decide to take action, but having done so, research the risks and take steps to reduce them. They do not go boldly in, but they do go in. The wealthiest entrepreneurs are, quite clearly, risk averse, but not risk avoiders.

Abraham Maslow is considered to be one of the key researchers in motivation and he came up with the idea of the hierarchy of needs. We have basic human survival and security needs that require satisfying before we look for higher goals such as self-realization. I have found that most wealthy entrepreneurs, despite their wealth, remain on this bottom rung. They are deeply insecure, believing that more money is the answer, so they keep going.

All their lives their focus was not only on making as much money as possible but on keeping it, investing it to make more money. They were not motivated by what they would buy with the money. If they own big houses it is usually in the belief that property is a good and, more importantly, safe investment. They typically will drive average cars, preferring to have their capital invested and producing a return.

You could argue that what we see as winners are in fact losers. I am suggesting that you learn from them the lessons of financial prudence, risk aversion but taking risks, leveraging their resources, keeping something back for a rainy day. Achieve financial freedom, but then move up Maslow's hierarchy to gain greater satisfaction.

Fear spurs people into action more than anything else I can think of. If you want to move fast or get other people to move fast and keep moving, fear is the key! The question then is, in what direction is the fear motivating us?

What can we do to control the direction? What can we do to manage the bad feeling? The answer is, take action, get and keep moving with a clearly defined goal.

Goals. Are they the right goals that you are going for? Too many people ask what your goals are and then look at how to get them. You first need to ask what is influencing your goals.

Ask lots of 'Why' questions. You may find that you are under the illusion of going for what you want.

An alcoholic's goal is to find their next drink. And, boy, are they motivated and fired up to achieve that goal. The goal should be to stop drinking alcohol. You need to be strong to focus on the long term and sacrifice the short term pleasure/satisfaction/ relief.

I ask people in business for their goals and they give me money related answers, usually vague but about income or wealth level. I then ask: 'Why, what for?' They surprisingly don't have much to say.

'What do you mean, does not everybody?' If you make £1million it should mean that you have produced £10million of value for other people. If you focus on supplying value of £10million to others you are more likely to make your £1million.

'What can I do to give £10million of value?' Different focus, different way of thinking.

What measures success? If it is just money then I am doing better than Jesus, Mother Theresa and Gandhi combined.

Consider the two goals of financial independence or material luxury. The first is a negative (away from threat), the second a positive (towards reward) motivation direction. Ask any dictator which one he has found works best, which one gets people moving quickest.

So FEAR: don't solve it or overcome it, harness it!

Imagine you had to keep poisonous snakes in the house until you achieved your goals. Would that help you become a great entrepreneurial success? If you are in business for yourself, the worst possible outcome is that you lose money. You are not in physical danger. Not unless, of course, you have not paid that dictator you were talking to.

Negative drivers can be making sure you do not do any of the following:

- letting your partner down.
- letting those you love down.
- letting your colleagues down
- letting your 'god' down.
- letting your friends down.
- letting yourself down.

A dream house in five years is too far off to spur you into action today. Negative thinking gets the urgency back into your daily motivation. Make sure you go one step towards your goals and one step away from your fears every day. Then you will have the benefit of both motivational forces working for you.

Negative thinking can stop you going into business for yourself. Right now you need to list the fears that you have of never making a go if it.

Positive versus negative thinking

If you believe everything is going to work out, you are likely to relax a little. If you believe that things can go wrong, you will prepare ahead of time for those contingencies.

Negative thoughts are not harmful, wallowing in them is. Moving away from them is the key. Here are some negative and positive thoughts. Which would get you moving most?

Positive	Negative
a new sports car	the house is on fire
a holiday in Hawaii	no money in old age
new clothes for your slimline figure	being obese with a heart problem
a Cuban cigar	lung cancer
a dream house	losing your current home
£millions	bankruptcy

Positive thinking leads to the comfort zone and that really reduces action.

It's 6pm on Friday night, you are exhausted, but still have a list of important things to do. Would you:

1 think of the Porsche at the end of the year and work another hour?

2 think of the mortgage going into default at the end of the month and work the extra hour?

3 think how nice a couple of beers with colleagues would be and leave for the pub?

Fear is your friend

In a country such as India there is no welfare state and millions of hungry people living in extreme poverty. It doesn't half motivate them to get work, and when they get work to keep it! There is no safety net to fall back on and India is currently one of the fastest growing economies in the world.

For business the greatest fear is insecurity. It denies you ever feeling that you are in a comfort zone. Wealthy entrepreneurs, however much money they have, consider it a safeguard against adverse conditions coming along.

The problem is that if you need a million euros to feel secure then the money is not really available to you. Hoarding loads of money is not that clever.

The best technique is to decide an amount of capital which, when reached, you will invest in a portfolio of investments. Have a distinct goal.

Most people would advise you to get rid of the negative thoughts and replace them with positive ones. I say the opposite. Get rid of comfort, relaxation and positive thoughts, and get a list of 'What would happen if you don'ts?'

The negative thoughts can generate a pity party, make you feel sorry for yourself, cause depression, low morale and low self-esteem. Fear these and move forward now.

Harnessing that negative energy

We all tend to move in the opposite direction to the perceived greatest threat. This negative power is a bit like dynamite: can get you through a mountain if used right; if used wrong, it can destroy you. You have got to know how to harness the energy. This means I don't want you to feel great, I want you to feel uncomfortable.

I once gave a lecture on motivation and put a flip chart on both the left-hand and right-hand sides of the front of the class. I asked the group on the right-hand side to write on their flip chart everything that motivated them positively, that they moved towards. I asked the group on the left-hand side to write on their charts things that moved them away.

After 20 minutes seven pages on the negative chart were used up and the positive chart had not filled one half of a page.

If I said you can have one hour of everything pleasant you could possibly imagine in return for five minutes of experiencing everything negative you could possibly imagine, what would you say? I have found 95% of people won't take up the offer. This suggests that keeping away from unpleasant things is more than ten times as powerful a human motivator as moving towards the goals of things we like. Puts a whole different perspective on goal setting, doesn't it?

The personal development industry for years has filled the shelves in bookshops and delegates on training courses with advice on positive thinking. 'Think positive' is the message. Sounds great, sounds logical. For years I read all the books, attended all the courses and applied the principles without achieving the desired results.

For this book I have read, in great detail, biographies of successful entrepreneurs and other famous people to discover their secrets, to learn if there are techniques I can learn from them and share. The interesting thing I found is that people who are successful at something don't do it the way in which most books tell you to. The theory and the practice are worlds apart.

Referring to successful entrepreneurs, you would expect the vast majority of them to be those with MBAs or chartered accountants, for example. Interestingly, most of these people were college drop outs (Bill Gates) or had never even got as far as higher education (Sir Richard Branson). I also noticed that most of the famously successful people whom I studied, both via the written word and personal contact, had negative motivational patterns.

These people are not positive at all, they are negative. I am not saying that positive thinking has no place. I am saying that it just is not as simple as that, and we need to stop and think, and stop believing all that we read. (Apart from my books!)

So what do I mean by negative thinking? Let us list some negative words:

> threat, no, not, never, rejection, bad, failure.

I know many people who learnt about the importance of backing up their computer files through having their files corrupted, me included. Now I back up regularly. Anticipate future threats and take measures to avert them now, when time is an ally, not when they become real and time has become the enemy. Think of what you can do if the following happens and decide a policy and action plan now, put things in place.

- Cash flow crisis.
  Get a credit line available now when you don't need it. There will be less credit available to you when you do.
- Your best customer closes down or relocates.
- A key member of staff resigns.
- Your website crashes.
- All your computer files are hit by a virus.
- A recession hits your market.

Entrepreneur interview: Paul Nuth

Paul is an independent business owner, managing and developing an international network of distributors offering a vast range of home delivered products. Paul is 53 years old, has two adult children and lives with his wife in Portsmouth.

Alex: What is your own career background?

Paul: I joined the Royal Navy straight from school with an interest in seeing the world and playing a range of sports. I was told I would never become an officer. In fact, I reached the rank of Lieutenant Commander and most latterly was serving with the Australian Navy.

I felt that it was time to make a move. I was also motivated to ensure that I would be financially secure for old age. I wanted to have my own business and the real objective was to become free, financially and of control mechanisms. Also to provide a good education and upbringing for my children. The idea of buying a business or a franchise did not appeal though and I had limited resources anyway.

It was at this time that I was introduced to one of the wealthiest men in Sydney who owned property and investment around the world. He was 63 and had been what I would call financially free since 27. He introduced me to an opportunity with an organization called IDA. I believed in taking advice on wealth only from people that had achieved it, so I listened attentively. I had found what I was looking for and I thought I could better develop the enormity of what I had seen back in Europe.

Although I started in Australia, I really got going in England. In the early 1990s there was quite a recession on and I was unemployed for a while and, in fact, got into debt to the tune of £70,000. I was on the edge of personal bankruptcy for quite a while. The ideal plan would have been to have a regular job while I built up my own business in my free time. In fact, within three years I had paid off this debt and had started to accumulate assets. You certainly have more choices when you have money. I was determined that lack of money would not decide where and how we spent retirement. From there I continued to build my own business while holding down a full-time job, recruiting more independent business owners in a system developed from the principle of network marketing.

The beauty was that IDA provided me with regular training and support from people that have started before you. They teach you how to become financially independent, and then in turn you teach others how to achieve the same goal. My success has come and is coming from following their advice. IDA has thousands of people who need not ever work again, and I have had direct access to all this knowledge. IDA provided an environment for anybody with the will to succeed in the industry that it was formed to support. It is led and populated by people that have done it. I had the will to succeed and was keen to listen to advice from wealthy people.

You build people, they build the business. If the desire is there, anybody can learn anything, but a supportive environment helps. Whatever problems you have will pass, it is your reaction to them that matters. My results were based on duplication and leverage in a system that works. The only real resource that I needed to add was my time. IDA has effectively given me a degree in behavioural psychology, taught me how to control motivation, be successful, overcome fears, etc.

I see people around me and they seem to anaesthetize themselves against thinking of the future by focusing on 'now' issues. Soap operas, football, computer games and the like can help in this. Every single successful person I studied had a clear dream that they focused on. I ask people: 'If you could take the rest of the year off, with no constraints on time or money what would you do?' They find it a hard question. I ask people: 'Does the thought of an extra income stream appeal?' Most are caught up in selling their time for money for 40 years and know little about how wealth is accumulated. The system seems to take away their hopes of a better future.

I continually read biographies of successful people and I listen to at least five personal development audio programmes per week. I believe the mind is a magnificent mechanism, but you have to program it. If you do not put in content for the future it can only refer to the past. I have taken longer than expected to get where I am. I have set goals and missed them three times but eventually got there.

Alex: What motivated you to be an entrepreneur?

Paul: To become financially free and own my own time.

Alex: How do you define success?

Paul: When I totally control my time. A happy balanced family.

Alex: What is the secret of success of an entrepreneur?

Paul:

- Be willing to define and do what it takes.
- When you set your goal, make it non-negotiable.
- Do it or not do it.
- You cannot build it on your own.
- Leverage your time.
- Fast is better.
- Have fun.

Like baking a cake you have got to put the right ingredients in, in the right way.

Alex: What advice would you give somebody starting out?

Paul:

- Determine why you are doing it and put it in writing.
- Don't negotiate the price (what it takes).
- Be willing to work.
- Enjoy the journey.

- Act with integrity.

Alex: How do you spot an opportunity?

Paul: Keep your antenna up, looking.

Alex: What would you have done differently if you could go back in time?

Paul: Do it faster!

Alex: How do you motivate yourself when things don't go to plan?

Paul:

- Read a book
- Listen to others.
- Inspirational music.

Three tips

1 Use fear to spur you into action, so as to avoid it.
2 Focus on your long-term more than short-term fears.
3 Think ahead.

Two tasks

1 Write a list of ten negative things that will or could happen if you do not take action on your entrepreneurial ambitions.
2 Think of three people who are successful, observe them to see if they are motivated negatively (away from bad things) or positively (towards good things).

07

going to plan?

In this chapter you will learn:
- that getting going is your top priority
- how to visualize success and create your own future
- how to use 'negative thinking' to pre-empt what might go wrong
- the magic formula
- that the best source of finance is customers

'Don't get it right, get it going!'

Michael Bloomberg

'As regards obstacles, the shortest distance between two points can be a curve.'

Bertolt Brecht

Types of company

One of the first decisions before you set sail is the form of legal entity under which you will operate. Depending in what country you are, there are just a few options. They are all, in essence, straightforward.

Incorporating is the favourite choice and usually the best option as this gives you limited liability to your debts, making you and the company separate legal entities. In other words, a creditor can sue only the company for its money and not the shareholders or directors. However, finance companies, banks and suppliers often seek personal guarantees or cash deals because of this.

A sole trader is the simplest type of company without any set-up time or costs; you just simply trade as yourself, although you are free to use a trading name different from your own if you wish.

A partnership can be advantageous in as much as your accounts are not public domain, which may be of value. When you take a loan, the bank will ask and usually insist on security or a personal guarantee. You are technically liable for anything any partner signs in the partnership name, so be aware. Some firms, like accountants and lawyers, have to be partnerships.

Normally, it is best to incorporate. There are many basic business books (e.g. another in this series, *Teach Yourself Setting Up a Small Business*) and guides from banks on the differences.

In all three cases you can choose to register for VAT, although if you expect to trade over a certain limit you have to register. Registering involves filling in a simple form. You can then reclaim all the VAT you pay on goods and services and you have to add VAT to all your invoices. If you are selling to other businesses this is great as your customer does not mind the charge because they can reclaim it. Because you can reclaim VAT on goods and services purchased by your business, your costs just went down. There is nothing complex you need to know about VAT; it is basically a very simple tax. The VAT office will give you every help, and provide you at the time of writing with free videos and seminars to explain what you have to do. You may prefer to employ a local bookkeeper to do this for you. You need to delegate and focus on what you are good at.

Thinking about the future

Bill Gates famously visualized a PC in every home. Walt Disney visualized Disneyland® clearly in his mind's eye and then endeavoured tirelessly to make it a reality. Ray Kroc visualized McDonald's restaurants in key property locations all over the world. When they had these ideas they were ridiculed and laughed at. If someone is laughing at your dreams feel good about it, that is how the champions started.

In addition, entrepreneurs have to have a clear vision of how they are going to survive and prosper in the short term. They can see potential customers going for their ideas. They can see staff being motivated by their leadership.

Most people I have met in business have tended to be really good at visualization for either the short term or long term. Entrepreneurs invariably do both. When this is not the case, arguably Walt Disney being a good example, successful entrepreneurs have had a partner with the other skill. In this scenario one is, if you like, the strategist and the other the tactician. The strategist is often the innovator, creator of new products and ideas. The tactician is the one who makes it happen. It takes two to tango!

The message is clear:

1 Establish whether you are more naturally focused on the short or long term. It is not hard to do this, you will probably instinctively know. Listen to your own language patterns, refer back to something you have written, clues will give away your natural inclinations. Look back at your career: what have been your key strengths and achievements? Were you best at short-term achievements or long-term planning. At school did you start thinking about your final exams at the beginning of the year or in the last few weeks? Ironically, one of the traits that I have noticed with many people in business is that they become more long-term focused as they get older. Reflecting on these thoughts may throw light on why you have excelled at some roles and not so much at others.

2 When you know what you are, if you do both well you are OK. If you are strongly oriented in one direction you need to make a choice between recruiting someone with the other talent or developing that talent yourself.

3 If you wish to develop the talent here is how to do it.

If you are good at long-term achieving:

a Close your eyes and think of where your business will be in five years. Concentrate on that for 30 seconds and then open your eyes.

b Write down what you saw in detail. Pay specific attention to the following:
- What location were the picture(s) in?
- Were the pictures clear or fuzzy?
- Were the pictures in colour or black and white?
- How large were they?
- Were they moving or still?
- What other significant things did you notice?

c Close your eyes and think of where your business will be in one month. Let the images form by themselves, just sit back and watch what comes into your mind's eye.

d With your eyes still closed go back to these images and change them so that they are all in the same style of the original images, using the bullet points above, all apart from changing their location. A line drawn between the points suggests your personal coding of time.

If you are good at short-term achieving:

a Close your eyes and think of where your business will be in one month. Concentrate on that for 30 seconds and then open your eyes.

b Write down what you saw in detail. Pay specific attention to the following:
- What location were the picture(s) in?
- Were the pictures clear or fuzzy?
- Were the pictures in colour or black and white?
- How large were they?
- Were they moving or still?

c Close your eyes and think of where your business will be in five years. Let the images form by themselves, just sit back and watch what comes into your mind's eye. They may come instantly or may take a while.

d With your eyes still closed go back to these images and change them so that they are in the same style as before, all apart from changing their location. A line drawn between the points suggests how you sort your personal calendar of experiences.

You now have an ability to focus clearly, literally, on both the short and long term. It is that easy. Make sure that the plan for your business has both elements in it.

Preparing the business plan

If you are raising money a business plan will be required from you. Many books and indeed the internet give lots of good advice on their preparation. Business plans tend to have a fairly formal layout and people get used to reading a standardized format, so I advise that you stick to it.

You need to start with what is called an executive summary, more commonly known in the USA as the elevator pitch. In other words make your pitch as though passing someone in an elevator. This means get to the point quickly, winning first their attention, then their interest and then their desire to know more. Detail can be kept in an appendix for reference. The key aspect is the accounts. Usually three years of projected profit and loss account, cash flow and balance sheet will be required, possibly more. If you are already trading your results to date need to be included.

The next most important area is the qualities and appropriateness of the management team.

The plan needs to pre-empt any question that a potential investor reading through your plan may ask. Ideally, if you are asked a question at a meeting your answer should be in the plan. If it is not in there I, for one, would consider your proposition no further. You clearly are not fully prepared for every eventuality. That might seem a bit harsh, but if you receive a hundred plans a day you have to be. Questions you will probably be asked to include: What would happen if ...

- a recession suddenly happened?
- your three key employees resigned and took your top client with them?
- you were ill for six weeks?
- the government gave you a tax audit?

- your bank called in the overdraft?
- your landlord wanted their premises back?
- your largest customer went into liquidation, owing you a small fortune?
- the sales budget did not happen?

Are you prepared for these eventualities? Would you know how to turn them to advantage? So many plans that I receive seem to assume that if you throw a big enough cheque book at marketing, sales will follow. Venture after venture goes down because of this thinking. Sometimes venture capitalists will continue their support, as in the case of Amazon where they funded extremely large losses for a long period, but only when they continue to see something with real long-term potential.

Part of your plan will include what is called a SWOT analysis, which covers key Strengths, Weaknesses, Opportunities and Threats. It gives a potential investor a quick synopsis of the opportunity. Type 'business plans' into an internet search engine and you will be able to access various examples, which are useful as a checklist for your own enterprise. Small-firm entrepreneurs who I meet seem to be always dismissive of their competitors, coming out with arrogant statements about how and why they are so much better than them. In practice, I think it is always prudent not to overestimate yourself and underestimate your competitors. That is definitely a habit of winners.

And the magic formula is S – C = P

Sales less costs equals profit. Business is as simple as this equation; everything in business boils down to this relationship. If you want to succeed in your new business, work to increase sales relative to costs: £10million pounds of sales with £10million of costs makes the same profit as someone who has not started yet! This seems obvious to me, but the papers are continually full of companies throwing away millions on trial marketing campaigns, clearly not really knowing what they are doing. The problem is often that there is a separation from the managers who make those decisions and the people whose money is being spent.

I once managed a large team of consultants who were always asking for expense accounts to entertain new prospective clients. I came up with what I call the 'double or quits' proposal. They have an unlimited expense account and put their expenses in as usual. When, and only when, business comes in from a client they have entertained, they are paid double the claim. It was a very effective tool in making entertainment an investment. I could not lose and some recruiters had a pay increase!

In most entrepreneur based businesses, costs literally come out of the owner's pocket. The owners are more inclined to be careful with their housekeeping. The so-called dot com boom in the 1990s was a break from this successful pattern. As the internet was getting going, greedy investors were happy to put billions in the hands of twenty-something technical experts. Few of these people had any business experience. The result was a boom fuelled by a gold-rush mentality. Internet companies got a bad name and then found it hard to raise capital. Some critics considered that these boom/bust companies were never proper companies in the first place and wrongly gave bad press to the potential of the internet start ups.

Think of a business as a giant bucket where the taps pour in liquid gold. Your objective is to have the taps on full while making sure that all the leaks are plugged. I see so many businesses where they have only one of these things working. A well plugged bucket without the taps on will not fill up. Taps on full, with lots of holes in the bucket will equally not fill the bucket up. I have seen so many owners rushing to get more sales to maintain the level in their leaky bucket, when what they should be doing is managing their costs more effectively. The way to start doing this is by questioning each and every one of them.

Here are a few golden rules:

1 **If you are going off course don't keep drifting.**

The purpose of a plan is far more than to raise money. Design it to be a compass that will steer you through every eventuality. You should be constantly referring to your plan. Your time as entrepreneur is your company's greatest asset. Staying until the ship goes down can take forever and deny you the next opportunity. Stay focused on your long-term goal. This sometimes means abandoning the direction you are going in. Entrepreneurs continually reinvent their companies and ideas. The main asset of the business is you, focus on that. If you are the asset, even liquidation cannot stop you from transferring it to your next venture. Set yourself a deadline for targets that have to be reached otherwise you will call it a day and move on. Do not be like the gambler who keeps throwing good time and money after bad. React to the feedback by changing tack. If something has failed, the danger is in kidding yourself. Don't spend years drifting to a slow inevitable end, hoping for that big break. Instead, take all that you have learned and make a better attempt next time. Each failure is a step to success. Read the biographies of any famous entrepreneurs and you will realize that the secret of mirroring their success is not to be found in studying how they succeeded but how they reacted to their failures. Think of a failure as consultancy worth £100,000.

2 **Keep tabs on statistics.**

Always know the statistics that are relevant to your business. Cash in and out, sources of sales enquiries, etc. To navigate your ship you have to have constant updates of a changing situation in order to make meaningful decisions.

3 **Opportunity seeking is constant.**

Non-entrepreneurs think that we find an idea and then run with it. In reality you need to look constantly for new opportunities, new improvements. It is an attitude of mind to look constantly. Remember that often a failure can be the creative grounds for the next launch.

4 **If you believe in it, launch it.**

Have you ever had a great idea and proudly told your friends of your innovation, then done nothing about it and actually watched somebody else do it and make it succeed? Entrepreneurs are not looking for their friends to admire their ideas and intellect. They are looking to change the world and make a pile of cash. If you keep throwing the die a six must come up eventually. The good news is you are allowed as many throws as you want.

On target for success

Goal setting is clearly a habit of highly successful people in business and outside. Daily, weekly, monthly, yearly, five yearly, successes know where they are headed and, guess what, they increase their chances of getting there. All planning requires is the decision to set goals, and some hard work and thinking. Plan what you want to achieve long term and work it back so that each day you are a step closer to your dreams. This book, for example, was written within three months and my first task was to plan every aspect and target for every day, week and month.

My initial plan showed that it just was not enough time, so I had to get creative to make it possible.

The bad news is that making a lot of money as an entrepreneur is the result of a great deal of hard work. The good news is that other people will do a great deal of the hard work. Entrepreneurs always have a ready supply of people wanting to work for them. I once worked for a gentleman called Michael Page, who became one of the wealthiest entrepreneurs in Britain. I was standing next to him when, for the first time, the company's shares went public on the London small firms exchange. As we listened to the trading his personal shares went up by over £1million. Now that was a quick million by anyone's standards!

Progress now

What are your top three long-term goals?

Why?

What would happen if you did achieve them?

What would happen if you did not achieve them?

Are you totally sure you don't want to change them?

Would you do whatever it takes to achieve them, even if meant sacrifices now?

Money as a goal

Let me explain my money goals. I think that money is like food, the hungrier I get the higher priority I give to eating. When I am completely full I consider concentrating on food to be a waste of time. I think people should have the target of being financially full. This means that they have enough to live on for the foreseeable future. In practice, this means having wealth that generates an income, which means that they don't have to work. For me, entrepreneurship is about creativity, independence about working at what I want to do. I passionately love my work. I would not change work to earn more money. In my opinion, anyone who does not love work will always be poor. Money is a small compensation for such a state of affairs.

I know other entrepreneurs have spent their whole life focusing on where the money is. They have always done what has to be done to maximize their financial return, uninterested in whether they are doing what they want to do. Such people develop an incredible eye for profit and will certainly do whatever it takes. They never seem to reach the real happiness, contentment and excitement I have in looking forward to every new day's work. Ironically, not letting their full talents develop can limit their potential. You have to decide your own values, drive and motivations. What exactly is it about being an entrepreneur that appeals to you?

Progress now

List in order the top five things that interest you in being an entrepreneur. This list may help you: financial freedom, wealth building, creativity, control own destiny, independence, develop own ideas, invent something, work from home, retire early ….

Good advice is to plan for dealing with failures right from the start. Few entrepreneurs do this but the great ones all did. Thinking 'it will never happen to me' is just not smart. A good general plans for every contingency so he or she can fight more battles another day. Failure in business is at worst losing a battle, and the war continues. At best it can be a wealth of opportunity, experience and knowledge.

Very wealthy entrepreneurs who I know seem to have a great deal of respect for their competitors and assume that around every corner they will be pulling off an attack. They are also self-critical, never satisfied with their own performance. This leads to them being lean mean machines. Those who wallow in self-admiration are, by definition, not focused on improving their efficiency and performance, believing they are already the best and as best as can be. This is a major difference, I have noticed, between those who lead their industries and those who remain average. Look at a random collection of brochures and websites of a hundred new enterprises and I guarantee you will see more self-love than descriptions of what they can do for you. Do not take your client base for granted. Having worked in sales for years, I have found that a customer base can take a long time to develop yet customers change loyalties in a second. Your competitors will probably ring them today with some new idea or promotions.

If you could go back five years ...

I asked many of the entrepreneurs whom I researched, 'If you could go back five years what would you do differently?' Successful entrepreneurs learnt by their mistakes and kept trying new things and making changes until things worked. The most common answer was 'to be more prudent with costs and have better skills in communicating'. Other skills they prefer to delegate to people they employ.

Many would-be entrepreneurs, when they acquire initial funding from whatever source buy themselves flashy cars and all the trimmings. They are directors now and want the status of that success. They can finally pay themselves what they are worth. This does not communicate useful messages to staff, so they fail to win their employees' real support. An entrepreneur is a success when he or she runs a business at a profit, however small. I have an expression for people who put on this front with no real substance behind. Nice party, no guests. I recommend that you make financial and professional independence a higher priority than social status, and focus on ideas that have a market you can reach. Start by redefining status as your opinion of yourself.

Getting started

If you have started your business and have made initial sales, however small, that is tremendous. You have proved there is a market for what you offer. You have moved from a theory, a dreamer to a realist.

Big Mistake Number 1: a business is about making a better quality product at the best price. Wrong. A business is more about processes than it is about quality products. Customers to a business are like petrol is to a car – absolutely vital to go anywhere, but there is a lot more to it. The car itself is a system of interacting parts working as a team in harmony and co-ordination. Similarly, your business, if it is an efficient machine, it will operate at an optimum.

About five in a thousand plans get funded. Those five also received many rejections and took at least six months before they were successful. One of the problems in the real world of starting a business is trying to eat and survive while you are designing the plan and presenting it to potential investors. You have to research and understand investment deals relative to the size you are seeking to be and the nature of your proposal.

Service providers may find it an easier business to start than suppliers of a product, as usually you can start small and build up. For example, if you are starting anything from a hairdresser to a management consultancy all you need to be able to start is your home telephone. A hairdresser would have the added advantage of immediate cash payments. If your idea is to develop a product it may require all sorts of research, development, testing and patenting before purchasing capital equipment, stock, staff and premises. Even then you can do a lot of this with no funding in your evenings and weekends while maintaining a regular salary. Ideally you need to be able to make, say, ten of the product, a prototype and then try to sell it and see what response you get.

All I am suggesting is that if you can avoid raising money do so. It is also good advice, more often than not, to develop as much as you can before raising money. The reason for this is obvious: the more you have proven the concept, the less the risk and the more likely you are to secure funding, and it will be on better terms.

Funding

There are three categories of funding available to an entrepreneur. I call them loans, equity and wealth reservoir.

Loans

Loans are paid for with interest. You will find that loans for business purposes are not as easy to get as personal loans for a new car or kitchen. A business carries an increased risk of default with it, so lenders are likely to demand some form of collateral to secure the loan if the business fails. Dreams, unfortunately, do not offer much by way of collateral. If the purpose of the loan is something tangible (i.e. vehicles, equipment, property) you will stand a better chance. If, however, it is for what I call fresh air investment (i.e. advertising, marketing, research), then it will be seen as more risky. Clearly the lender has got less to repossess!

If you have collateral to put up for a loan do not assume that being made an offer is a vote of confidence in your business plan. It just means that it is no longer their risk. Banks, in

Britain at least, have changed their philosophies to businesses. An old banking principle is to lend one against every one put up by the company. In other words, you put up £50,000 cash and they will match it. Sometimes this is done with the support of a government scheme. At the time of writing, the British government has a scheme, potentially worth up to £200,000, giving certain guarantees to the bank if the loan defaults. Check with your bank for any government-backed scheme, local or central, currently in operation.

Another principle is what has been called balance sheet lending. Put simply, banks will lend according to the value of your balance sheet.

Both philosophies have given banks substantial bad debts. These philosophies also ignore the viability of the business. The problem with funding entrepreneurs is that there is little relationship between people with commercially viable ideas and how much security they offer. In the early days, companies like Microsoft®, Virgin Group, Marks & Spencer just did not have much collateral to offer until they established a track record of success. Therefore, the banks' philosophies would have missed out on great opportunities.

So look at your proposal from the point of view of the bank. How do you differentiate the next Bill Gates/Paul Allen team from the thousands of other hopefuls. There is a naïvety among, particularly young, would-be entrepreneurs that if you can persuade a bank manager how good your idea is, they will back it. Taking risk is the specialism of another type of financial institution.

Equity: venture capital explained

Venture capitalists financially and in other ways support businesses usually for a mixture of ordinary equity and loans. They are taking high risks in return for high potential payoffs. They will thus want to see considerable growth and an exit strategy, usually within three to five years.

Before approaching a venture capitalist, the first thing you will need is a business plan. The beauty of having a plan and getting professional advice is that it forces you to write down why you think your business is special. I have been a consultant to many growing enterprises on a range of issues. It is interesting what they want of me. I get requests like: 'Our staff need to be more motivated. Can you look at them for us?'; 'We are below target.

Can you do some sales training?'; 'Do you offer any team building programmes?'; 'Our financiers have asked about our marketing strategy. Do you know of anyone who could do that for us?' The requests tell me that the underlying problem is:

- They don't know where they are going.
- They don't know why or how to get there.

Any venture capitalist will need to be totally convinced that you know exactly where you are going and that you have the management team that can take it there. If you have any doubts on these matters address them before seeking funding.

A business is like a person in as much as it is a separate legal entity. Like a person it needs a direction, a goal, a purpose, a reason for being. Both need money to survive, but most goals, to be really fulfilling and worthwhile, need more than that.

So when I first look at the business I like to clarify where exactly the owners want it to go, and how they intend to get there. Next, I need to know how it differentiates itself from its competition. These are really basic business questions, but in practice few business owners have the answers. That is why they can become so much better entrepreneurs. Business gurus come up with the latest management fad. Managers are constantly looking for some new clever techniques to run their businesses. Very successful entrepreneurs seem to have mastered a few basic techniques. Business is simple, don't make it complicated. The more complicated the more chance for something to go wrong.

Venture capitalists put in money in return for a share of the business. They can be broken down into two distinct groupings.

The first group consists of wealthy individuals who, sometimes through a club, invest directly in companies. Typically this would be for amounts up to say £250,000. At this level the enterprise is valued and they take a minority stake for their investment. They rarely want to control the enterprise although they certainly will want to keep in close touch with how their investment is doing. Many of these types of investors often have business skills and contacts to offer as well.

These people are also sometimes called, 'business angels' and may be family, friends or colleagues of the business owner. Failing this you can network with such people by attending events, seminars and meetings. You can also use one of many business angel networks whose business is to make introductions, and they keep a database of potential investors.

In the UK they are joined through the National Business Angels Network. This type of investor tends to prefer to invest in a local company in their locality or in an industry about which they know something or have spotted as offering growth opportunities. These networks often require a registration fee plus a percentage from 2% of the money raised as their fee. Be careful of claims as to how likely they are to be successful, and if they seem more interested in the registration fee than their completion bonus.

You might prefer to use a firm of professional accountants or lawyers to find a venture capitalist. Many firms will not be active in this market, but others will. They will often work on a contingency basis, no deal no fee, and offer a great many support services, such as accounting or business plan preparation. They also have a list of high net worth individuals as their clients. A potential investor is also likely to be more sold on looking at a business plan that has been gone through and represented by a professional firm with a reputation at stake.

The biggest cost, in practice, to raising capital is your time spent doing it. Until you are successful this is non-productive work which could be used elsewhere. On the positive side the discipline of writing a business plan and selling it to potential investors gets you to look really closely at every aspect of your business. In practice, when I have been down this route I have improved my plan in light of the comments and questions of the people I have visited in search of funding. Unpaid-for consultancy can be considered a worthwhile investment return in itself.

The second group comprises the institutional venture capitalists. These deal typically, though not necessarily, with larger amounts of money and the deals become more sophisticated, part loan, part equity, so that the management team can retain overall control.

When you are looking for a large amount of funding the time investment in raising the capital is more worth it. As a general rule, the larger the amount the easier it can be to raise. This is because the work in assessing a proposal is much the same irrespective of the deal size. Venture capitalists cover their risk by gambling on the high potential payoffs of one of the ventures making it really big. They also syndicate their loans with other venturers. Again in the UK a comprehensive listing can be obtained by the British Venture Capital Association (BVCA). They will send you a book listing their members and their website (www.bvca.co.uk) is full of good advice. Different institutions tend to specialize is different amounts and different sectors of the economy. Again, though, you may well do better by employing an intermediary. People in the investment business tend to prefer to deal with someone they know. They also receive thousands of speculative business plans, so an established firm of accountants with which they have done business in the past is going to get far more attention than an individual about whom they know nothing.

Investors are buying the value of the company in the future. They will want a valuation then according to your accounts and also an exit route to realize their investment. Then, of prime importance is the management team that will make the plan happen. Great ideas for businesses are ten a penny. Management teams which can make them happen are rare. I will share with you some practical ways of funding in Chapter 11.

Wealth reservoir

This is without any doubt my preferred funding route. It is based on funding your business by using your creativity and ingenuity. It is the route that most successful firms took. I think there are good reasons for this.

- It gets you into the habit of thrift and keeping overheads low, which is a vital ingredient for success.
- Your time is spent developing the business.
- Pressure is on you to perform and this helps innovation.
- There is nobody on your back.
- There is no interest to pay or profits to share.
- You grow from the strong foundation of a proven market.

So what is this wealth reservoir? It is what I call the entrepreneur mindset, the attitude of using your brain and creativity to exploit resources that are already there and not fully utilized. This skill is not just used for product ideas. The advantage is that you do not have to give out shares or pay interest. You have a wealth reservoir, an abundance of resources. As soon as you can adopt this belief you will start to see a path forward, stepping stones towards your goals.

Another source of your wealth reservoir is your established competitors. They will know the industry you are in and have many resources other than finance to offer. Large players often recognize that the best way to recruit innovative talent is to find start-ups in their industry. This then secures their future, protecting them from what could have been a threat.

One of the faults of entrepreneurs is thinking that raising money is the success of their business. In practice, it is just a start. That money needs to be managed very well; it will soon run out if an increasing stream of sales revenue does not replace it. What might appear to be a large amount of money on an individual basis, in a business can be quite small.

How to make your own luck

Many people accuse successful entrepreneurs of being lucky. I think they took specific actions in order to get that luck. If someone wins the lottery by selecting a random group of numbers this is pure luck outside their control. However, when someone wins at cards, chess or backgammon, for example, I think their 'luck' has come from years of studying the game. I think that someone who accumulates great fortunes by investing in stocks and shares has done so by years of studying such investment. Along the way people have made the right investment by accident. These are the types that started out in a growing market, where true investors make profits whatever the market conditions. It is not luck, it is study. Aristotle Onassis was not lucky with his shipping investments; he religiously, daily studied what was happening in his industry.

Therefore, I suggest that whatever industry you are in you subscribe to trade and professional publications, set up a selective internet newsletter, attend forums and exhibitions and keep informed. This way you will make informed decisions and significantly increase your fair share of the luck. Confidence is a belief in your own abilities. The best way to maintain it is to constantly take action to increase your abilities. Energy exerted in business creates wealth. The more focused the energy the more wealth is created.

Marketing your way to sales

Marketing has been described to me as making the phone ring and sales as closing a deal on answering it. Sales is about going out there with your product and making deals. It is therefore focused on your company's needs. Marketing on the other hand is resources put into finding out what consumers will pay for and how to exploit that knowledge. If the marketing is good quality, sales plays a far more minor role, so be a marketing person before a salesperson.

Entrepreneurs have a dream and understandably cannot wait to see it turn to reality. They are so caught up in their passion that they have forgotten a basic principle of marketing. People pay money for what they want to buy, however irrational. For example, if you look at the market for children's toys, innovations become crazes: yo-yos with flashing lights and Pokémon® cards, for example. Production could not keep pace with demand. What creates or could create the mad rush to retailers is the constant focus of entrepreneurs. Your idea could be the next craze.

To keep customers, ask and keep asking yourself what I call 'product down-to-earth' questions:

- Are my customers satisfied?
- Have they been given reason to be loyal to me?
- What can I do to improve my products?
- Are my new product ideas good in the customer's eyes?
- Is my idea as original as I think?
- Is it worth anything?
- Will it sell?
- Will it be copied or stolen by competitors?
- How do I reach the market?
- How much finance will I need to develop it?

Balancing ideas and action to best effect

Entrepreneurs' minds are creative and therefore single-minded focus often does not come naturally to them. What is natural is to keep thinking of ideas. Once you have decided your goals are clearly defined, you need to keep to them. This might mean several tweaks to get them just right, that is fine. It is also fine to re-evaluate them as you go. What is not fine is trying to do many things all at once. Get one thing really working and then progress to the next; this is the repeated behaviour of most of the successful entrepreneurs I have studied. Running one business with limited resources is a major challenge. Running two is not doubling your chances of success, it is eliminating them.

Moving on

Many entrepreneurs start with just themselves and build from there. One of the pitfalls that they commonly get into is not replacing their gut decision making with processes. If they or you have a vision to one day be a big company they need to start with that in mind. In practice, this means that you have to think of your company as a big multinational at its earliest stage.

The more people you employ the more controls and decisions you will need to delegate. Therefore what you need to do is to write a policy on every process so that things are controlled as you grow and new people need not reinvent any wheels, for example a policy on expenditure. As owner you will have been prudent travelling standard class, staying in cheap rooms and eating sandwiches for lunch. Employees tend to think differently; they tend to be quite keen on maximizing the expenses they can get away with. In fact, in many companies they expect it and take it for granted. Once you have a large organization it will be more difficult to change habits. It is so much easier to start off as you mean to go on. Again the golden rule: think ahead and make decisions now, not when the pressure is on. When you establish an efficient way to do something, record it as policy. These documents must be accessible to your staff. This way no staff member can claim ignorance and the documents will save you a lot of management time in repeating the rules.

Each job role needs to be recorded in a manual so that you are not dependent on the person in that role. If they leave it will be easier to bring the next recruit up to speed. Every issue or problem they come up with can be referenced. This way you are a learning organization that does not re-invent the wheel constantly for every new employee. If something works, record it and get others to do it that way. Business is a system for making money, entrepreneurs tend to focus on innovating products and services, sales and marketing. These are the skills that are necessary to get something off the ground. The next stage requires different skills. It also requires delegation and bringing in people who can specialize in functions as you grow. The second stage is quite exciting as it involves much more efficiency, whereas initially the entrepreneur does everything.

The case for planning

Nobody plans to fail, but if you fail to plan you probably will. A long-term focus is essential for success. This includes considering every contingency and deciding ahead of time what to do if it happens. It gives you direction and makes decision making along the way easier.

The benefits of planning are perhaps best made through an analogy. Two couples left Southampton harbour for a month's sailing holiday. They had filled the boat with provisions and decided to just sail where they pleased each day and not be tied down to a rigid timetable. Besides, it saved a lot of boring time planning and added an adventure element. Was the holiday a success? How could you know? What criteria could you measure it against? Did everyone do what they individually wanted to do? Did the four people work as a team? Were their options restricted by not having the charts and other equipment for certain waters? Did they find that something essential had not been packed? Was provision made for mishap? Were the costs divided equally and fairly? Were there any arguments as to what to do and who would do what each day?

When the sea gets rough in the middle of the night is not the time to find out you do not have essential equipment and to decide whose shift it is. Yet this is exactly how many people manage their business and still expect to be successful.

Progress now

What advantage could you take now of opportunities that are available to everyone where you live?

Find out what you can do and then provide it yourself. When you get more orders than you can manage, subcontract the work. This enables you to grow in response to customer demand while maintaining flexibility and avoiding risk. When growth continues and is sustained, think about permanent members of staff. They will be the cheaper option but carry all the responsibility and risk. This may seem obvious, but too many entrepreneurs develop their plan, recruit a team and then launch the whole team onto the market. Then they find out that the market did not respond in quite the way or as fast as they thought it would. This is the most common approach by people using other people's money. You may know there is a market for something, but you still have to inform that market and add the cost of this to your price and to your funding requirements. You have to perhaps break current loyalties or re-educate customers into needing your product.

Progress now

Write a plan for your business that explains why and how it will work, on one page.

Three tips

1 Business is practical not intellectual. Plan, but don't make it a work of art.
2 Perfection only comes from regular customer feedback.
3 Get beyond break-even point as soon as possible. Cut corners to do so.

Two tasks

1 Write the exact amount of your money goals and by when you need to achieve them in one line.
2 Take your one-page plan and on a second page break it down into ten steps.

08

turning knowledge into entrepreneurial advantage

In this chapter you will learn:
- why you need to be careful of expert advice
- how to do an 'asset audit'
- how and why to build assets and reduce liabilities
- the skill of asking ODQs (opportunity directional questions)
- how to generate new ideas that will build your business

'The secret of business is to know something that nobody else knows.'

Aristotle Onassis

'Knowledge rests not upon truth alone, but upon error also.'

Carl Gustav Jung

Advice: take it or leave it?

The thing about knowledge is knowing how genuine it is. This applies to any knowledge not just in business. I suggest you become very sceptical. Think of those adverts on television for slimming products: any statistician will point out to you the weakness in their claims. They show you the successes of people who tried their programme and subsequently lost weight. They prove it, with before-and-after pictures. They then bring genuine successful customers onto the set to verify the success claims.

Let me tell you something. If you tell 1,000 overweight people that if they wear only blue clothes for a month they will lose weight, 10 or so probably will. If you now invite those 10 to appear on television, sure enough they can honestly verify that they followed the programme and, hey presto, they are now thinner. You will have a growing market for blue clothes.

What the adverts have not done is parade the people in front of you who tried the programme and it did not work (990 in the above example). Neither have they reported what happened to all the people who tried the system: success, failure and no change.

They have also assumed that the people who lost weight did so because of the programme; they do not know if this was the reason. Maybe those people did other things that were effective, not even knowing what it was that worked. Have you ever found that your weight has changed in either direction and you have no rational explanation for it? I certainly have, and I was not consciously following any programme.

They also tend to avoid any short- or long-term, positive or negative side effects. Saccharine was once a marvellous product for slimmers, sweetness without calories, until the long-term toxic effect on digestive organs was identified.

If you develop a group rapport and then hype people up, you can whisk them into a state of belief in something. Any scientist who has conducted experiments with placebos will tell you that if the brain really believes something there is a substantial chance of it becoming true. People are cured of illnesses every day by being given placebos. Now scientists organize two control groups: one group is given the real new medicine and the other is given the placebo. No group member knows to which group he or she belongs.

This section is designed to make you a little more sceptical of what you are told. Do not take any knowledge at face value, and certainly not from someone with a vested interest. If you disagree with this advice I would just like to say, buying 100 copies of this book will make you 100 times richer!

Quality advice that is value for money

Be wary of expert advice. I know of many people who failed on the basis of expert advice. There are two types of experts. The first type is often found at a social gathering; bring up a subject and there seems to be an instant expert on it. The second type is a genuine expert, convincing because of their qualifications and track record in the area being sought. There is a great tendency of people to answer any question you ask them. Hardly anyone will say those magic words, 'I do not know the answer to that one'.

My advice is to seek guidance, when you need it, from three independent 'experts' and be careful not to let them know what you think the answer is or that you have talked to other experts. Advice that confers from three experts has a high chance of being good advice. Even then the majority are not necessarily right.

Experts charge high rates, usually by the hour, for their advice, good or bad. There are, however, various ways to get this for free. The first and easiest of these is via the Internet. You can surf a whole range of information, and check it with various other sources. Second, you can email experts from their websites and put your questions to them. Invariably they will answer your question in the hope of winning your respect and making you a client. At the same time they are also developing their name awareness and public relations image. You can even email me directly. Depending on what country you are in, there are government institutions, central and local, working as charities to give citizens free advice. One of the entrepreneurs I interviewed said she went to the Citizens Advice Bureau with a complicated legal challenge she was facing. Apparently she received, free of charge, the advice of a retired partner of a major British legal firm. His advice, which she took, saved her business at a time of crisis.

Banks have a whole range of information on specific challenges relating to entrepreneurial businesses, which they will give you free of charge. If you are researching a subject your local library will have well-trained staff who will be only too pleased to find information and advice on virtually any subject or issue, again for free.

There is a whole range of professional and trade associations that will provide free services to members. These are worth joining. In the UK the Institute of Directors, for example, offers a great many resources to its members. The Federation of Small Businesses for a reasonable annual membership fee will provide you with advice from top professionals.

Take advice only from someone who has got practical experience in the area of your enquiry. If I have a plumbing problem I get advice only from plumbers, not from neighbours or other individuals with good intentions. If I want advice on running my own business I am selective regarding what I take on board from the bank manager. After all, someone who works for a major multinational conglomerate with a regular monthly salary cannot identify directly with a sole trader. They deal with many entrepreneurs and have good advice from that perspective, which is different.

Do not take advice from someone who has got a vested interest unless that interest is totally in line with your own. Potential suppliers of services are looking to make sales. Their job is to sell to you and provide the arguments in favour of what they offer.

Be very careful about people around you encouraging you to take their advice, which is really suiting their personal outcomes not yours. People from large companies usually heed this as they are used to an environment where this is the norm. Being an employee, by definition, is working for someone else, so naturally the employer's outcomes will come first. I have yet to meet a manager who comes to the conclusion that the interests of the company are to make them redundant. They usually find reasons to make different decisions.

What knowledge do you require to be a successful entrepreneur?

You need to know:

- how to sell something for more than it costs you
- how to write a business plan
- your industry
- your market
- processes
- competitors
- what could go wrong
- the future outlook
- how to raise money
- how to set prices.

Knowing where to find knowledge quickly and cheaply for your particular business is essential. Knowledge is the key ingredient in decision making. Your decisions are limited by the knowledge you have. You have to learn to use those people and resources around you that already have that knowledge. Remember that knowledge only becomes power when acted upon and so you need to balance knowledge with action to be effective as an entrepreneur. A well-researched business plan will not bring in customers, that research has to be used to target your sales and marketing efforts.

Knowledge of the law

I find it interesting that Bill Gates, Sir Richard Branson and Howard Hughes all had lawyers in the family. To be an entrepreneur you need a streetwise knowledge of the law. Not the 'passing exams' type of knowledge of the law, but the practical knowledge of what exactly happens if someone does not pay you or breaks a contract. What, in reality, can you do about it? The law may be on your side but getting paid is a different matter. A patent or copyright might make you feel that you have secured your ideas, but how long would it take and how much would it cost to sue someone? Chasing money through the courts can take months or years. It is practical knowledge that is important. That is why entrepreneurs are more focused on cash inflows/outflows than sales/costs.

Be mean with your signature and always read small print; because there is so much of it, it can come back to haunt you too easily. Don't be afraid to renegotiate a standard contract or take your business elsewhere. Be aware of any statutes that will apply irrespective of anything agreed in a contract.

There are certain aspects of the law with which you have to familiarize yourself, at least the basic principles, for example: contracts of employment, terms and conditions of doing business, company reporting. But don't waste valuable time on trying to become a lawyer.

Knowing about money

All you need to know about money is your bank balance: how much money is going out and how much is coming in over the coming weeks. Everything else should be delegated.

Entrepreneurs don't suffer vanity. The ones who really make it big, spend a lot less on luxury goods than you might think. On the contrary, they invariably keep their drawing to a survival minimum until their business is well established. Even when they become very wealthy their habit of thrift persists. Thrift came to them really through their upbringing. For example, while he was still a child Paul Getty recorded every transaction.

Part of being thrifty is knowing exactly where you stand financially at any point.

Don't spend as though you have made your success before you have. Ask a successful entrepreneur: 'What is in your bank account right now? What is about to come in and go out?', and they know. In fact, on interviewing a wealthy entrepreneur he stated, 'When I started in business my only objective was to get as much money in my bank account as possible.' He tracked it daily.

Know the difference between an asset and a liability

Entrepreneurs think in simple terms. An asset is something that increases your wealth, a liability is something that reduces your wealth. The object of business, then, is to increase assets and minimize liabilities. It is that simple. In your business establish for everything whether it is an asset or a liability. Ask what you can do to increase the wealth earning properties of this asset.

What can you do to reduce the wealth draining of these liabilities?

Take an audit as follows:

- What assets do you have and how much do they make for you?
- How could they make you more money?
- What can you do to acquire more assets?
- What around you could become an asset?

I have defined a liability as something that costs you money. These you want to reduce as long as it does not impact on revenue.

- What liabilities do you have and how much do they cost you?
- How could they be reduced?
- How could they be eliminated?

Some items have an element of both asset and liability. For example, a sales representative costing £70,000 per annum in salary and related costs brings in sales of £150,000 per annum. I would define this employee as an asset bringing in £80,000. A bookkeeper, on the other, hand costing £17,000 per annum in salary and related costs is a liability. This exercise clarifies who is an asset and who is a liability, and who you should look after to ensure their loyalty and continued performance. This does not mean you do not look after your bookkeeper but monitor their productivity relative to cost. The two people in this example show that you should be less concerned with the £70k salary than with the £17k one.

To the established business, things should be clearer. An entrepreneurial business being new involves developing assets, i.e. new sales staff.

Progress now

Are the following assets or liabilities, or do they have an element of both?

property, motor cars, computers, stationery, shares, royalties

It is interesting to note that how entrepreneurs think about money is quite different from their corporate counterparts and professional moneymen. Assets to accountants and bankers are things they can repossess, things that offer security. Think about it: in a major international company the report and accounts would list the assets as property, fixtures and fittings, goodwill, money owed, computers, other equipment. Do these things make money or cost money to run?

What are your assets

On the audit you need to put a capital value on each asset. Remember to a recruitment agency an introduction fee would be about £5,000 for an average salary of an employee. You can double this for initial training. Therefore you need to value each staff member at this figure. Also your contacts and customers can be assets in this way. Who do you know who could become an income source and has also got a value?

People whom I have defined as liabilities are usually quite necessary to the business. Therefore, the gains to be made are not just on reducing their costs but also in making them more efficient. What value are they adding to the organization? Can it be done cheaper or for the same money? Can we make them more productive?

Progress now

Complete the following chart for your business. A few examples have been included.

Asset audit

Item	Estimated value	Possible value	Action
Key people:			
Me	100,000	200,000	Improve time management
Susan	75,000	100,000	Training course
Sales Manager			
Tim	35,000	75,000	Manage & motivate
Telesales			
Products	35,000	50,000	Market differently

Ideas	?	?	?
Contacts	?	?	?
Database	?	?	?

Liability audit

What are your liabilities, and what can be done to reduce them without reducing revenue or incurring other liabilities?

Rent
Salaries
Stationery
Advertising

Keeping your finger on the pulse

Many entrepreneurs are so caught up in the day-to-day challenges that they have no time to sit down and think. If they did so, they could have foreseen many of the events that become news. The future is predictable, it is just a matter of reading all the information that is around you. In the 'Information Age' there is more information around us than ever before.

People phone me often and say, 'Alex, you keep well informed. Is there going to be a recession?' My answer is yes, and I have always been right. Why? Because that is how the trade cycle works; what goes up then comes down. I also know that thinking there might be a recession coming makes people sharper entrepreneurs. Pressure produces performance. The point is, if you assume there is going to be a recession, you will take action now, when the pressure is not on, to secure your business and prosper from the situation. In practice, there is always a recession coming; we just do not know how soon.

I find it interesting that the same people never ask me if I think there is a boom coming. Their outlook seems to be that in a boom we are OK, just worry about the recessions. Upturns in the economy need as much planning to take advantage of the opportunities. Whatever the conditions in front, you need to be ahead of the game, sensitive to what is happening and to be able to interpret it. You do not have to be right every time, the important thing is to be prepared for whatever comes.

Once you start becoming a leader, making the news, you then have started to control your destiny. Like the surfer riding waves, you have to harness the energy of what is there, predict what is coming and react quickly. An unforeseen wave is what will knock you down. Note it is not the wave in itself but the fact that you did not see it coming which threatens you.

I therefore suggest that you invest time to keep well informed of whatever industry you are in. Sign up for some relevant internet newsletters, subscribe to any trade magazines, attend seminars and talks, join business groups. While you read keep asking yourself what I call ODQs: Opportunity Directional Questions. For example:

- Where is this all leading?
- How does this affect me?
- How could I benefit from this?
- What does not exist now but there is clearly an emerging demand for?
- What opportunities are advances in technology releasing?
- If I had £1million to invest right now, what would I do with it?

What ODQs do you think people like Bill Gates ask themselves on a daily basis? Remember, questions determine the focus of your mind. By deliberately setting questions you take control. Left to its own devices, your mind will tend to wander aimlessly; you need to harness its power.

Knowing the importance of difference

Being a creative entrepreneur means being a non-conformist. That is to say not accepting that the way things are is the way they should be or are going to be. We get so familiar with the things around us that we start to accept them. It is when we are in a fresh environment that we realize how much we took for granted. I suggest you read Bill Bryson to train your mind in doing this. He is an American with an English wife who has spent a significant amount of time in both countries. His book *Notes from a Small Island* sees England from an American viewpoint, while *The Lost Continent* sees America from an English point of view. I certainly have to thank Bill for my improved ability to see my own country and society a little differently. I read his books and I am inspired with no end of ideas.

People, though, do not like to change, and be careful of thinking, just because you have something that will improve people's lives, that there is a market for it. A market is what people will spend money on. If it is new then there is a strong chance that they have got to break an old spending habit first. Then you have to train them in the new habit of consuming what you provide, to ensure your repeat sales and benefits from loyalty. If you are starting out alone it may help to join a group of similar minded people. Look locally and you may find all sorts of associations and people meeting regularly. You can also subscribe to online networks.

Where the ideas come from

Inspiration for ideas often comes while not at work. This is because of the different perspective and mindset you are in.

Progress now

1 Think of something that you may find on the beach.
2 Apply any ideas, shapes, textures, thoughts, associated with that item to the new idea of operating a restaurant.
3 Consider the raw idea generated above and make it more commercially viable.

For the exercise above I thought of sand. Sand drops through your hand very easily. So I thought of having an egg timer on each table and when people sit down they turn the egg timer over. The restaurant promises to serve the customer before the sand has run through the egg timer or the customer will get a free bottle of house wine.

Commercial advantages:

- No real cost
- Advertising theme on promising to be served in less time than it takes to boil an egg.
- Novelty, fun atmosphere created in restaurant.
- People come for chance to get free wine.
- Free publicity in local papers and other media as it is news.
- Waiting staff can see who should be served next.

- Logo and number on printed egg cups which people can take with them and use when booking a table.

Here's another example: deck chairs. Now deck chairs are handy because they can be stacked and quickly prepared for use. They offer the flexibility of being able to use any amount of them at a time and they are relatively easy to store. I would apply the idea of deck chairs to a restaurant by financing each table. Investors would own shares in a particular table. The table would cost around £5,000 according to size and location in the restaurant. The investor would receive 25% of all the net takings for that table, as a sort of rental income. They have a secure, immediate and continual return for their investment. It would also be relatively easy to sell their investment. The restaurateur has multiple sources of finance.

Commercial advantages to be exploited:

- This idea focuses investors and the restaurateur on income per table. Both parties will constantly ask the question: 'How can we increase table income?'
- This leads to the idea that a restaurant need not restrict itself to selling food and drink at a table. What else might people be interested in buying while eating? How about having their car washed and polished?
- The restaurateur has a good formula for expansion of the business model.
- The customers could also rent the table by the quarter hour, and eat and drink all that they want. The rate for a quarter hour would vary according to demand. That way the potential income from busy periods could be maximized and custom during low periods be increased.
- Waiters from the restaurant could be contracted out to serve customers dinner at home. A list could be kept of contract waiters/chefs who are charged out to prepare any meal from their menu at the customer's home. A restaurant has limited capacity for sales because of the number of tables. Suddenly, like the deck chairs, the number of potential tables is greatly increased!

These ideas are crude and need refining. Then they need further refining when you actually launch them with the advantage of the feedback that you get. People find creating something from a blank space to be hard but improving a basic idea is easy. These techniques do nothing more than jump-start you.

Armchair entrepreneurs dream of one day having that magical idea like 'cats eyes' on which they can make their fortune. Ideas are the relatively easy part, the talent is in turning ideas into cash from customers.

Know thy future self

Imagine at a future time, you are on stage telling your success story so that others can be inspired. Take a moment to consider what you would say. How would you feel about that? Write that story now. Tell the audience about your proudest achievements. Explain how you got through your darkest moments.

Now make a decision to make that speech. Then keep going, whatever it takes, to get to that stage. How long it takes is not the key issue nor how you get there. Know why you are embarking on the entrepreneur route and make sure the reasons are compelling. Start and then make a decision to finish what you have started.

- What do you believe are the main traits of an entrepreneur?
- What would you like them to be?
- What does not happen fast enough?
- What happens too fast?

People who dream of being an entrepreneur and never have a go are usually very creative. They have to be creative to imagine inside their head a whole range of things so powerfully influencing which will stop them from going for their dream. In order to stop putting your ideas into practice you have to qualify as an exceptionally creative person.

Now think about having a go on your own. I want to know how you get yourself not to. Close your eyes. What images are there? Are you making negative images, say large pictures of terrible things, people with loud voices telling you not to do it? Is that your technique?

I have found that those who do have a go are similar in what they do internally to get going. To cross that bridge from dreams and ideas to commercial reality, they focus on what it would be like when it all goes right. They actually have a place for images of failure but they see themselves, really, working their way through these obstacles.

The three types of entrepreneurs

1 Create ideas, think of problems, plan a path around them, succeed.
2 Create ideas, do not think of problems, get started, fail.
3 Create ideas, think of problems, avoid starting, fail.

Creating ideas is easy, everyone can do that with some basic techniques of which there are many throughout this book. The next challenge is to think of any potential problems. The final stage is to work out a path around them. This is how top entrepreneurs do it. It is a very easy process, anyone can follow it.

Know your advantages

Economists like to talk of economies of scale bringing advantages as companies become larger. Less seems to have been written on what I would call 'acorn advantages'. These are the advantages of being a small growth company. Consider the following:

Growth company	Large company
simple management structure	complex management
all managers deal direct with customers	few managers deal with customers
personal service	meet with bureaucracy
call anytime	voicemail jail, rarely get through
all staff produce or sell	many admin functions
quick decisions	slow decisions
lead from the front	head office decisions

It depends on your industry, but whatever it is there will be economies of scale and also acorn advantages. It is important that you can recognize both in order to help your decision making. In fact, so important have acorn advantages become that many large companies have gone to great lengths to build autonomous small companies with minimal head office functions to maintain the energy and advantages of being small.

Of course, if you are really clever you can use franchising or network marketing and take the advantages of being both big and small, like McDonald's and Amway have done, both organizations producing a substantial number of very wealthy people.

Learning from others

Experience is valuable when the lessons are learnt and behaviours and decision making changed. Even better than this is to learn from the experience of others. It is an excellent short cut saving a lot of time and pain.

Wisdom comes with age and experience, but only if one chooses to learn from the experiences. Otherwise we just repeat things. Many famous entrepreneurs went bust several times before making a great success. Some still went bust after making their fortune and then made another one. This shows that the real value of their enterprise was not in the tangible assets but in their skills, developed through learning from their experiences.

Most entrepreneurs seem to have really hit success in their fifties or later, showing just how long was their learning curve. Yet they did not give up; they continued to pursue their dream. No doubt they had days when they felt like throwing in the towel. One of my objectives with this book is to accelerate your journey to being a better entrepreneur by taking tips and advice from those who have gone before you.

People asking me for my advice on entrepreneurs are most interested in the initial transition from being a full-time employee to getting their idea off the ground, and establishing a firm foundation in which to grow.

Progress now

Think of a small business in your locality that you use.

Which three advantages of being small are they failing to exploit?

Entrepreneur interview: David Leyshon

David is owner/MD of CBSbutler.

Alex: What is your career background?

David: I was brought up on my parents' farm and had an entrepreneurial streak then, and was always looking for more ways to sell the produce. I was also academically focused and went to university where I played rugby and had a good time generally. I was not sure what I really wanted to do.

I qualified as a geologist followed by a few graduate trainee jobs, eventually falling into the recruitment industry. It was a developing, exciting sector and a place where I could make a lot of money very quickly. It appealed to my entrepreneurial side and I quickly made lots of commission.

I went from success to success and an opportunity came up to manage the UK and Dutch operations by my then MD breaking away and inviting me to join him. I had a lot of fun, though also made and spent a lot of money! Approaching my late twenties I took my long-term career ambitions more seriously. This led to me joining a larger more stable American organization called Butler; they had been around for decades and were listed on NASDAQ.

The European MD was a good mentor to help me develop. After a few years though the business ran into problems and a lot of businesses in the group were sold off to survive. The MD was removed and I was offered the job at 30. I wished to turn this to my advantage and tried a management buy out. This was rejected so I encouraged them to invest in the business.

The investment was promised but never really happened, so I looked for another move. Then the telecoms recruitment market took a dive and head office was desperately cash short. In 2003 I made another pitch for a management buy out. We stretched ourselves but managed the buy out without losing shares externally. We grew in sales and profits, and six months later bought another small company.

Today we are now running at £20million sales and £1million profit with 50 staff. Our goal is an exit over the next five years, either by trade sale or AIM listing.

Alex: How do you define success?

David: For me it is financial security, independence and to achieve business goals. I want to grow a sustainable business, something to be proud of. I am looking for £5million in the bank.

I aim to be able to retire early and then would like to invest in start ups and be a consultant to pass on my guidance in how to grow a business quickly. I also have a range of external interests, especially travel and history.

Alex: What advice would you give somebody starting out?

David: Consult the right people. Do your research thoroughly especially if you are going into a new area. Sometimes you need to move fast in business, but going in blind is taking unnecessary risks. I believe in a good business plan and model, and someone strong on the financial side.

Complement your skills: if you are strong on the sales side find someone who is strong on the financial/admin side and then maximize their strengths.

Seek out a good mentor at an early stage to learn from. Someone that you respect for their success. Learning from them is better than learning through your own mistakes. Surround yourself with success.

Alex: How do you spot an opportunity?

David: You need to be alert, constantly speaking with people, reviewing all the business press. Our management team are tasked once a fortnight to spot opportunities in their sector. Spotting a trend, brainstorming with colleagues. At CBSbutler we have an innovation forum and reward ideas. Knowledge then needs turning into opportunities.

Alex: What would you have done differently if you could go back in time?

David: I would have studied business early on to give me a good grounding. I suggest to people starting out to take a night school course or similar.

Alex: What made you want to become an entrepreneur?

David: I never set out to be an entrepreneur. My need to be independent and my 'hatred' of corporate bureaucracy and politics were the drivers. I don't fit into that environment, I would rebel. I need to set my own agenda and live by my own decisions, to have freedom and be in charge of my own destiny. When I was younger I could not wait for success. I wanted to achieve high earnings very quickly, I could not wait for a structured career advancement programme.

Alex: How do you motivate yourself when things don't go to plan?

David: Well they do go wrong all the time. I realize that business is all about facing problems and I address them. Even in the good times there are constant challenges, problems and setbacks. I believe that unless you are getting these then you are not advancing. I keep focused, positive, work hard, prioritize and know that I will bounce back having been through it many times. I take a positive out of every situation. As a leader I know people will look to me for help, I have an excellent FD who has many good ideas, practical skills and who has been crucial to the support of the business.

Three tips

1 Be thrifty in all that you do.
2 Always look for leverage.
3 Keep moving forward.

Two tasks

1 Reflect over the last week until you learn two things of value.
2 Join Club Entrepreneur (www.clubentrepreneur.co.uk).

09

better skills than your competitors

In this chapter you will learn:

- that learning from others is faster and less painful
- how to apply skills from other aspects of your life
- that you must get the most out of all of your assets
- how to develop your skill of focus
- the skills you must be good at

'A wise woman always learns, a wiser woman lets wise women do the learning for her and heeds their advice.'

Alex McMillan

'Don't borrow, buy what you want, when you can afford it.'

Austin Reynolds

Learning for business success

Business is not an intellectual exercise. There are intellectual entrepreneurs: for example, the founders of Google™ and eBay® were well educated. The vast majority, though, are not, practicality and action being the key required skills.

Most successful entrepreneurs become successful from their late fifties. Those who start up in the fifty-plus age group have far higher success rates. This suggests that there is a great deal to learn about running your own business. By virtue of a specific set of circumstances encountered while growing up, some rare individuals instinctively do the right things from early on. Sir Richard Branson, Bill Gates and Sir Alan Sugar are examples. They usually don't know what makes them successful, they just follow their instincts.

Where there is success, there are behaviours, attitudes, patterns that led to that success. Therefore, there is a recipe that once found can be duplicated. This book is that recipe with the intention of saving you years of hard knocks to learn through your own experience what works and what does not.

Unfortunately, would-be entrepreneurs are mostly strongly independent with a self-confident belief in themselves. All good qualities, which tends to mean that they are destined to learn the hard way.

Most learning in business comes from feedback, it is iterative. You try something and get feedback and in light of this improve your offering the second time around.

Skills from other aspects of your life

Sensei Paul Elliott has built up a thriving karate school and develops in his students valuable skills, which are useful in life in many ways. He has coached many adults and children to black belt level and has built a business that is his passion. He is living his dream.

He teaches how to:

- be totally sensitive as to what is going on around you
- conquer ego and vanity
- be disciplined
- be respectful
- be humble
- be well behaved
- take a fall without being hurt
- fight while being on the ground
- keep fighting after several blows
- fight against someone of higher skill or advantage
- change your style, and why
- never give up
- keep fighting fit
- avoid fights.

Pretty good stuff for an entrepreneur, don't you think? Every one of these skills is vital for success as an entrepreneur. Not surprisingly, many of his students are successful entrepreneurs. You could learn more of the skills of running a business from karate school than from business school. I know you will have other skills in your life that the lessons can be directly useful in your business, if you think to apply them. You have far more of the skills that you need than you think.

Skills in 'grasping the nettle'

Who has not had an opportunity come their way and talked and thought about it until the opportunity has gone. That is the thing about opportunities: they tend to have a short shelf life. You need to analyse and make full and proper judgement, but recognize when this is done and the time for action has arrived. I have seen too many would-be entrepreneurs researching, developing and thinking until they missed the boat! Hesitation is as bad as not taking enough time to weigh up the options. Work on refining your judgement skills as to make an effective balance between not being too hasty or hesitating.

Skills in getting the best out of everything

You have £10,000 to invest. You go to three well-established banks.

- The first one offers you 10% interest.
- The second offers 8% interest.
- The third offers 4% interest.
- The fourth offers no interest at all.
- The fifth would charge you 10% interest to look after your money.

How would you spread your investment among these banks?

I would put it all in the bank paying 10% and look forward in year two to receiving 10% on the first year's interest as well. Now I think most of you would do the same. If you were extremely risk averse and not trusting of banks you might spread it equally among the four to reduce the possible downside. I cannot even imagine why anybody would make a deposit in bank 5. This is a very easy principle that works, but people don't apply it in their businesses.

In your business you have a whole range of resources: money, contacts, goodwill, client database, computers, website, people, premises, motor cars, ideas, market intelligence, locations. My question is what rate of return are you getting from these resources? Which bank have you invested them in?

Progress now

1 Write a list of all the resources of any nature, you currently have in your business.

2 Assess, as a percentage, whether you are getting a full return, part return, zero return or negative return from this resource.

3 Decide what you can do to maximize the return from each resource.

4 Repeat this exercise every month, ensuring that the returns from each resource are included in your new resource list.

5 Now take a moment to think of the three resources you have at your disposal but have omitted from the list above.

Market research has its uses, but often what the public say to you is quite different from what they will do. For example, 20 years ago how many people in England would have responded positively to the suggestion of a new type of restaurant, cheap and clean, where you eat out of cardboard boxes with your fingers instead of using plates, knives and forks? Who would have thought five years ago that the tea drinking British would flock to coffee shops?

Skills in developing good habits

There are two aspects to developing good habits: breaking redundant or destructive habits and forming new useful ones. Forming new habits is easier. The beauty of habits is just that, once they are formed they happen automatically without any conscious effort. For example, let us say that you wanted to keep a positive focus and eradicate those down periods when things get on top of you.

Progress now

Write down or use a computer to type the following in whatever you deem to be an attractive colour, print size and typeface.

Success focus

Five things that are really good news at the moment:

1

2

3

4

5

My three targets for this week:

1

2

3

One thing that I will shortly give myself as a reward for accomplishing the above:

Now attach this to the wall where you work. At the start of the week fill in the answers and each day refer to them briefly, doing nothing more than reading through once. At the start of each new week take it down and repeat the process. I guarantee if you do this rather simple exercise you will maintain a consistently positive outlook.

Shall I tell you why the exercise above works? On interviewing very successful entrepreneurs I found that they all did something effectively like this. I asked them: 'How do you keep yourself motivated consistently, irrespective of the highs and the lows?' They responded that they would keep focusing on what is going right and on something that they feel good about which is coming up soon. It is that simple to take control of your habits.

Progress now

Taking the simple concept above, how else could you use this idea to assist you in your business?

Skills in information management

Established businesses have a great deal of information at their disposal, statistics about their business, client databases, all their experience and lessons so far. Entrepreneurs face uncertainty if they have no track record and limited resources. New products or ideas do not have trends that can be analysed so easily. For this they need to be in touch with their potential market. The internet has changed this factor dramatically, allowing free access, apart from your time, to a multitude of research material.

Skills in managing capital

Only take on debt if it is being invested for an expected higher return. That is where you can make the money earn a better rate of return than you are paying. Never spend a penny on anything that is not mission critical while you are in debt. Every penny saved is a penny invested in your business.

Prepare for every eventuality you can think of. However well you do this, you will still find yourself facing something completely unexpected. The way to deal with this is to have some reserve ready to tide you over a lean period. Referring to the game of Monopoly® this principle holds true. You need to be able to take the cost of one or two unlucky throws of the dice in order to survive while the other players approach your investments. It is a simple idea, it holds true and you need to practise it.

Skills in managing expenses

Expenses have a habit of rising up to the same amount as our sales income. So many companies I see only investigate and monitor costs when a cool wind blows. Cost discipline is more important during the good times when the pressure is off. Because the pressure is off, it is no longer your main focus. If you make it your focus from the start the pressure will never be on so much for you as for your competitors. Entrepreneurs make the mistake of getting carried away with their own success, a recipe for future failure.

Some people, when given a contract by a large corporation, assume that the deal is 'take it or leave it on our terms'. Trust me, this is not the case. I regularly inspect terms, propose changes and shop around until I find someone who will deal on my terms. How? Just don't accept what they say and keep not accepting it, be stubborn and persistent and you shall prevail. To be an entrepreneur you have to learn to fight your corner, and fight for every penny.

If your costs are £20,000 and your sales are £19,000 a month are you in profit or loss? Loss. Now, if you could trim 10% off your costs without affecting sales where would you be? Profit. Business is simple, don't make it hard: this is one of the major messages I have learnt from successful entrepreneurs. The secret of their success sometimes seems to be that there is no secret, and knowing this, they just get on with it, instead of pursuing magic complex formulas from the latest management guru.

A good entrepreneur cannot reduce costs by 10% because every expenditure was justified on the above basis ahead of time unless needs have changed. Therefore, the trick is to look at cost saving behaviour. Here are examples from entrepreneurs I have interviewed.

- Instead of a serviced office convert your garage.
- Instead of buying new laptops and PCs buy at government auctions.
- Travel economy class.
- Use the phone to communicate if travel can be avoided.
- Send an email rather than make a phone call.
- Incentivize staff with bonuses linked to results.
- Avoid mobile phones unless absolutely essential.
- Use email instead of paper post.
- Utilize all the free advertising and promotional methods available to you before spending.

- Drive used cars or use public transport.
- Buy your office furniture second hand.
- Whenever possible employ staff based at home.
- Know about and take any government assistance available.
- Focus on one thing at a time, get that up and running then focus on the next thing.

Skills in standing apart

A trait of the self-made rich is that they tend to move in the opposite direction from which most investors move. Paul Getty, the oil billionaire, was a classic example of this. Throughout his business career he constantly went against the crowd. He bought in a down market, sold in a booming market, invested in countries that his competitors were pulling out of, expanded during recessions.

Using your skills to be free

To a lot of people money means worry and fear of the lack of it. Therefore, I think that wanting to be financially free is a good goal for an entrepreneur even if that is not the main goal. This worry and fear often means that when people make money they store it up in every possible way to be secure against every eventuality that could happen. If a person has known extreme poverty this desire is even stronger. In the UK many of our greatest contributors to creating enterprising businesses and to our national wealth come from the Asian community, a community which knows, understands and feels only too vividly what a poor economy without a welfare state means. Members of this community understand that if you have not got something put by for a rainy day, you go hungry, literally.

Some entrepreneurs who I have met seem to think that life's purpose is a competition to see how much money you can amass. Therefore, what from this point is the motivation to make money? The main ones I come across are power, status, greed and financial security, but the most common and best one is really loving what you do, which usually means controlling your own destiny, while amassing money is a pleasant extra side effect. As a recruiter I used to ask people: 'If you won £1million on the lottery tomorrow would you change your job?' If the answer is 'yes' I consider them to be in the wrong job.

Interestingly most entrepreneurs of whom I ask this question would continue what they are doing and the money would give them more opportunities in what they are doing. There comes a point, quite soon actually, when people have no further cause to worry about money and having everything they want.

Does McDonald's have the best skills in baking the best burgers?

Entrepreneurs see a business as a machine to make money. If the machine works well they then duplicate it and make more money. It is, in essence, to them a system. Entrepreneurs focus far less on that magical product that will just catch the public's imagination and sell like hot cakes. Think of your business enterprise as designing a system to make money. Many inventors and entrepreneurs go wrong because they think it is all about coming up with a winning product; that is 5% of the answer at most.

McDonald's entrepreneur Ray Kroc bought the original restaurant from the two McDonald brothers, and was obsessed with details and processes. He listed every process in the operation until it was as efficient as possible. He designed a business system. When it was finished he duplicated profit by duplicating the winning formula. His target was to own as much property as possible; he was not interested in burgers.

Sir Richard Branson is one of the world's most famous and successful record producers. Was he a music lover, a musician who wanted to run his own label? No. He was in touch with what musicians could offer and what teenagers wanted to buy and matched the two in a business system called Virgin. Too much interest in the product takes your focus off the business. If the priority is profits the focus must be on producing and getting to market your product in an efficient manner. He had the same access to musicians that anyone else had.

Skills in reading people

A common mistake for someone new in business is assuming that people are logical, rational and will make buying decisions according to their best interests. It just does not work that way.

Progress now

Go to your local largest retailer (Sainsbury's, Wal-Mart, Mammouth, for example) and instead of shopping and focusing on products focus on the shoppers. Just stand in one key spot with a commanding view and look at people as they make decisions to buy things. Look specifically for how they walk, stop, plan their route through the shop, backtrack, pause, are influenced by merchandising or not, talk to other shoppers, talk to staff, put things back, put things in their trolley. How closely do they look at prices? Do couples stay together or separate?

- What different patterns do you notice emerging?
- Are there any differences according to socio-economic groupings?
- Are there clear stereotypes evident? For example, do older people do things differently from young people?
- Do men shop differently from women?
- How logical and rational do you now think people are on buying decisions?

Skills in constantly improving efficiency

Progress now

Does anything frustrate you?

Is there an aspect of the world around you that could in your opinion be better?

What would you like to see done about it?

How could you do something about it at a profit?

Every aspect of every enterprise can be improved, and then improved again. That is a belief worth adopting because it will get you constantly to look for improvement. Even after you have just improved a system you immediately start criticizing to find the next level of improvement. Start by looking at a market and seeing how the current suppliers operate. If you can spot an improvement somewhere you have got yourself an opportunity. Entrepreneurs don't just create new products and services, they look to produce the same things at less unit cost.

Look for waste: waste in time, materials, finance, energy, manpower and market advantages. Organizations as they grow tend to develop excesses. These are usually in terms of things that were once useful but no longer serve a purpose and nobody notices. Early in my career I was a management accountant responsible for producing a large document of more than 30 separate pages produced monthly and distributed to all directors and other senior managers.

I did a quick survey to find out which return was read and used the most. I found out some interesting and unexpected results.

- Nobody read all 30 pages.
- Assumptions about the figures varied between managers.
- Nine of the managers never read the report at all.
- Twelve pages were read by nobody.

I made a report to my Financial Director with a proposed new format. He was dismissive and told me to work only on what he gave me. I had just lost my virginity to the world of office politics. In future I kept my ideas to myself. When he suggested anything I told him how good I thought it was. I eventually left and decided that when I had my own business I was going to encourage new ideas, always be looking to be more efficient and even encourage criticism of myself. In fact, I then worked for an organization that actively encouraged ideas and allowed staff to carry them out. My point is that if you pick an inefficient industry there are always going to be opportunities to improve on providing the same product. Those with a large chunk of existing market share are likely to be focused on it and thus miss new markets emerging.

Many people in business think they are cleverer than they are and this can be used to great advantage by the entrepreneur. Success understandably encourages this trait. This is excellent news: the more they think like this the less they look for new ideas. That means they will stop progressing and provide opportunities for entrepreneurs.

You, of course, must guard against behaving like this yourself. It is the blindfold that covers the entrepreneur spirit. Again we all have the entrepreneur gift; we have to think more of unfolding and releasing what is already there.

Skills in time management

The most efficient skill of an entrepreneur is in managing their time effectively. To do everything you have to do needs a 100-hour long day! Therefore you have to be efficient in every possible way.

Mary runs her own business and her added value to the business is estimated at £20,000 per month. Each hour of her time is worth £100. The value of each hour's work depends upon the level at which she is working. If she always tries to work at a higher pay rate, she will add more value to her enterprise.

1	taking action to make deals	£500 per hour
2	creating and developing	£400 per hour
3	on telephone calls	£100 per hour
4	meeting people	£100 per hour
5	training new staff	£75 per hour
6	emailing	£50 per hour
7	meeting sales reps	£25 per hour
8	surfing the internet for information	£10 per hour
9	filing	£5 per hour
10	looking for lost papers	£1 per hour
11	waiting to be put through	£1 per hour

Replace Mary's 11 tasks with those that you do in a typical week. Put them in order of importance. Note in your diary how much time you spend on each and total it up for the week. Multiply it out and the total represents your contribution to the business. Now set a target to eradicate, delegate, reduce time spent on the items lower down the list, and spend that time on items higher up the list. Your target therefore is to add at least £500 of value per hour consistently.

Time management has more relevance to the entrepreneur because when he or she starts he will usually be working alone, or certainly with a small number of people, and therefore is responsible for all aspects of the company. Changing hats from accountant, salesperson, recruiter, manufacturer, etc. is going to make impossible demands on time. When you grow, labour becomes more specialized and thus more efficient.

This means that you have to be very disciplined. To do this you have to work back your long-term vision to a quarterly, monthly, weekly then daily objective list. This way you know that at the end of every day you have moved that much closer to your goal. This is the simplest and most effective way to make sure that you are productive and not just busy.

I record this information on a document that I refer to daily. The day's targets I write on a separate piece of paper at the beginning of each day. Each morning I read through my long-term goals, then I refer to the 'How to' section, which has a page for the current quarter then 13 pages for each week of the quarter. The week pages I complete first thing Monday morning so that my week is focused on where I want to get to.

It is very motivating to see how I am consistently moving forwards to success. If I have any decisions to make I always make them with reference to my 'success controller'. That makes them more scientific and less vulnerable to emotional sways.

Skills in drawing out good ideas from the people around you

> **Progress now**
>
> Next week do something different, anything at all, for example dress differently. You will be pleasantly surprised how breaking one minor habit gives you the advantage of a new perspective and the ability to break bigger habits.

When you are thinking start by ignoring boring concepts such as possibility. I asked a telesales person the other day if she could have any product at all, however unreasonable, what would she ask for? She answered as follows.

'I would like a phone system that had a screen with four sections on it. The display would have on it in real time what the other person was saying, top left, and thinking, bottom left. In addition, suggested answers to their questions, top right, and suggested questions to ask, bottom right.'

If you could make such a product there is clearly a market for it, of at least one. I think that many people would happily invest in such a device. With accurate digital electronics and sophisticated software abilities it is possible to go a long way towards developing that device. Subtle changes in voice tone could be identified and meanings printed on screen. Verbal and non-verbal voice patterns could be analysed in real time.

Progress now

Ask five people around you:

'If you could buy any product at all that does not exist yet, what would you buy? Be as unreasonable as you like.'

People will respond with all sorts of weird ideas. This is the raw material, which you can then sculpt into a workable commercial prospect.

Skills in letting people go if you have to

Staff can be your greatest but also your highest risk asset. They can perform badly, be off ill, need constant supervision, have emotional problems, let you down and arrive late, resign, sell your secrets to competitors or go on strike. At the end of each month there is one thing secure about them, they will want their salaries. If you have achieved only half the sales that month they are unlikely to be happy with half salaries.

I suggest that when you employ staff, particularly at the beginning of the life of a new venture, if it doesn't work out in some way, they will get another job while you go into liquidation. Their concept of loyalty is linked directly to a pay cheque. From your perspective they are an investment. Think very carefully before making an offer and if it does not work out you have to terminate the employment quickly.

At interview both you and they are likely to make promises you do not keep. Nearly every manager I have met has had experiences of people not living up to the potential they showed at interview. Nearly every employee I have ever met has a story of broken promises.

Skills in cold calling

When starting a new venture you are going to have to attract customers from a cold start. I have trained many professional sales people, and wrote my first book on sales, and cold calling is the thing they dread most. Part of this is the balance in their mind of success to failure. You can make 100 calls before you have a success. So your mind is registering that 99% of your time is unproductive and thus giving you a growing feeling of rejection and failure.

I have found a simple concept that totally changes this set up.

How many appointments turn into a deal?   X
How much is the value of the average deal?   Y
How many calls on average to get an appointment?   Z
Then each call is worth X multiplied by Y divided by Z

For example, if your average deal size is £6,000 (Y) and one in three visits (X) is turned into a deal and it takes on average 100 calls (Z) to make an appointment, the value of each call is worth £20. If you focus and get your people to focus on this figure then their mind will be focusing on making more £20s, and to do that you make more calls which leads to more deals. If on the other hand they make 90 calls and feel they have achieved nothing for their work, their motivation level will seriously drop. I took this idea a step further and invented something called the Points Award scheme. In this scheme I put a points value on every piece of work and achievement. Bonuses were then paid according to points. This way every task that everyone in the organization does is respected, valued and encouraged. You can do this for yourself.

Sell to people who are prospects for what you have to sell. It is always easier to sell to people who have already bought a similar product. A new book is sold to people who have bought books before. A new style of training shoe will appeal to people who have previously bought training shoes. Sounds obvious but millions are spent daily by entrepreneurs re-learning these lessons the hard way.

Sales, selling and salesperson skills

Many people have a fear of selling, and many of those people are working in selling! I have found, in practice, that this fear can be overcome in a few minutes.

What are the top three things people do not like about receiving sales calls, and immediately go on the defensive and resist?

1 Lies: for example, this is a courtesy call. You have been specially picked. We specialize in people just like you. You have won a holiday for two in Hawaii.

2 Script reading.

3 Pushiness.

The top three things people do like from sales calls which often encourages them to place orders are:

1 Honesty and coming straight to the point: 'I am calling to try to persuade you to buy from me.'

2 Listening and answering questions. People prefer to talk and be listened to than listen.

3 Relevance: there is something in it for them.

It amazes me how quickly sales people drop price. They clearly believe that this is the way to secure a deal. More thought needs to be given to the perceived value for money of your product. By discounting you are in danger of reducing its perceived value. Your profit is determined by your margin multiplied by the number of sales. If you halve the margin you now have to double sales. Notice I use the word 'perceived'. What are you doing to raise the value of your product, relative to alternatives, in your customers' mind? Focus on this and you will set a price in their mind. The golden rule is, if in doubt put prices up and sales will probably go up, not just in revenue but also in volume terms.

Skills in turning ideas into products that sell

Here is an exercise to train you to think about prospects from a marketing person's point of view.

Progress now: *Example*

You have invented a new machine that will cost about £5, a homing device to find anything you lose, using invisible marking. Lost mobile phones, keys, handbags, wallets, watches, glasses can be located immediately.

Your task is to think of ten ideas of to whom you can sell your invention.

Example ideas

1 *People who are constantly losing such items. Therefore, I would immediately want to approach sellers of mobile phones, spectacles and watches.*

2 *Insurance companies might have listings available in some form of people who lose things (because they make claims).*

3 *Insurance brokers' offices might be a good prospect.*

4 *Professions that might have a specialized use for such a device, for example security guards with a variety of keys, to detect one set from a bunch.*

5 *The device could be used for locating people easily within a building.*

6 *People who do not know each other can identify one another at a meeting place.*

7 *Sell it to my personal contacts in order to get some initial cash and feedback.*

8 *Ask my network of contacts for their ideas.*

9 *Talk to motor vehicle retailers about buying in bulk and giving the device away to each customer as a promotion of their services.*

10 *Approach the RAC (Royal Automobile Club) to promote it. Their interest could be in reducing the time wasting calls they get from people who cannot get access to their car.*

Now it's your turn.

Progress now

You have noticed while driving that the vast majority of cars on the road carry no passengers. It occurs to you that you could set up an agency to organize lifts around the country. What you need is people travelling and people wanting lifts or things delivered to register with you. Your vision is of a major distribution company, and the beauty is that you would not have to seek an investor to buy vehicles. You consider that computers are so sophisticated now you can buy a database matching service linking offers to wants. You charge 15% arrangement fee to the vehicle owner. You produce a price list, which they adhere to.

Having got the systems set up, your challenge is that you have no drivers nor customers to match together.

I want ten ideas as to how you can practically get the business off the ground.

Skills in spotting future trends

Many entrepreneurs start by taking what they did when employed by a big company and offering these services. Others start a business which is really based on a hobby. These are good motivations, as they tend to have passion, enthusiasm, knowledge and experience associated with them. However, they are missing one crucial element: your focus to make money should be on what customers are going to buy in the future. Ask yourself this question and then ask how you can use your talents and experience to ride this wave.

Find something that is on the increase. Visualize yourself five years into the future. What do you expect your industry to look like? If you like, start by going back five years and write down ten things that changed during that time. Where is society heading? What overwhelming trends are rising in force and going to make major changes in how people spend their money? I do not think this is hard to do, but it has to be done. Make sure that your passion is matched by a set of customers.

Progress now

For what do you think there will be an increase in demand? How can you benefit from this trend?

A skill taken from Bruce Lee

In the opening sequences to one of my favourite films, Bruce Lee taps a trainee on the head saying, 'Don't think, feel'. In martial arts combat, your focus needs to be external specifically on the opponent and at the same time all around you. In business you also need awareness all the time of any potential threat around you. As soon as you start thinking your focus lost. Apply this philosophy and you will go far with marketing. You must be sensitive to how the customer will react and instinctively be there fast to meet their needs. As soon as you start thinking of what attack to use, you are going to be second. The bloody nose can come quicker in martial arts, which is one of the reasons that I think that karate is excellent training for business.

In this world of rising technology, major changes are constantly happening. The internet does not recognize individual countries. Therefore marketing people need a totally different perspective. The development in telecomms means that we are increasingly moving in to a world of mobile intelligence. Anyone who has a job which is basically processing zeros and ones will be replaced by technology. All of these factors are going to make major changes every month for at least the next ten years. If technological advancement stopped totally tomorrow it would take at least this long to absorb all the improvements that have been made already but have not been fully introduced yet. All of this means that there has been no time or place more opportune than right now.

The skill of mastery of illusion

When they are growing, entrepreneurs are often limited by working capital. A growing company by definition has always got a cash flow drag. One of the practical ways around this is to contract out some of the work until you are bigger. For example, you have orders in for whatever it is that you do but cannot satisfy them because you cannot afford to employ the staff. Why not subcontract the work to a competitor for a percentage off the top? This client will still be bringing the business in to you.

Skills in persistent motivation

In business, people need a lot of training and motivation to get over failure or something not working. The natural inclination is clearly to give up. I find that engineers seem to have a much better mindset. For example, have you ever watched a mechanic fix a car? They gather information and make a judgement about what action has to be taken. They try it and it does not work.

Do they give up? No. They keep trying something else until it does work. On the way they seem to find that the problem becomes more and more interesting.

Scientists and engineers consider experimentation and getting lots of things wrong to be the natural path to success. I used to work for a major pharmaceutical company. We had whole teams of people conducting research which had produced no direct commercially valuable results for years.

A significant skill is being able to remain enthusiastic while enduring failure (and enough cash flow to see you through it). Have you ever noticed that whatever knock you take, time heals? This is because the recorded memory of the experience becomes further and further away, literally. Your brain will probably code time with images of recent past or future quite near to you, and events long in the past or future further away. So all you have to do with a negative memory of a knock is to push the images in your mind far away to where you keep the five-years-ago memories.

While you are at it, why not bring forward and relive three really positive experiences that you had over the last five years and two of the best jokes you have ever heard? With the images well away from you, the negative feelings will also be well away. You can concentrate on the valuable learnings and opportunities that the experience gave you. Just ask a couple of well-directed questions and your unconscious mind will burrow away while you do something else, then interrupt you with the answers when it is ready.

Progress now

On which skills do you need to concentrate to personally develop the most as an entrepreneur?

Entrepreneur interview: Emyr Williams

Alex: What is your career background?

Emyr: I left school at 16 and worked on the family farm. I then went off to agricultural college and did a Marketing course before going to London to make my fortune. My first position was telephone selling subscriptions, a hard job but gave me the opportunity to learn. Nine months later, I moved to another publishing company in direct marketing, where I was made redundant. I stayed in publishing though, eventually becoming a director of a company that was quoted on AIM. After three years I left to try and build something myself.

'Business Bricks' was an email newsletter for start ups and small businesses. I looked for a partner. I literally sat down and made a list of what I thought I was good at and the skills I needed from a business partner. He ticked the blank boxes and had other attributes to me. We are now currently running the website www.bytestart.co.uk with ezines which have become among the highest visited in the industry. It is all growing fast and we have hit all targets which we set on a six monthly basis.

Alex: How do you define success?

Emyr: Success to me is enjoying life, being a good person and to make £1million pounds. I measure myself by how much money I am earning and its rate of increase.

Alex: What advice would you give somebody starting out?

Emyr:

- Don't underestimate how long it takes. If you are starting from scratch and not done it before you need to understand how long it takes to get things going. Business has to evolve at natural pace.

- If you have raised money don't spend it all in the first six months.

- Get used to rejection and failures. Don't be afraid of getting things wrong. Toughen up and plough ahead.

- Make as many friends as you can. When networking, find out how you can help them as they will then be more likely to come back and help you. People come back to me years down the line.

- Celebrate success. If you have a good quarter celebrate it, treat yourself, so you can remember the good times when things are tough. By doing so I trained myself to focus on success, it eliminates negative thoughts. So if I have to make some cold calls, it does not bother me because I am focusing on the success I am going for.

Alex: How do you spot an opportunity?

Emyr: Let the market guide you. A gap in the market might be for a good reason, nobody wants it. The market will tell you if it is a good product. A personal experience of something you cannot find is a good start. I also consider that if a business is in a competitive market then this is a good thing, as it shows there are paying customers available. You just have to find your niche.

Alex: What would you have done differently if you could go back in time?

Emyr: I would change nothing. Everything that has happened helped create who I am today. It has given me the experiences, knowledge, contacts and skills.

Alex: What made you want to become an entrepreneur?

Emyr: My father; he always worked for himself and this gave me an innate desire to be my own boss. He instilled the value of hard work and integrity in my early years. I always wanted to run a multinational company, not necessarily for myself but working for others put me in this direction. I also always wanted to make a million pounds and enjoy the journey. The thought of retirement scares me, I never imagine not working in some way. I love being in business, doing deals and meeting interesting people.

Three tips

1 Focus on your strengths.
2 Keep up to date on your sector.
3 Buy an MP3 and fill it with business and motivational material.

Two tasks

1 Write down two dozen resources available to you.
2 Delegate something which is not in your skill set.

Please note that the author with Dr Howard Bailey, an expert on learning in the business education sector has developed a game called 'Start Up' to help you acquire the practical skills needed to become successful in your own business, and is available from www.ClubEntrepreneur.co.uk.

10

streetwise sales and marketing

In this chapter you will learn:

- the first step to sales is finding a market
- to talk to as many people as possible
- who to contact and what to say to them
- how to do marketing without a budget
- 100 result producing questions for every situation

'The fight is won or lost far away from witnesses – behind the lines, in the gym and out there on the road, long before I dance under those lights.'

Muhammad Ali

'You can have everything in life that you want if you will just help enough other people get what they want.'

Zig Ziglar

This chapter offers some tips to help you develop sales. The appendix to this chapter is a reference source of 100 questions in 10 areas to ask a prospect, customer and yourself in order to increase sales.

Market research

Before you start selling you should have clarified the market that you are approaching and best pricing policy. When you have done this remember that market research is not a one-off activity. It happens with every sale, enquiry and click on your website. You continually hone and change your offer to meet customer needs in a way that will make you most profit. That builds a strong element of safety into your business.

In writing business plans would-be entrepreneurs often estimate sales. When they come into contact with the real world they find the market does not behave as rationally as they thought. They start to realize how illogical people are and how strong brand loyalty is. Often, reaching that market can also present problems.

You need to address these issues before you start selling.

Streetwise promotion

Promotion is informing a prospective customer about and then persuading them to take up your offer. This covers branding, the building of a consistent identity and set of values associated with your offer. In practice, it might mean wearing printed Polo shirts bearing your company name and logo (sell them to get others to promote you), car stickers, websites, directory listings, sponsorships, giving free talks. The list is as endless as the ideas you can generate. I have found that trying different methods is the most effective way to truly find out what works best. Then stick to it.

Streetwise selling

Promotional activity may, if you are lucky, get customers to contact you. Winners, though, don't like to wait, they like to get a head start over their competitors. So I suggest that you get on your phone and you get in your car and talk to as many people as possible.

Here is a simple (because selling is simple) process to follow that will lead to success.

1 Before you make contact, ensure that you are contacting a worthwhile prospect.
2 Before you make contact ensure you are in an enthusiastic, motivated, positive mood. Be prepared for more rejection than acceptance.
3 Before you make contact ensure you know all the benefits of your offer. Here I mean the benefits of owning the product, not a listing of its features.
4 Develop rapport with the person. People need to buy you before buying your offer.
5 Ask questions to find out their personal needs.
6 Do more listening than talking.
7 Tell the prospect about the benefits offered by your product which match their needs. Do not mention benefits that do not match their needs.
8 Ask them if they agree it meets their needs.
9 If they pause, probe or make objections, address their concerns.
10 Ask for their business.

Remember, as an entrepreneur you have a scarcity of resources so always use creativity to leverage your efforts. For example, a client visit is selling to one person in an hour; a free talk might be selling to 100 people in the same time.

Networking

Networking groups have spread like mushrooms around the UK and the world; so they obviously work for a lot of people. Basically their formula is simple. They meet typically very early in the morning, once a week, all stand up and introduce themselves to each other and try to refer their contacts to each other. Thus the contact database is far bigger than the membership. They will let only one person in from each professional area to avoid conflicts of interest. Some will insist that if you can't make the meeting you have to send someone else. For this they can charge about £500 per annum. I have met many people who have won much business via networking groups; they clearly work.

When I went to my first network group, I paid £15 and was in a room of about 200 people in central London. There were speakers and various activities to get people talking to each other. I said to my close friend, Rupinder, who was with me: 'Why have we paid £15 to be introduced to the person next to us when we could have gone to any pub or coffee shop, bus stop, rail station or shop and talk for free to the person next to us? Aren't you getting bored with all these people making sales pitches to us, and as soon as they see we are clearly not prospective customers moving on?'

I network everywhere I go, I did it from when I was a child and never attended a course on it, or paid someone to network for me. I have always been successful at it and made countless clients and long-term friends through it. I just cheat and consider everywhere to be a networking club.

To share that success is easy. Ask yourself when you meet a stranger: 'What do they do that I like and what do they do that I don't like?' Trust me, they will feel the same, so just do it first.

- Have a genuine interest in meeting people.
- Have an open mind.
- Think more about what you can do for them than what they can do for you.
- Realize that good rapport with three people is more valuable than a passing acquaintance with 30.

Online selling

Websites, links on other people's websites, ezines, a big subject covered in the specialist press: the web provides a vast range of cost effective, efficient, non-stop marketing potential. Exploit it.

Streetwise marketing

The biggest spend when you start your own business is usually marketing. Every advertiser is ready to take money off you.

However, the true entrepreneur is creative and wins new business without a budget.

How to gain new business without a budget

I once met the Marketing Director of a major British plc, told him about the business I was building up and asked his advice. He asked, 'What budget do you have?' I replied, 'I don't have a budget.' 'Well you can't do any marketing then,' was his response. Actually I could probably get you more business for the price of an hour's consultation than he could with a £10,000 budget. So read on.

Entrepreneurship is about doing things differently, better and more efficiently, with new ideas, imagination and innovation. It's about changing the world for the better and receiving profit for doing it. As a start up you are in a race to breakeven point and what makes you faster is cutting unnecessary expenses.

Whatever your business, I can guarantee that there are at least 50 ways to promote it for free and 50 ways for a token amount. There will even be ways in which you can be paid to promote it. One good idea is usually enough.

What exactly is streetwise marketing and how does it work?

Streetwise marketing is about low cost, no cost or receiving an income for your marketing. It starts before the business does. You need to have a passion, drive and energy for what you are about to launch. All the articles, books and seminars tell you this is essential. This is true, but that alone is not enough!

People part with cash to satisfy a need that they have, not to make your dreams come true. Actually they don't care what your goals and dreams are. Do you care what my dreams are? What motivates me to write this book? Or are you focused on 'what is in it for you'?

The streetwise marketer starts by asking: 'What do I keep hearing and/or observing people say that they want and will pay for, which I can provide?'

When you get answers you then match them to what you have a passion and the enthusiasm to provide, NOT THE OTHER WAY AROUND.

The next stage

The streetwise marketer then asks: 'What is so special about what I offer in the eyes of the prospective customer?'

When you have a good answer ask: 'How can I reach this market without spending money?'

You are now on the road to riches.

Surf the web or attend any networking group and you find that most people don't do it this way, which means that you will now have an easy path to prosperity.

If you have to spend all your money developing your ideas and products so that come launch time the coffers are empty, worry not.

So you want some examples of answers to the last question above. Let me give you some methods that work for me. First, you are reading one!

- I sell books, booklets and audio CDs, rather than give out brochures. Whatever you are doing this is likely to be an option for you too.
- Providing an electronic newsletter (ezine) is essential.
- I give free talks to customers with an audience but no budget; you can too. You will sell products and services, win referrals and gain new subscriptions to your ezine. Don't go to networking events, offer to talk at them. They will market you to all their members before the event has even started.
- Offer related online businesses a commission for every one of your products they sell, rather than pay them for advertising. There is no cost to them or you, you both make money without risk.

There are many, many more ideas that will work for you; get started now. If you want some more ideas just come to our next Entrepreneurs Club meeting as our guest. The path to success means applying simple ideas and following the easy path instead of the one everyone else is following. So right now ask these two questions above of your own business, and email me at alex@clubentrepreneur.co.uk telling me what worked for you so I can share it.

Or, if you prefer I could give you the phone number of the Marketing Director I met!

Three tips

1 Let the market tell you what to supply.
2 Sell at every opportunity.
3 Buy my book *Advanced Selling for Beginners*.

Two tasks

1 Sell something today.
2 Start your own monthly electronic newsletter (ezine).

Appendix

This section focuses on the value of questions, offering 100 tried and tested questions to help you increase sales.

Question: How many professionals does it take to service my requirements?

Answer: How many can you afford?

Sales tips: Always look to increase sales to a customer. Sell more to existing customers.

Questions focus the mind of the person being asked. They determine which 'files' in our unconscious are accessed. For example, if I asked you the name of your first school that file would be searched for and when found the name would pop into your conscious mind. Questions also determine our mood, how we feel, by triggering memories and associations. How would you feel if you had just won the lottery? They are very powerful and it is hard to resist their influence. Try not to answer the following questions:

1 10 + 2 = ?
2 Stockholm is the capital of?
3 A collie is a breed of?

Chances are that you are thinking of 12 Swedish dogs.

See the power? It is that easy. I asked you to resist answering and gave you boring, meaningless content. Imagine the increase of power without those two elements.

All of the questions in this section are used regularly by very successful sales people to great effect. We could explain why and go in to great detail. Instead I suggest that you just try the questions with the knowledge that they work. Remember though, English is a language where how you say a word will have an effect, so ask with passion, meaning, interest, respect, enthusiasm, whatever is appropriate.

You will note that most of the 100 questions are to be asked of yourself. This is because it is mainly you who holds yourself back from achieving your potential. You are the constant in all of your sales contacts.

Many of the questions below have specific NLP (Neuro-Linguistic Programming – The Psychology of Success) techniques in them. Some of them contain advanced language patterns. Most though are simple, unsophisticated yet work time and time again.

NLP is the modelling process of extracting simplicity from complexity. It is important to remember that selling is simple. So often when people are not achieving the results they desire, they need to become less sophisticated and get back to basics.

Nearly all prospects will present you, metaphorically speaking, with a silver platter piled high with bundles of £20 notes, to which you can help yourself. All you have to do is listen and take some when invited to.

'The important thing is not to stop questioning.'
Albert Einstein

Converting prospects to customers is easy, they have always been ready to spend money. People like spending money, in fact they are obsessed with it. (At the time of writing the British government has just released statistics saying that the average debt per head in Britain is over £5,000. That means as a nation we have just spent £200billion of money we don't even have!)

They are out there, just waiting for you to get your act together and communicate your message clearly, with enthusiasm, and match it to their needs.

Asking good quality questions then, at the appropriate time is essential to achieve your sales potential. Start with yourself questioning motivation, focus, goal setting, deciding on the best approach.

Having good answers to these types of questions is essential before progressing to your prospects. The rewards of using good quality questions are:

- Controlling the conversation.
- Letting the other person talk more.
- Obtaining information.
- Obtaining decision and commitment.
- Putting the future customer into a buying mood.
- Generating attention and interest.
- Qualifying the buyer.
- Establishing rapport.
- Checking out your assumptions.
- Eliminating or differentiating from the competition.
- Demonstrating that you are listening.
- Helping you to listen.
- Building credibility.
- Knowing the customers and their business.
- Identifying needs.
- Identifying decision makers, influencers, processes and styles.
- Identifying NLP and other patterns of prospects.
- Finding hot buttons.
- Triggering positive associations.
- Obtaining personal information.
- Closing the sale.
- Testing if the sale can be closed.
- Generating other sales leads.

The following 100 questions are designed more as a reference resource. As a learning tool, find a question that you like and use it constantly for a week. Next week try a new one. That way you will be changing habits according to what works. These 100 questions have been researched from successful entrepreneurs and sales professionals to be the ones that have greatest effect.

Ten questions that test your sales and marketing plan

1 Do I know exactly why I am doing this?
2 Is this the best route towards my goals?
3 What would happen if everything went to plan?
4 What would happen if everything did not go to plan?
5 Am I working to my or someone else's goals?
6 Who can I help achieve their goals?
7 If I had a better set of objectives, what would they be?
8 Who can help me achieve my goals?
9 What target shall I set myself for today?
10 What will I wish I had done two hours from now?

Ten questions that get you focused

1 What would make me happiest if I achieved it today?
2 Who would benefit most by what I offer?
3 Where are the quickest results to be found?
4 What is the most valuable thing I can do right now?
5 What action should I take now?
6 What question would I like to know the answer to?
7 Who am I letting down by not calling them now?
8 What or who is closest to making me money?
9 What are my priorities?
10 Can I spend more time with prospects offering higher returns?

Ten questions to make you feel great and fired up

1 What three things are really great in my life right now?
2 What would I spend an extra £1,000 on right now?
3 What gift can I give myself?
4 What motivational music could I play on the way to work?
5 What would I treat myself to if I hit target this month?
6 What are my six greatest ever successes in sales?
7 How much is even one good lead potentially worth to me?
8 Would I like to be rich? Why exactly?
9 What would fire me up if I achieved it in the next 15 minutes?
10 What fuels my burning desire to succeed?

Ten questions that increase efficiency

1 How can I do what I do for more people with less work and for a better price?
2 What will I do better next time because of this experience?
3 What resources could I leverage better?
4 What is my most unproductive time in the day?
5 What is a better way to do this?
6 What can I change to move faster?
7 How can I save time?
8 What do the best performers in my mrket do differently from me?
9 If I employed me, what would I have me focus on?
10 Who do I know that has good ideas?

Ten questions that help at cold calling

1 Who haven't I called recently?
2 What different approach is worth trying?
3 What would I respond positively to if someone called me?
4 Who are the ten people I would most want business from?
5 Who could help me?
6 Who holds the budget?
7 Who is most worth talking to?
8 What is the ideal customer profile I am looking for?
9 What can I say that is different and gets attention fast?
10 What can make my phone call memorable to the other party?

Ten questions that get to the core

1 What is the hidden opportunity here?
2 What could go wrong that I can prepare for now?
3 How motivated am I really?
4 Do you have any questions?
5 What did I notice about myself today?
6 What is really important to my prospects?
7 What motivates me the most?
8 What metaphors is he/she using?
9 What problem can I solve?
10 Is he/she using more visual, auditory or feeling words?

Ten questions that improve your approach

1 Am I selling from the customer's perspective?
2 Do I know at least 30 benefits of a prospect choosing me?
3 Are my prices high enough?
4 Am I providing what people want to buy in the way they want to buy it?
5 Do I truly believe that what I offer adds value to customers?
6 Am I using all my advantages to the full?
7 Have I asked my prospects what approach works with them?
8 What is my weakest area in sales that I can work on?
9 In what way am I ignorant?
10 What can I do to excel?

Ten questions that gather information

1 Can you think of one special time when you purchased something and everything went really well?
2 Describe to me the perfect supplier?
3 What is your ultimate objective?
4 Tell me, what headaches have you got, that I might be the Anadin™ for?
5 Fancy a cappuccino?
6 How can I help you?
7 How interested are you on a scale from 1 to 10?
8 What can I say that you would like to hear?
9 What would I have to do to win your confidence?
10 Can I ask you for some advice?

Ten questions that move you towards a deal

1 What would you do if you were me?
2 What would we have to do to be even better than your current suppliers?
3 Do you have a 'contingencies' budget?
4 What is the key question you need to ask me?
5 What is the one thing I could offer that would get you interested?
6 If I could address all the issues you have, would you go ahead and place an order with me?
7 How can we best move forward?
8 What is your decision making process?
9 What, if anything, stops you from going ahead?
10 What could I do now to secure an order from you?

Ten questions that close the deal

1 Shall we go ahead then?
2 Are you in a position to go ahead if you like what I have to say?
3 Who else do you know who might be interested in this?
4 If I agree to what you ask can you agree a deal now?
5 Do you want the standard or deluxe version?
6 You agree that this represents real value for money, don't you?
7 Can you see all the benefits to you of what I am offering?
8 Is there anything important to you that I have not covered?
9 How does that sound?
10 Are all your criteria met by what I have proposed?

Progress now

Put a fresh pad of paper by your desk. Record during the day, after each call, the questions you found yourself asking. Where can improvements be made?

Listen to questions that people ask you, make a note and use any good ones.

Listen to professional journalists interviewing people in the news. What probing questions do these professionals use? How can you apply them?

Make a list of the five questions that, if you had the answer to them, could increase your income by 25%. Now think of the ideal outcome you want and think of five questions that, if you can find the answers, will lead you to it. When you have the questions, keep asking them. Stick them on your wall.

Think of who you admire most for his or her business success. If you could get an audience with them what three questions would you ask them?

success mentor

'Knowledge speaks, but wisdom listens.'

Jimi Hendrix

'Opportunities multiply as they are seized.'

Sun Tzu

I suggest that all entrepreneurs should find themselves a mentor. Someone who has been there, done it, whose words of wisdom and advice can be listened to and then actioned. Start by heeding the useful tips in this chapter. I am often inspired, motivated and given valuable ideas and support by people around me. One of those key people to me is Raj Malhotra, who seems always to have the ability with whatever is the appropriate resource at the time. The return I receive from him is a major asset to me. I therefore suggest that you find your own Raj, avoid arrogance and take good advice regularly.

Progress now

Pick one of the following hot tips and make it your focus for the week. Then pick another, and so on …

- Only buy at bargain prices.
- Know the difference between an investment and a cost.
- Turn your garage into an office.
- Live within your means.
- Cash is king.
- Recruit the best and set them up to be outstanding.
- Train an elite team.
- Establish a corporate and team identity and culture.
- Have a microscope and a telescope.
- Catch the success virus.
- Make negative words illegal.
- Be decisive but explore all the options and implications first.
- Be flexible, see from multiple perspectives.
- Think ahead .
- Play Monopoly® for real money.
- Always have a plan B.
- Harness your whole concentration upon one goal.
- Provide what people want to buy.
- Get free publicity and advertising.
- Spread the word.
- If in doubt raise prices.

- Be in the right place at the right time.
- Think opportunity.
- Ask a lot of 'why' questions.
- Move fast.
- Keep it simple.
- Do what has to be done.
- Keep to your strength areas, you have advantages here.
- Take a trip to the US of A.

Only buy at bargain prices

If it is not a bargain, haggle, shop around, do without, take other routes, wait until it is a bargain. In negotiation time and waiting is, more often than not, a powerful influencing tool so never be in a hurry when buying. In practice, when we shop around, we are inevitability then offered the same or a similar thing for a better deal. Refer to the life stories of Paul Getty and Warren Buffet and see how these billionaires have mastered this principle.

Know the difference between an investment and a cost

Poorly performing entrepreneurs do not understand the difference between a cost and an investment. Investments are things that you want more of, because they make an eventual and regular contribution to profit. Costs, on the other hand, reduce profit and need keeping to a minimum without adversely affecting operations. Look at your own business in the last month and differentiate costs from investments.

Turn your garage into an office

When studying entrepreneurs I hear time and again something that sounded quite strange to me at first. Running a business profitably is all about keeping costs down. There is a clue in this. Business is simple and runs to the equation: Sales – Costs = Profits.

The wise also realize that there is a difference between good and bad costs. A good cost is one that directly increases sales or the potential for sales. Any other cost is something that threatens you. At some point during a business life cycle cash inflows will go down for whatever reason. If your minimum cost base is less than your competitors' you will probably outlast them. The more cost the quicker you will be threatened.

In the 1980s in Britain there was an airline called Air Europe. Since inception its report and accounts showed a significant growth in both sales and profits for every single year. Then the First Gulf War happened and it went bust. I went to the auction in its ex-offices near Gatwick Airport. I knew them well as the company had been a major client of a business I owned at the time. The luxurious furniture, three-piece suites, thick pile carpets went for less than a tenth of what would have been the original price. Long-lasting entrepreneurs are the ones who buy for this price at the auction. Air Europe's nest egg against a down turn consisted of wasteful and needless luxuries.

Air Europe personnel were very enterprising, but this top-quality airline suffered from vanity which eventually caught up with them, and they are no longer in business.

I buy my PCs, laptops, carpets, furniture second hand or from places like IKEA, which are focused on functionality rather than charging premiums for designer labels.

Mind the pennies and the pounds will look after themselves.

Live within your means

I have noticed that most people instead of accumulating wealth are getting into debt. Therefore, as part of the club I run, I try to help people reorganize their lives with some sensible financial planning, according to their goals. The big spenders are not the rich, they know how to keep hold of their money and not be tempted against their best interests. Big spenders tend to be people doing it on credit who are satisfying their short-term desires for a much increased long-term cost.

Cash is king

When it comes to accounting, entrepreneurs seem to focus their attention on cash flow. They see their business in cash flow terms even when it becomes larger. They concentrate on increasing cash in and reducing cash out. When it comes to the balance sheet they think of assets as things that produce income, and liabilities as things that cost them money. Accountants see property, fixtures and fittings, and motor vehicles as assets. As these things cost money to run entrepreneurs see them as liabilities. Key people are not valued in the accounts. The Virgin Group's accounts will show Richard Branson's PC as an asset but not him. If I had him advising my enterprises I would consider him to be a very valuable asset that I would use to the full.

Recruit the best and set them up to be outstanding

Make it difficult to get a job with your company, through a rigorous recruitment process. Then don't try to get the best staff by relying on paying the highest salaries. The harder it is to get a job with your company the more elitist it will become and the more demand there will be for people to work for you. When they get through this procedure they will also value the job far more and be far less inclined to leave. People naturally value things according to how much effort it took to achieve them. Think of the organizations you know that you consider to be leading in their field and then look at how they recruit.

The toughest recruitment process I have come across is to join the British Army Special Forces: they have the reputation of being the world's most elite force. How have they done this? They recruit the very best and then have by far the best training programme.

How many members of the Special Forces, do you think, could be tempted to join another division with the lure of a higher salary? Look at Microsoft®, Virgin Group or, more relevantly, perhaps companies with which you are familiar in your industry. Believe me, having run a headhunting business for years I know exactly which types of company it is easy to pull people out of and which types hard. I have often said to managers to never fear headhunters because with all their techniques they cannot persuade staff to leave – only the manager can do that!

How do you make yours a tough recruitment process? Various ways: many interviews, panel interviews, aptitude and personality tests, assessment days, gruelling and professional interviewing and selection. The best way is to use an outside organization to carry out the short list assessments. This, in itself, sends a message to would-be applicants of just how seriously you take your recruitment process. It ups the value of a job with you in their eyes. I have found that the better employers often pay less than their average counterparts. I conclude that professional recruitment is an investment and salaries are mainly a cost. Identify the exact profile of the people you wish to recruit and keep looking until you have found them.

Look at Bill Gates's career and it is quite clear from the start that he went to great lengths to recruit the best quality staff. He even bought whole companies when he could not headhunt the key staff directly. Training should also be for you as well as for your staff. Paul Getty learnt foreign languages to help in his business dealings.

Train an elite team

Training is often something that is considered important but not urgent and thus keeps getting postponed. Again this comes back to my earlier observation of the most successful entrepreneurs balancing long-term and short-term needs. Training, when selected carefully, is not a cost but an investment with a long-term return. It gives you an edge over your competition. It can make you more efficient in any of the functions of your business. It is also motivational to staff. American entrepreneurs have a far greater record here than their British counterparts. Americans spend enormous amounts, by British standards, both corporately and individually.

Training return is limited by the quality of the staff being trained. You should initially spend time clarifying your recruitment policy and processes. Recruit the best and you will also get the bonus of a better return from the training you give them.

Establish a corporate and team identity and culture

It is clear that entrepreneurial companies which really go places identify a strong team and corporate culture early on, and then recruit people whose personalities match that culture and identity. This they put before job competencies, as skill training will be a lot easier than personality changing. There seems to be the view that if people really fit in with the team the company can easily train them in any skills they are missing.

Progress now

Think of the five companies that you admire the most for whatever reason. They may be of any size or in any industry.

Now write down the five things that you admire the most about these companies.

What policies, ideas can you apply to your enterprise from this list?

Have a microscope and a telescope

Focus on what is immediately in front of you *and* on the horizon. Entrepreneurs of any type and at any level of financial success tend to talk about what they are going to do rather than what they have achieved. This includes entrepreneurs already beyond retirement age. Their focus is clearly future orientated and perhaps this gives a clue as to how they see new opportunities and don't get bogged down in old ways of doing things. It also casts light on how they manage to keep positive when experiencing failures. The failures as soon as they are past become out of focus, literally. Obviously we can learn important lessons from the past but often successful entrepreneurs beat those who started with so much more experience, knowledge and resources. This implies that whereas good can come from experience, it can also limit us.

In looking at failed entrepreneurs, experienced executives point out their lack of industry experience. It is also true that an entrepreneur's future focus can also have a negative side. It has become clear to me that the entrepreneur who steams ahead, is the one who can draw on the good from the past, and also focus on the good in the future? I find that entrepreneurs can be very flexible and look from many different perspectives before coming to decisions. The optimism of the salesperson is blended with the pessimism of the accountant. The long-term view of the strategist and visionary is blended with the practicality of and action of the 'now' person.

Catch the success virus

Destiny will deliver to you a certain amount of good and bad luck. I don't know about you but I want more than my fair share, so I fix the odds in my favour. Here is how.

How much do you want to be a millionaire? If I asked you to take a risk on the roulette wheel, bet £1,000 and if 22 comes up I will give you £1million, otherwise you lose, would you take the bet?

If I said gamble £10,000 and if anything other than 22 comes up I will pay you £1million would you now take the bet?

If I said that if anything but 22 comes up I will pay you £10million, but if 22 comes up I will shoot you, would you take the bet?

What do your answers and thinking tell you about your attitude to risk?

Let me tell you what a self-made millionaire would do. Find another game where they could determine the stakes, the odds and have a strong influence on the outcome, to play money-making games without even being there. Entrepreneurs don't play roulette, they have not got time for games of chance. Losers play roulette and gamble. Entrepreneurs design their own game, reduce the odds of them losing, increase the odds of them winning and cover for the downside. The entrepreneur would either receive a royalty on inventing the game or own the casino!

So what do you have to change in order to become an entrepreneur?

Success is contagious, hang around it and you will catch it!

Make negative words illegal

In one of my training sessions I put up two flipcharts and ask the delegates to write positive words on one flipchart and negative words on the other.

Then I got them to talk to each other in various contexts using the words from one of the boards alternately. The result is simple and dramatic. The delegates who are hearing the negative words rapidly decline in mood. Those hearing positive words rapidly begin to smile, laugh and are full of energy, and all that is associated with positive thinking.

Words that we hear generate internal pictures and sounds which in turn, determine our feelings. Therefore, what I do and have done for many clients is to get them to do two things. This tip is free, simple and always works.

1 Surround the workplace walls with positive pictures, suggestions, quotes and words.
2 Open a negative word box. Every time someone uses a negative word they have to put £1 into a box and then they have to repeat what they said but in a positive way.

This, incidentally, is how hypnosis works, gently making suggestions that are reaching your unconscious continually. As we have stimulus all around us 'hypnotizing' our mood and how we feel, why not take control and make the stimulus one that makes us feel good, encourages ideas, action and energy.

Be decisive but explore all the options and implications first

When you can you must learn how to wait and be patient, wait for something good, the right deal to turn up. Ascertain anything that could go wrong and make your decision on as much information as you can. Take as much time making important decisions as you can, but don't hang around too long or opportunity will be lost.

Be flexible, see from multiple perspectives

Keep trying different approaches until you are successful. Looking at a challenge from a different point of view often produces ideas. Ask other people their opinion. Look at everything first from the customer's point of view.

Think ahead

Always think ahead and think about anything that could go wrong in the future. This is deliberately making yourself think negatively. Now you have time on your side to work out what to do. You can even take it a step further and figure out how you could benefit from the event transpiring. Everything that happens in business has a positive side and the easiest way to exploit it is to think ahead of time.

Play Monopoly® for real money

I find it interesting that Bill Gates in his younger days was an avid player of Monopoly®. I have heard many wealthy entrepreneurs refer to the principles that need to be applied to this game. Looking closer we can learn and apply a lot of these principles. For example, certain players will always go for the dark blue (e.g. Mayfair and Park Lane in the London edition) set, but these people very rarely win.

In fact, more often than not, the winner is the person who 'owns' the orange set, where the balance of investment to return is not too hard to build, and the returns are worthwhile. It does not cripple you as you are building it up. It allows you to build some wealth and then from that higher standpoint the dark blue set seems a worthwhile investment.

The brown set is handy to generate cash flow but with only two properties it would take forever to generate reasonable wealth. The stations offer four properties with a reasonable frequent return without any building costs. You will never win on this set alone but they can finance you as you go along, keeping the cash flowing.

Chance and Community Chest again is realistic to life. The wise player knows all the cards that can come up and sets something aside for the worst scenario. The best way to learn from Monopoly® is to play with friends for real money. That way the lessons will be logged into your unconscious as you are getting real business experience.

Always have a plan B

Successful entrepreneurs are always thinking ahead and considering every scenario. The biographies of Aristotle Onassis, John D Rockefeller and Paul Getty clearly show this trait again and again. So often when their opponents thought they had been caught out, these entrepreneurs would clearly show that they had made contingency plans for exactly the situation they had got into. Onassis, for example, was pursued by the CIA, for good reasons, when he admitted to organizing a strike in the Hamburg boatyard that was working on his ship. The CIA case failed. Another time he was whaling off the Chilean coast and the CIA arranged for Onassis's boats to be impounded. It later transpired, whereas the CIA thought they had ruined Onassis, that his insurance contract with Lloyds had a clause in it predicting this possibility with a very large payoff. He made an incredible profit by foreseeing this possible scenario.

So in your business ask yourself what could go wrong in the next three months. When you have that information, ask what you can do now to prepare for it, or even make opportunity from it.

Harness your whole concentration upon one goal

If you have five things to achieve, the more you can do them sequentially the more success you will have. Attending to five things at once usually means that none of them is achieved. If you focus your mind on one goal your thinking can, by definition, be much clearer and you will arrive at quicker, better answers.

Provide what people want to buy

Entrepreneurs have a real passion for their ideas and products. This does not mean that the buying public will. Products have to be sold and people buy things when they perceive a need for them relative to competitors. What people want or should want can be very different from what they will part with money for. The best products are those that were initiated by seeing a need in the market place and then supplying it, not the other way around. People pay for what they want to have, not what you want to give them. You can influence what they want though.

Get free publicity and advertising

Before you raise finance to spend a small fortune on promoting your business, seek and exploit all the free ways first. You can write articles for online and offline periodicals, give radio or television interviews, give a free seminar at an association. There are always lots of ways depending on what you are offering. Find at least five before you spend a penny on advertising.

Spread the word

The most effective marketing is word of mouth and personal recommendation. It is the most reliable and the cheapest. People who are recommended are also less likely to haggle on price, being already convinced of quality and service.

If in doubt raise prices

There are three reasons why, if you are in doubt, you should raise your prices.

1 Most people associate price with quality.
2 It can give you more profit even if volume drops.
3 Volume may go up.

Be in the right place at the right time

Having studied entrepreneurs in detail, it is clear that there are certain golden rules that are discussed throughout this book. There are traits that allow an enterprise to be launched and developed from the first stages to profit. The really big stars seem to have an additional ability to be in the right place at the right time. Many artists, for example, die penniless only for their work to be acclaimed as masterpieces much too late for them to benefit from it.

To be in the right place at the right time as a business entrepreneur is to not invent and take your goods to market, but to do it the other way around. In other words, find out what people might have a need for if it were to exist and then go away and invent it. That is how you make sure that you are in the right place at the right time.

There are clearly some times and places in world history that are more appropriate. For example, being born into a communist society would not benefit an entrepreneur. A good time in Britain was immediately after the Second World War because everything had been destroyed and needed rebuilding again. There was limited capital available but your competitors were in the same boat. This was the time that the young Charles Forte opened a milk bar, building what became a major hotel and restaurant group.

These good times keep coming around: you are in one now; change always creates new needs. The fastest to recognize and exploit these needs make a fortune.

> **Progress now**
>
> What three major changes have happened around you in the last year?
>
> What new needs do they create?
>
> Which of these are you in a position to exploit?

Think opportunity

Always look for opportunity. For example, when negotiating with a supplier can you put any other business their way? How about more favourable terms in return for their brochures in your office, or a link on your website?

Ask a lot of 'why' questions

'Why' questions get you in the habit of challenging the current status quo and this process leads to you seeing opportunities. The opportunities were always there, it is just that you could not see them until you started to ask some 'why' questions.

Move fast

Put deadlines before quality. Get something to market fast then continually improve it. If you wait for perfection the market will have moved on. Microsoft® has spent years developing and improving a PC operating system for common use. Their earlier versions were absolutely riddled with bugs, breakdowns and totally meaningless error messages. They still offered more than their competitors and customer feedback led to enhancements.

Business is about deadlines. This is doubly hard for an entrepreneur getting established with limited resources. Meeting deadlines is an essential step to success.

Keep it simple

This is a very well-worn principle in business and I came across it being put into active use by all the entrepreneurs I know of. Business is not an intellectual exercise, don't make it one.

Do what has to be done

As your own boss you are free to decide what to do each day. Most of us, naturally, will focus on what we want to do. Instead, ask yourself what needs to be done with priority in order to meet your goals, and focus on doing the answer.

Keep to your strength areas, you have advantages here

Know your strength areas and keep to them. Everything else look to delegate, as soon as possible. Your time is precious and in short supply. Maintain its usefulness at maximum output. Doing the accounts yourself, for example, is not a thrifty habit, it is a lavish one. What will take you a week and not be done properly can be done in two hours by a professional accountant.

Take a trip to the US of A

The United States is the greatest source of new ideas being put into practice in the world. Their society was largely founded on the principle of entrepreneurship. Many people became millionaires in Europe by seeing great ideas in action in the USA and bringing them home. Many more were inspired by just how creative and imaginative Americans are. Nowhere in the world are people encouraged and free to dream more than in the USA. If you want an idea of how big Americans can dream take a visit to Walt DisneyWorld® Resort in Florida and the next day visit the Kennedy Space Center. Think of all the big companies now in the world that have come from the internet age. How many can you think of that are not American?

Progress now

Forget answers, think of questions for now. Design ten questions, however unreasonable and unrealistic, to which you would like answers.

Two tasks

1 Find a personal mentor, someone who has entrepreneurial expertise.
2 Turn the advice from your mentor into action and then results.

12

the Time Bank

In this chapter you will learn:
- that TIME for an entrepreneur stands for Totally Inadequate Minutes Everyday
- how to take a loan out from the TIME BANK
- that time is your most important resource
- that the entrepreneur's job is to manage resources not just be one

'*Once a day is gone you can never get it back again*'
Richard Lowden, Eurodrive Car Rental

'*I wasted time and now doth time waste me.*'
William Shakespeare

Time – we all know it flies, but who is the pilot?

Minutes are probably worth more than money, so spend them wisely. People about to embark on their new business typically consider the resource that is in short supply to be finance. To put it simply, they believe they are short of cash and securing finance is the key to their success.

They are wrong, time and time again. For finance you have endless options, not just the loans or equity that textbooks talk about.

I advocate paying interest for a bank loan or releasing equity only in extreme circumstances. They are the finance sources of last, not first resort. But that is another story for another time.

Time stands for 'Totally Inadequate Minutes Everyday', and is the most vital resource in your business. Your eventual success is totally about how you spend your time; use it wisely and leverage it. Imagine you could freeze time, for everybody and everything else. Just you are able to work, while the world is kept in stasis. Wouldn't that help?

'What we love to do we find time to do. So focus on loving profit!'

What would a Time Bank offer and how could we take out a loan?

A Time Bank would offer constant and never ending ideas, techniques, short cuts on how you can practically, realistically get a loan of extra hours through paying up front through the nose. In short 'Time Leverage'.

'How long a minute is depends on which side of the toilet door you are on.'

Here is a small selection of products from the Time Bank.

- adverts placed on other people's websites, at no cost to you
- how to set up third party resellers

- the franchising option
- the network marketing option
- joint ventures
- students looking for unpaid work experience
- free consultants via government small firms.
- better technology
- better systems
- improved administration
- contracting out
- cutting corners
- software to speed up the process
- commission only sales agents
- a risk reversal marketing strategy
- an ezine to all your previous customers

183
the Time Bank

12

Progress now

Ask these four time saving questions every day.

- What can I change to achieve more in less time?
- What am I currently doing that could be done by someone else?
- Am I fully exploiting technology?
- What is most important to spend my time on?

If there was a Time Bank every sensible entrepreneur would be at its door looking and happy to borrow 10,000 hours and pay back with interest at the end of the year. At that time, with the business built to the next level, your time is freed up, it is less mission critical. That is, if you are streetwise enough to have leveraged your resources in the year.

Most new entrepreneurs pay for time through the nose, by working all hours and trying to do everything themselves. They cannot delegate and thus under utilize the skills of those they employ. Big mistake. 'Through the nose' tends to mean payroll. In practice, you are more likely to lose time through extra time spent on recruitment, training, managing and motivating.

Worse, the government will want a bonus called 'employer's national insurance' for the privilege of letting you do this, and will give you a library full of legislation to read and abide by. Try finding the time for that and you are lost before you start! So, keep asking those time leverage questions and act on the answers!

Other people

I once asked a training group, at Hillcroft College for women, completing the Certificate in Business Start Up for the Institute for Leadership Management: 'What are the skills you require to be successful as an entrepreneur?' I wrote their answers all over the walls as they produced more than 50. I then asked, 'Think of an entrepreneur you know personally or a famous one. How many of these skills do you think they have?'

There was a great sigh of relief as realization struck that they need not learn more than 50 skills to be successful. If you don't like maths and accounting find a partner who does or employ a bookkeeper. You must constantly delegate and find ways to have others help you. Entrepreneurship is not about dong it yourself, it is about better manipulating the resources around you, using other people's money, skills, assets, ideas, qualifications, etc.

Entrepreneurs often don't have the budgets, departments, etc. that their large competitors have. You must be creative, always thinking of ways to get things done. Don't try to do it all, it will take for ever and you will get very stressed with the inevitable multi-tasking you find yourself doing. You probably will not have a budget or a place for people to work from, especially in these days of virtual businesses.

So, ask yourself questions like: 'Who can help me with this and how can I motivate them without a budget?'

There may be many answers to the question. You could offer a generous performance bonus. You could offer shares. You could do something for them in return.

Another question to ask is: 'Who else has got an interest in me succeeding?'

If you will employ people local and central government and all their agencies could be interested. Phone your local authority's economic department and ask them what they can do to help you.

Other assets

An asset I have already defined as something that makes you money. I will now define what I call a 'golden asset' as something that makes money for you without your involvement.

An example of the former is something you sell to a customer personally. An example of the latter is someone or something that, while you were asleep, bought something from you. Ironically, as if to make the point, while I was writing this I received a paypal payment for a downloadable CD from my website.

So the question to ask is: 'What golden assets can I acquire?'

Your answers may include: websites, ezines, anything with software, sales agents, affiliate deals, viral marketing.

Get out of employee mode where you are used to all income coming directly from the work you do. As an entrepreneur your role is to manipulate resources all around you in the most efficient, leveraged way to exploit a commercial opportunity.

For this book I conducted much research on successful entrepreneurs. One of the factors that kept coming up is that they tend to be very good judges of people. Entrepreneurs don't need to be talented, if they can spot it in others and then motivate and lead that talent.

Most famous entrepreneurs left school at 16 and I think being in the 'real world' developed their 'people skills' before those who did not join the world of work until after further or higher education. Interestingly those graduates often come to apply for jobs along with those who left school at 16, as the television programme *The Apprentice* in North America and the UK has shown. Graduates, frankly, are not a rare resource. Why study for a degree yourself when you can recruit graduates? You as entrepreneur exploit their talent while they, probably under parental advice, are seeking to secure a good job with a typical employee mindset. As a qualified teacher I am not suggesting that you shouldn't invest in learning. I am suggesting that a lot of learning happens in and outside of academic institutions. Do both!

You can develop your business skills in a formal way, but don't see your talent as a skill you sell for money. Develop your skills in managing and developing and turning assets around you into golden assets.

Entrepreneur interview: Richard Lowden

Richard Lowden is founder and MD of Eurodrive® Car Rental (www.eurodrive.com), which is a franchising group with multiple branches throughout the UK. He is 36 years old and lives with his wife Kim and two children, Chay and Aria, in Milton Keynes.

Alex: What is your career background?

Richard: I was inspired by my father who was a very successful businessman. I also had the career of Richard Branson as a role model, whom I later met. My first enterprise was when my father was closing down a pottery with a warehouse full of products. I told him that I would sell them for him and then did, to retailers such as garden centres and direct to the public via car boot sales. I was 13 years old. I had also in childhood worked in my sister's riding school where I learnt a great deal about the administrative side of running a business. I was motivated to become an entrepreneur by an overwhelming passion for success.

I could not wait to leave school and with a passion for success worked initially in a sales capacity. My final employee position was with a major car rental company. It was here that I saw tremendous scope for improvements. I thoroughly researched every aspect of the industry. Even the name Eurodrive was based upon where I wanted to be in ten years. I was 21 and my only financial resource was my Barclaycard with a £500 limit. I left work and persuaded four investors to back me. I also negotiated contracts with Ford, Vauxhall and Peugeot, each of which were over £1million deals. I even got free demonstration vehicles from them. I also had to negotiate various other things such as an insurer. The year was 1993 and I had an overwhelming challenge to deliver what I had promised.

I intended to be a completely franchised group and open branches all around the UK. My philosophy is that a franchisee is the customer and I did not want the potential conflict of interest with company owned outlets. The first franchise was going to be the hardest. I learnt to take franchises in as groups which overcame the initial, nobody wanting to be first, obstacle.

In business anyone can have an idea, it is going out there and making that idea work is what separates people like Richard Branson from the crowd. People are happy to advertise and mailshot, but you really have to go out there and fight for it to make something work. My major problem though was getting people to take me seriously at 22 years of age. I never gave up. I never rest on my laurels. I never take no for an answer.

A few years later we were firmly established and I was in the position to make attractive offers to the investors for their shares. The market is always changing and you cannot control it, so you have to predict and prepare for those changes. Our original business plan just would not work on today's market. For example, we were one of the first in our industry to exploit the web and always try to put systems in place that will cater for the future rather that where we are today. Now with 85 operations, the company is funding its own growth and still returning growing profits. I have had attractive offers to sell but I intend to make it the most recognized, best quality car rental company on an international basis.

Our website is an interesting case. Our statistics showed that we were getting a vast quantity of requests for quotes but only a very small percentage of the subsequent bookings. We made one simple change offering surfers the option of having their quote emailed to them, making it simple to order. There was a dramatic overnight change in orders, a small fortune was created just by this one seemingly minor improvement. Some companies think that the customer is king; I think he is God, cash flow is king.

I have also found that a high level of integrity is important. We always have been transparent to our customers and there are no hidden extras when you rent a car from us. Simple, straightforward, honest. We think of our franchisees as customers. I demand exceptional service; if I cannot find it, we set it up in-house.

Alex: How do you define success?

Richard: Success is a measure other people give you. For me it will be when we are acknowledged as the world's leading car rental company.

Alex: What is the secret of success of an entrepreneur?

Richard: The ability to never give up. To take any form of rejection or knock back as a valuable lesson.

Alex: What advice would you give somebody starting out?

Richard:

1 Research what you are going to do thoroughly, being careful of people not telling you the truth.
2 Whatever funding you think you need, double it. Cash is paramount.
3 When you hit problems deal with them.
4 Make sure your credit is good.
5 Surround yourself with people that are talented in an area you are not.

Alex: How do you spot an opportunity?

Richard: Keep your eyes open all of the time.

Alex: What would you have done differently if you could go back in time?

Richard: Nothing. Every mistake I made I learnt from and progressed.

Alex: How do you motivate yourself when things don't go to plan?

Richard: Ask myself how I can turn this to advantage.

Three tips

1 Move so fast, you sweep past your problems hardly noticing them.
2 Focus most of your time on the customer.
3 A stitch in time saves nine, plan ahead.

Two tasks

1 When you are in the gym, network as well.
2 Delegate all you can, to everyone you can.

13 the happy entrepreneur

In this chapter you will learn:
- business and home life need to be in balance for true success
- why keeping fit will help you progress and prosper
- to be optimistic but keep paying into a pension scheme
- that success is more about giving than taking
- the tough times can be rewarding if you believe and focus on the goal

'If you suddenly lost all your material possessions would you still be happy? I would!'

Sensei Paul Elliott

'Whatever you are, be a good one.'

Abraham Lincoln

What makes a happy entrepreneur?

Being a happy entrepreneur means making sure that all aspects of your life are happy as your success and wealth continue to grow. Some costs are not worth it: your health, your life partner and family are three of them. Proceed wisely and these other aspects can be integrated, grow and flower with you.

Earlier in the book I talk about the idea of picking role models. Care needs to be taken. When you pick any model to learn their secrets, check first if they had or have happy lives. Many of the entrepreneurs I researched had other aspects of their lives that were abysmal failures, even in their own words. Many of the traits of successful entrepreneurs may have come through negative experiences. For example, thrift is a common virtue in every entrepreneur I have studied and one I strongly recommend. This is often created through an experience of hardship and is thus natural to them. If someone has a reference experience to extreme poverty in childhood, when their impressions of the world are being formed, this can also make them feel very insecure and inferior.

This insecurity part of their subconscious develops an overwhelming obsession to hoard as much money as possible in order to feel safe. The irony is that they never reach this position of safety; it is like the carrot in front of the donkey, when they move forward it moves forward. So they keep working hard hoarding more and more money, never achieving true happiness. Sometimes on this path they become unpopular and find that they have few friends and are increasingly alone.

Imagine somebody holding you off the edge of a tall building by your feet. Think about how motivated you are to get to safety. This is how these people are motivated to save money (safety) all the time. The reality of life is that we are more motivated to avoid the unpleasant than to acquire the pleasant. That is why people who are motivated as entrepreneurs, to make money to spend on houses and yachts, tend not to do as well. They are unlikely by nature and habit to be thrifty and have a motivation that is on full power constantly.

So if your goal is to make a lot of money, model this behaviour and you will attain riches, but not necessarily happiness. If you need a lot of money to feel secure and safe, a good therapist or personal coach could be a lot more effective. Make happiness your overriding goal, for you and your family, and design a destiny for yourself that is really fulfilling and deeply satisfying. That way all types of riches will flow towards you.

Perceived failure can lead to depression, and this often leads to heavy drinking or other types of denial behaviour. I say perceived because this all depends on how you define success and failure. If success is defined as getting up again each time life knocks you down, you will avoid the negative spiral. Sometimes keeping your business going is putting more money into a bottomless pit. Good money after bad. Not accepting failure is the real failure. Let there be no mistake, the entrepreneur route can have some downs as well as ups along the way.

Remember those at home

Keep your family informed of what is going on. Many think that they have to protect their partner and children if appropriate from anything negative in the world. A good motive certainly. Yet they also love you and need to feel they are supporting you during both the ups and downs. In fact if you share openly with them they can be a fount of support, ideas, encouragements and be with you all the way. Many parent entrepreneurs may find they are making compromises, they are unsettled with such things as leaving children with a nanny. Children must come first otherwise you will not be happy with yourself.

I have met many entrepreneurs working all hours away from home, making lots of money and saying the motive is to give the children a better future. They do not even believe it themselves. You must make sure that whatever your personal circumstances, when you look at goals your whole life and other people in it are fully considered.

On the other hand the family can actively participate and feel a part of the business. In Asian culture this family model for the business is the norm and solves a lot of the initial challenges of the entrepreneur, such as who minds the shop or phone when you are away. Statistics for the UK show a large number of wealthy Asian entrepreneurs. This is well known, but what is less known is that a high percentage of these are women. Asian communities often have very strong family ties, a willingness for working long arduous hours, an attitude of thrift, practicality, a 'roll up sleeves and do any task' attitude and an eye for an opportunity which are ideal qualities for entrepreneurship.

Whatever your personal situation and background you will have people around you that are more affected by you becoming an entrepreneur than an employee. Those that live with you will be affected by your late working hours and perhaps stress over cash flow etc. Keep a tight rein on costs and focus on early sales. When you have a good quarter keep a reserve for a rainy day. Those around you can be a great source of support and help you with various tasks. If things do become challenging, work together to move forward. Address challenges early on, remembering that if what you are doing is not working, change is required.

Keep fit and make a fortune

When I have done goal setting workshops it amazes me how many people in their twenties smoke and drink heavily, and list starting a pension scheme as a key goal. Being financially secure in your old age won't do you much good if your body does not last the distance. Entrepreneurs, no doubt, have to pay a price for their freedom to put their ideas into practice. That price should not include their health or that of their loved ones.

Stress is literally burnt out of our systems with exercise. In many other ways our mind and imagination works better the fitter we are. To launch and build an enterprise you are going to have to work hard, be constantly motivated and full of energy. I do not know how anyone can do this without maintaining a high level of personal fitness and health.

A common pattern for dealing with stress is to replace a workout in the gym, with a quick gin and tonic before dinner or a couple of pints on the way home. Smoking is another habit that relieves stress but at a terrible long-term price. This lifestyle leads to declining health, accelerated ageing and a whole range of health problems. No goal is worth this price.

The way to get healthy is to define being in the gym as part of your working hours. Budget for it in your timetable and consider it part of what you do to build your business. For all sorts of complex physiological reasons the period after a workout is very productive thinking-wise. This is when many entrepreneurs get their best inspiration. For each hour invested in the gym the return is an extra two hours of productivity the next day. The fact that you will live longer, happier and healthier is a good bonus!

Here are some tips that can change how you feel without any cost in terms of money or time.

1 Replace all drinks with water for two weeks, and notice how much better you feel.
2 Start off each day with three slow and deep breaths.
3 Take a short break and go away for a long weekend each quarter. However, do something that decreases stimulus to the senses not increases it.
4 Build more walking into your habitual routines. For example, park the car two minutes away from your destination. Simple walking improves weight control, reduces stress, improves mood and gives more energy.

My baby

Entrepreneurs tend to think of their business as their baby. If it is attacked they react accordingly. Yet the idea behind an enterprise never comes to an end, it transforms into its next life cycle. Like a baby growing up, it learns from mistakes and keeps changing its form, as it builds experience. Even liquidation is only a transformation if you allow it to be. This experience is a million-dollar asset, don't throw it away. It only needs converting into hard cash.

Companies fail not entrepreneurs, entrepreneurs evolve continually from the knowledge. The worst thing that can possibly happen to you is bankruptcy, and this means that you no longer have any debts and can start something afresh with the added resources of all the knowledge gained. The reality of this scenario is much less frightening than the one people conjure up in their imaginations, fuelled by taking advice from people who do not know what they are talking about. If your personal and business relationships are built on trust and integrity they will remain for the long term.

Plan for retirement

Many entrepreneurs do not bother with paying into a pension scheme for themselves, believing that their business is their pension. Entrepreneurs certainly have the advantage, should they wish, of not having to retire. I will work on new ideas forever, it is what I do and I love it. Therefore the feeling of insecurity during old age does not affect entrepreneurs as much as it does an employee, who is effectively going to be fired one day.

Paying in to a sound pension scheme is a good idea for two reasons.

1 Excellent entrepreneurs work from the assumption that if something could go wrong it will, and plan accordingly. This is good entrepreneurship.
2 Whatever else happens, money in your pension scheme will be secure.

Stay in touch with your spiritual side

During an entrepreneur's career there are many challenges to overcome. Your salary is not secure as an entrepreneur. Sometimes what you have spent years building can come under threat. Survival instincts take over and this has tempted some to borrow from the employee pension fund, withhold payments to suppliers, and take advantage of others unfairly. Employees largely get paid for serving time. To an entrepreneur this in itself counts for little.

These pressures can test you, the weak will succumb to the easy path. The right path requires strength of character and a high sense of honesty, integrity and responsibility to others. Real entrepreneurs are more about giving than taking. Being more tuned in to the needs of others gives them an advantage in seeing opportunities. If you are just looking for opportunities for your own gain then you will never realize true satisfaction and happiness. That is why I believe ultimately a real entrepreneur is a very spiritual person. Managing costs effectively does not mean that you have to begrudge every pound that you pay to staff. These people certainly exist. I used to work for someone who always got depressed when payroll time arrived, even when the business was very prosperous.

If you are married it is important that your spouse is very supportive of you. If you are the main earner this is even more so. I find it very warming just how many wealthy entrepreneurs have impeccable virtues, never tell a lie and spend a lot of their time helping others.

Risk taking culture

The USA seems to have the most supportive entrepreneurial culture in the world, encouraging risk taking and getting people off again after a failure. The venture capital industry was launched there. Having a go and failing in the USA seems to be a lot more acceptable than in the UK. Many British entrepreneurs are quite jealous of that. In life it is mostly through our failures that we learn. From my research, few self-made millionaires have not known complete failure of their enterprises. US law does not threaten your home as easily as it does currently in the UK, but these rules are under review as clearly, this discourages enterprise. The USA is my target for a specific study, as Americans are an incredibly creative people who seem to have values, beliefs, attitudes and thinking styles that generate practical ideas.

In the UK, if you fail you are actually not allowed by law to be a director of a company for one year (it used to be three years). This does not mean, however, that you cannot operate a business. You can even continue to operate the business in which you went bankrupt. At the time of writing this legislation is under review. From an economics point of view, we are totally dependent on new ideas to survive and compete in an ever-changing world.

Making the world a better place

When was the last time your thoughts were focused on what you could do for somebody else, without any benefit to yourself?

- If you see a stick, bottle or something like that in the middle of the road, would you remove it?
- If you saw litter on the road would you pick it up and put it in a dustbin?
- If you looked all day could you find not even one cigarette butt discarded on the pavement, street or road?
- Would you feel safe late at night waiting for a bus alone in your capital city?
- If you lost your wallet in the street would you be totally confident that it would be returned via the authorities?
- Are you 100% confident that if you buy something that you would not be short changed?

There are many people in the world who can answer 'yes' to all of those questions. On a trip to Prague with my father I was astounded to see no litter anywhere. A friend returning from Tokyo told me how the local paper had placed wallets full of cash all over the city streets and all of them were handed in!

My point is that although we may feel proud of our national achievements, whatever nation that is, there is still vast scope for improving society, making it a better place for current and future generations to live in. Entrepreneurs need to have a heart and a conscience, as these are the people who make changes. It is important, therefore, to realize that you have a great responsibility for your actions. There is a world of difference between someone driven by a passion for something that they know will work and has a commercial opportunity, and someone just going for profit. Economists talk of profit maximization as the main motive of companies. Unfortunately, along with a great deal of good we have also now got polluted rivers, cities and food, and even the ozone layer around the planet has been damaged and is continuing to be damaged. Profit alone is not a good enough motive.

The above questions also ascertain to some degree the quality of entrepreneur you are. Are you focused on others or yourself? The focusing on others I have found makes better sales and marketing professionals. This focus enables them to have great empathy and connectedness with customers and thus make better decisions.

Positive environment: the quick tick test

Here is a practical test to see how much positive thinking and energy is around you. You will need a pen, some paper and a clipboard. Write three headings along the top of each sheet of paper as follows: Positive   Indifferent   Negative.

Next time you are, say, having a coffee or waiting in the airport, for each person who passes you put a tick in one of the three columns. Judge which one by looking at the person's body language: smiling, frowning; upright, slouched; fast, slow, etc. When you have done this for 100 people, total up your three columns. You can repeat the exercise in different locations, times of the day, days of the week, and months of the year to get more data. For example, I notice a significant difference in people before Christmas compared with immediately afterwards.

Doing this in the street, I have found that more than 85% of people walking past have a negative energy focus. People who look happy, excited, enthusiastic, smiling are very much in the minority. I have also found, particularly from my experience in managing sales teams, that whatever the dominant mood of a group, its newcomers will rapidly adopt the group's mood, regardless of the mood they started with.

Negative people are allergic to positive energy and they have many effective weapons in their arsenal to destroy positive energy thoughts, ideas and dreams. My first advice is to avoid them like the plague and surround yourself with positive people so that you are absorbing positive suggestions and influence.

How do you keep going through the tough parts

I remember talking to my father about the Second World War; he served in the RAF on Lancasters in Bomber Command. It was a long war where the odds were stacked against Britain. We can look back on what was happening from the standpoint of knowing the outcome. The participants did not know the outcome. My father stayed in the RAF for a total of 42 years and therefore was very experienced in military matters. What fascinated me was, how did he and everybody else keep going? He told me, 'despite all the terrible things that were happening and the odds against us we just knew that we were going to win through. We had to learn, recover, innovate faster, and above all keep going.' Clearly Winston Churchill's now famous speech about fighting them on the beaches reflected this view.

This is the attitude, an unswerving belief and determination, that you need to adopt for your success. It is within you, proven by how it was found in everybody in Britain during the war. They thought that failure was so horrible to contemplate that it could not be allowed to happen, no matter what. Do not mix up losing the war with losing battles. In business you may lose many battles, even whole companies. These are just battles, you learn from them and come back more effective than before.

The war accelerated the spirit of enterprise in everyone, the development of ideas such as radar, the Spitfire, the Anderson shelter, and blowing up dams with bouncing bombs! On the home front we learnt how to utilize our resources better to be self-sufficient in food, how to make factories double their output when the experienced men had been drafted into the forces. You see, with the right incentive we all can be incredibly innovative, enterprising, industrious and determined.

Progress now

What unacceptable pressures on your life are there? What action can you take or changes can you make now to bring them into alignment?

Entrepreneur interview: Sensei Paul Elliott

Sensei Paul has founded, runs and is expanding a group of karate schools around the south of England. He is 53 and lives with his wife and two children in Sussex. See www.wadoryu.co.uk

Alex: What is your career background?

Sensei Paul: I was originally a trainee electrician with Hawker Siddeley, and later worked for a smaller company. In 1980 I opened my first karate club in Sussex with a small group while maintaining full-time employment. Society can hold you back in a way, for example school focuses you on full-time jobs for careers. It was not until ten years later that I was really fed up working for somebody else. I really wanted to be my own boss and work at something I really loved and found worthwhile. In fact teaching, and helping others was a major motivation in itself. I get a real buzz from teaching, and I am teaching my hobby. I was thinking about this at a time my company was bought by a larger group which also made the job less appealing. Initially I had a small income from the club and also did some freelance work as an electrical expert.

I realized from the start that I had to sell myself and worked non-stop at all sorts of ideas to promote the club. I had to inform people of its existence to get them there and then to maintain interest to keep them coming and spread a good reputation. I had posters put up, leaflets distributed, including on cars, newspaper advertising and visited adult education centres. I took a lot of action to promote myself and offered a variety of services. I have now opened other clubs around the south and am looking for instructors further afield.

In 1997 I opened a shop, with a partner, that turned out to be a disaster for me. I was left responsible for debt that was not really mine. I could have pursued it legally but I knew that my energy was more productively utilized in building a karate school. Negative energy needs to be let go and replaced with positive attitude.

I am always looking at new things. For example, I set up a separate club for children and used teaching methods that were more applicable. In fact, I have many children that I have trained to black belt. I am developing a web page with one of my members and producing videos with another. I am also developing healing courses, which is another side of the martial arts, using the chi energy. I am a healer member of the National Federation of Spiritual Healing.

How I run the club with my team is very different. I do a great deal of research and also put many variations in the syllabus. This helps me maintain my interest and this attracts people to the club. I teach skills and techniques, for example in how to talk your way out of a fight, or calm a situation down. You have to be patient with a business. I set up a new club once and had one person for three months. Then it grew to twenty!

Wado Ryu means the way of peace and this is the focus of the discipline. For example, pressure points can be used in self-defence techniques. They can also be used in healing, such as acupressure. Karate is all about control of internal energies. I have this term 'energy vampires' that suck out your energy. There are negative people, situations and objects that can drain your energy.

Alex: How do you define success?

Sensei Paul: Being happy at what you do. If you suddenly lost all your material possessions would you still be happy? I would.

Alex: What advice would you give somebody starting out?

Sensei Paul:

1 You have got to take a gamble and trust that you can do it.
2 Be wary of taking on a partner.
3 Don't get in a rut doing things the same way. Try something else.
4 Don't do everything yourself. Look for advice.
5 Don't worry about security. The companies that I had secure jobs with have all gone now!
6 Minimize the risks. Take any safeguards. I have medical insurance, for example.

Alex: How do you motivate yourself when things go wrong?
Sensei Paul: One door closes, others open.

Alex: How do you spot an opportunity?
Sensei Paul: Ideas just come, particularly during quiet times or meditation. I constantly ask myself what to do next. If you try to think of ideas they might never come; if you have a clear mind, ideas come.

Three tips

1 Enjoy it!
2 Keep all aspects of your life in balance.
3 Occasionally take a short away break.

Two tasks

1 Write down what you are best at and like doing the most. Focus on that.
2 Make one improvement in your lifestyle, however small.

14

going for it!

In this chapter you will learn:
- why your top goal must be financial freedom
- that success is a decision, yours
- that desire is the main driver
- that if you focus on one thing you will get it
- various sources and methods of raising finance

'*Empty pockets never held anyone back. Only empty heads and empty hearts can do that.*'

Norman Vincent Peale

'*Never, never, never, never give up.*'

Winston Churchill

Two of the most common questions I am asked by aspiring entrepreneurs are:

1 How do you get started while providing for yourself and perhaps a family?
2 How can you raise enough finance to get your business off the ground if the bank turns you down?

Focus

In working out their goals, many people seem to focus on houses, holidays, cars, etc. It is more effective to focus on financial freedom as your goal. All the other things will come anyway. You are financially free when you have created enough wealth so that your income from it, without depleting capital, is sufficient to live on. In this situation you never have to worry about money, ever again. Luxury goods deplete wealth and should never hamper your progress towards financial freedom or take it away from you.

You tend to get what you focus on and the material things can be achieved by raising mortgages, loans and credit cards. I think that having a lovely house with a larger mortgage, a car on loan and a holiday paid for by credit card is celebrating success before it has happened and does not lead to happiness. This is conditioning your mind to reward yourself without success, and this sets up bad habits that at best will hold you back, at worst put you out of business.

So have houses, cars, holidays as part of your dream building, but make sure that you reward yourself when you can really afford them by paying cash and by remaining financially free. Once you are financially free you never want to risk losing this position. Focusing on being financially free is more supportive to running your business. It keeps your mind on cutting costs, making sales, creating new ideas, growing and investing; this is what counts. Your goals are the driving force that will keep your motivation fired up, whatever the conditions.

Goals can seem sometimes too big a target, too far off. The thing to remember is that goal like a house: it is made up of individual parts, every brick you build is one step closer to the house. Every step forward in your business is a step in the right direction. Always focus on achieving the next step. It will be easy to focus on and not be an overwhelming target. We can see clearly what is close to us. Do something every day to take you closer to your goal.

The success decision

Entrepreneurship is a state of mind, an attitude and a decision. So one of the secrets is taking control of your thoughts, making them work towards your goals. Most people are a slave of their thoughts, their thoughts take them randomly through life. They feel depressed and they don't even know why. Feeling good is a thought. Don't believe me, try this.

Progress now

Think of three things that are great in your life right now.

To learn you should pay more attention, from challenging what you already know, do or believe in to seeing what else comes in. Changing some of the routine things we do teaches us how to break patterns and allow in new choices. We can think in a different way.

Progress now

Think of something you do habitually. Now change it.

Motivation

If I set you the challenge of making a million in the next three months could you do it?

If you had three months in which to make a million, or you would lose all contact with your family and friends, could you do it?

Most people say no to the first and yes to the second. If this is you, my next question is what changed?

See, motivation is easy. It all depends on your desire and how much you want something.

Customer focus

Many people I have coached and trained in sales have needed their focus changing, from their commission to the needs of the prospect. Prospects will tell you their needs freely and provide you with commercial opportunities. If you are walking in with a specific product to sell, you will focus on how to move your prospect's conversation to your offer. It is better selling to just listen and then offer something that truly addresses their needs. People looking for commission focus on their offer. There is no 'empathy bond' created, the bond that transfers knowledge.

Some of you stop growing because you believe you have not got enough brains. Hey, use other people's brains! Business is a team sport. Knowledge is easy to acquire. Anything you want to know just type it in the search engine of your web browser. It is that simple.

Sales channels

There is always more than one way to sell your merchandise. Here are some avenues for your consideration.

- Set up a group of sales agents.
- Employ commissioned sales representatives.
- Organize other companies to be resellers.
- Give free talks, presentations or demonstrations.
- Offer your products to a network marketing company or set one up yourself.

Free resources around you

You are surrounded by great wealth, all is available for you to use freely. Have you taken your share yet? Here are some sources for consideration.

- local library
- friends
- personal contacts
- government offices
- tax rebate if starting on low income
- brains of friends
- living room
- location
- competitors
- potential suppliers

What stops you going for it?

Barriers to entry in any particular industry vary but the most common responses I get from people who have not started yet are: supporting my family and the mortgage, lack of finance, lack of suitable staff, lack of an established name. They are all excuses for not overcoming fear of some sort. Recognize this, and identify and work on those fears.

Finance raising for the entrepreneurial firm is hard. Retained profits are clearly the main source and thus there is even more of a case for thrift, to make sure every penny made can be reinvested. Many entrepreneurs are caught in the dilemma of having a full order book, which they are turning away, due to lack of finance to produce.

Fear is the biggest stopper: fear of losing your house, poverty, criticism, failure. My boss once said to me: 'If the pressure comes on get your head down and work.' A good technique for two reasons.

1 If your mind is occupied with working you have not got spare capacity for worry.
2 By taking action it is fairly obvious that your work is going to progress you beyond your current challenges.

Pricing

I have noticed many times that when considering price, people will focus more on a discount than they do on the absolute price. They will also judge quality from the original price not the discounted one. Their attention is on how much money is off.

So if you want £25 for an item, ask for £35 and offer them a special £10 discount. Their mind immediately focuses on the £10 saving on a £35 level of quality item. It is an illusion, as the basis for the £35 price was not established in the first place.

So when you are buying, only consider the asking price. Be wary of making judgements on what the price used to be. If there were buyers at this price they would not be offering a discount!

One thing at a time

Be wary of having five great ideas and going for all of them. Focusing on one, making it work and then moving on to the next is a much more practical strategy destined for success.

If you are starting a new enterprise, that very newness can put off both potential customers and suppliers. The latter look for cash payments until you have established yourself. To a potential customer, your being new means that your service is more unpredictable than an established player. Naturally, how important these points are depends on your type of business.

The beauty about owning your own business is that you can run it the way you want. Business history is full of radical ideas, well out of the ordinary, that worked. There are even more failures. The ideas have got to work.

I once knew an organization where the owner was constantly frustrated at the bickering about unfairness of the salary scheme. He came out with an interesting solution: he put everybody, including directors and managers, on the same salary! You can guess what happened. Those who got a rise were highly motivated and those who got a cut left over the coming months. Surprisingly, the organization prospered with a total absence of hierarchy. I think he felt that if the original managers were worth their salaries, he would not have had to deal with such unrest in the ranks!

Don't give up

Many entrepreneurs who have made a great fortune claim to have struggled for years. In fact, weeks before their big breakthrough came they debated with themselves regularly on giving up. They often think that if they had given up, they would have never known just how near they were to a fortune. So often great success is just around the corner.

Networking

Think about all the people you could possibly contact to get your sales of the ground.

Progress now

1 Write a list of 100 names of people you know. How well you know them or in what capacity is irrelevant. Consider first family, relatives, friends, colleagues, ex-colleagues, club members, neighbours, people you have bought something from.

2 Write a second list of 100 people, this time names of those you have met through the above list.

You now have your starting point for networking.

3 Go through the list, giving careful consideration to each name and in what way they could help you in your venture.

4 Phone them, tell them your plans and how you see them fitting into them, and ask if they can help. Whether they do or don't show interest, ask them for two referrals. Also ask them for their ideas.

Know what you are up against?

Carry out your own survey of competitors. Phone them with a sales enquiry.

- How many rings before they answered?
- How pleasant out of ten was the greeting?
- Were you left hanging on?
- Did they ask your name or number?
- Did they really want your business?

If you make sure that your employees perform better than the above, you will rise above them.

The most crucial resource in any business is its people. At the beginning, one mistake and the enterprise can be out for the count before it has had its fair chance. Therefore people, as a resource, have to be managed effectively. The entrepreneur has to take total responsibility.

Practicality of raising money

Good entrepreneurs apply their creativity to minimizing the financial resources they will need to get their venture underway. They will live on a survival budget, work all hours from home, convert the garage and buy second hand. This way they can slowly build up sales with a minimum of overheads, learning as they go, getting the business model right, and grow from there.

Sometimes, though, depending on the nature of the venture this method might work but raising significant finance can make what would happen in five years happen in one year. Books on business will advise you that there are two main sources of finance: debt or equity. This means that you get a loan and pay interest or sell shares in return for a cash investment. In practice, both sources have benefits and disadvantages. For many entrepreneurs the loan route will be limited unless they have considerable assets to secure the loan.

Do not be naïve. If you walk in to a bank with a fantastic plan for a business, you will probably be turned down. At some point you will be asked how much equity you have in your house; this is their primary interest. This secures their loan if the business fails. As their statistics will clearly indicate, only one in a hundred businesses survives the first year. So expect to be rejected; they, after all, will not share in your capital gain if you make it big. Why should they finance your dream? There are, however, sometimes schemes available such as guaranteed security from the government for a loan.

That is where venture capitalists come in. These can be private investors, known as business angels, or institutions. If you go down this route your main cost can be all the time you spend researching, developing, visiting, presenting and negotiating with these people. You have to become an expert in something you will probably only do once. That is why I recommend going to a medium to large firm of accountants or lawyers which specialize in this area. They usually work on a percentage of money raised. They also do a great deal of the work and can give good advice on a whole range of things such as patents and contracts.

Now I am going to tell you the streetwise ways to finance your business that the business school books don't tell you about.

Factoring/invoice discounting

Factoring is a great idea for growth companies with continually increasing needs for working capital. Basically the concept is simple. The finance company will give you what is effectively a secured loan on your invoices out. To an entrepreneurial company the debtor balance is always growing and thus always causing more of a strain. Factoring will give you a percentage of your invoices on issue and charge you an overdraft-type interest rate. They will also now provide you with full credit control and legal services. If your business is paying out for contract labour on a weekly basis and being paid on 30 to 90 day terms, factoring can be the difference between being in or out of business. Bear in mind, if you grow your overdraft size automatically goes up with your invoicing level.

Again, look closely at the small print of the agreement you will be signing. They often want personal guarantees and initial deposits, both of which I have negotiated out of a deal in the past so I know that you can achieve the same.

Grants and awards

Contact your bank manager, the Department of Trade and Industry, Business Link, the Training and Enterprise Council, the European Commission, your MP, Euro MP, Chamber of Commerce, local networking group, trade or professional association and your accountant for information. Big companies sometimes have a programme to support entrepreneurs: Shell and IBM have done so in the past. There are many grants available particularly if you are set up in a relatively less developed part of the country. They are clearly worth pursuing but sometimes the research and application process can be time consuming with no guaranteed result. Time that could have been spent productively.

Retained contracts

Whatever business you are trying to launch, this method is always worth consideration. The technique basically rests on who will buy from you when you are up and running? Visit prospective customers and sign them up to a contract, where they pay one-third as an initial retainer for you to start work. (You never let them know just how dependent you are on the upfront payment.) Aristotle Onassis was a master of this technique. He started his shipping career by getting a contract for delivery and then taking that to a bank in order to get a loan to buy a ship! Thus he was able to offer collateral.

Supplier credit

When you have worked out your business plan, you will know what you need the money for. If you can negotiate 90-day terms with suppliers this could solve or considerably reduce your financial requirements. Those 90-days will allow you to get your own sales up and running. Find suppliers who need orders. Once you are trading, your suppliers can be kept at bay with promises of future orders. Bear in mind that to pursue their money would, in practice, take at least another 90 days anyway. Ideally, rather than just not pay creditors, negotiate the terms, keeping their goodwill, offering them your long-term business as you grow.

Loan back

Banks, often with a government scheme supporting them, will probably lend to an entrepreneur on a 1:1 basis. This means for every £10,000 of cash the business puts up, the bank will equal it. Assuming you have not got an initial sum, one way to achieve this is as follows. Say you wanted to raise £50,000. You take in a partner who invests £50,000 in the business. You go to the bank with this and they give you £50,000. You now give back the original stake to the investor over a period, with a bonus in terms of shares for their trouble. You are off! In practice, you may work this principle with more finesse than the bare outline of the idea above.

Fast-growth businesses, by definition, need a lot of investment to keep the momentum going. I have been in the situation of having an overloaded order book without the finance to employ the staff to carry out the work. It is a very frustrating and real problem. You turn it away or take the risk of overtrading. That is going bust, caused by trying to keep up with rising sales while cash flow is becoming overstrained.

Contingency payments

Advertise by paying the advertiser commission on sales. For example, instead of buying advertising space, negotiate a deal where the company can market your products for a cut. This way you have no advertising spend and a steady income stream without any incumbent fixed costs. Whatever your product or service, there will be hundreds of webmasters interested in such a proposal. Pick sites which have the type of traffic that would be interested in what you offer.

Supplier funding

This method is producing to order. Market your goods and services whatever they are and produce them to order, thereby avoiding the necessity to manufacture and hold inventory. You may have to work very fast, so make sure you are prepared.

Who else has got an interest in me succeeding?

Ask yourself the above question. When you have the answers, and there will be many, ask yourself how you can use this knowledge to help the enterprise. Issuing shares to family and friends can be better than just asking for loans. This way they participate in the profits if all goes to plan and you do not have a debt if it does not. Later, when raising further venture capital, it could look good to have more than you as a shareholder.

Credit cards

Because credit cards companies get a percentage from the retailer every time you use one and charge you interest, they are extremely lucrative for the issuer. The large amount of fraud and defaults is tiny compared with the huge profits they make. Therefore they go overboard trying to give out as many as possible.

Many major companies started in this way, for example Cisco Systems. The advantage is that by getting as many cards as possible you can finance a significant amount of purchases.

Unlike the bank, credit card companies don't require you to spend one day a month preparing a report on how well you are doing.

The interest rate will be high but you have given away no equity and it can get you off the ground with little fuss. They are, however, in your personal name, so pay them off as a priority. I know many entrepreneurs who keep several credit cards so that they can go a couple of months without drawing salary if they need to, or acquire something immediately when an opportunity arises.

Reverse financing

Another way of solving this demand for funding is to look at the challenge inside out.

In other words, instead of bringing capital into the company, take the company to the capital. You can approach an existing larger company that is well funded, and offer your enterprise together with you as a package. Part of the deal is that they can have majority control and even a formula to buy out your minority interest geared to performance.

This way you can use their corporate resources and infrastructure without any extra spend: they will have an established name, contacts and markets. Your venture is now far more secure and has a far greater chance of success. They have control both of the shareholding and of financial decisions. Therefore their investment too is a lot less risky. It is essential that the partnership is made with an organization that has synergy with your enterprise. Specifically the partnership can further exploit resources that they already have.

You become MD, or whatever your preferred role/skill is, and with your team you make it happen. Another advantage of the small and large companies working together is that a larger organization will have more muscle to help you get through things like recession or other temporary challenges that arise.

This is an ideal option if your objective is a capital gain. You are more interested in the value of your shareholding than the percentage. You could also use this route to sell out and have a significant cash resource for your next venture.

Franchising

Be a franchisor. This way the managers of all the branches effectively bankroll the whole operation. Franchising is a possibility when you have a business model that can be duplicated easily to autonomous units. The main danger is having franchisees who, being owners, want to call the tune all the time. You cannot control a franchisee in the same way as you can control an employed manager. Many small companies have become large this way, without the need to raise large amounts of capital.

Progress now

With reference to your last five years, and to what you want to achieve in the next five years, consider very carefully the following statement.

'It is not what talent you have got, it is how you use it that counts.'

Three tips

1 Start each day with physical exercise.
2 Write the next day's 'to achieve' list before you go to bed.
3 Expect success, and keep going for it until you are proved right.

Two tasks

1 Join a gym, get a fitness regime going, this week.
2 Get a business going on eBay®.

15

letting the genie out of the lamp

In this chapter you will learn:
- how to spot a gap in the market
- how to build a reputation for excellent customer service
- how to progress from failure
- once the genie is out, what to wish for
- how to build your own 'Enterprise Island'

'If we all did the things we are capable of doing, we would literally astound ourselves.'

Thomas A Edison

'Most people give up just when they're about to achieve success.'

Ross Perot

Going forward

The natural entrepreneurial spirit of corporate staff is often lying dormant. All they need to do is revitalize it. This usually means setting up their own business. For a corporation to encourage entrepreneurship, and many do, there must be no punishment in any form to anyone who makes a mistake, or fails. If there is, personnel will seek to stay with the safe and secure. In fact, when working with individual goals it should be made company policy that every employee should fail at something. And then say what they learnt from it. This way they have to think of new ideas as part of their job.

Venture capitalists know that for every ten new ideas they invest in, most of them will not make it. Yet the one that becomes, say, a Google® is worth all the others. It is like this with ideas. More often than not it is the failed ideas that lead to further work on the same idea that eventually creates something that works. Failure is the essential process that allows success. So if you have a corporate culture that punishes failure, you will not develop a breed of corporate entrepreneurs. This holding back of entrepreneurial instincts gives rise to many new companies each year. At some point the entrepreneur in employees says 'enough' and decides to pursue their dreams.

Can you tell me why it was not an established, well-financed, multinational retailing organization which developed the ideas that Jeff Bezos had for Amazon. So often it is people from outside an industry who come up with the idea. So one of the problems you have is this: your strength area is the industry/profession with which you are familiar. You have bought into your business many of the established ways of doing things, which can hamper new perspectives. To be innovative the trick is to challenge all your assumptions and ask a whole series of question beginning with 'Why ...'. Challenge everything.

It is clear that to be a good entrepreneur you must have a balance of different traits. For example, you must be both optimistic and pessimistic. Most people seem to have one trait and believe that people are one or the other.

Optimism is valuable in visualizing a potential market for your idea and to provide the daily drive to keep you going through thick and thin. Pessimism defends you against things that could come up. Think ahead of time and rack your brains for everything that could go wrong. Then structure your business accordingly. A common defence is to ensure that the cost base is as low as possible. The lower it is the longer you will withstand a cold wind. Also, of course, your profitability will be higher, not to mention the competitive advantage you will have.

In the north of England there is an expression, 'Where there's muck there's brass'. This basically means that money is made in the non-glamorous areas. Why? Because nobody wants to work there and this discourages new entrants. In business you make money when you supply what people need. This sounds obvious but many keep failing by doing what they want and then looking for a market for it.

Mind the gap

Anyone who travels on the London underground hears these three words often just before the doors open. Like those travellers, entrepreneurs always need to be spotting gaps. It always makes me think of moving people from one place to another. Predicting gaps that are emerging is where there is most opportunity.

A gap to an entrepreneur must be defined as something that is not being supplied, or supplied well, which can or will satisfy a frustrated need. The same product at a better price through more efficiency of production might be the gap you are looking for. Often if there is something not currently available it could be because nobody wants it. You might be in a long list of entrepreneurs who stumbled upon this idea only to then lose your risk capital. So be mindful of any gap and examine any opportunity thoroughly in terms of costs and realistic sales, and how those sales can be made.

Innovate to prosper

People often think that entrepreneurs focus their ideas purely on creating new products or services. Ideas and innovation are equally important in running the business itself. If you have an idea to produce an existing product in a way that is far more efficient, you can compete for sales on price. The enterprise might be founded on a manufacturing process that the consumer is not even aware of. Ford Motor Company in its relatively early days turned its innovation and ideas not just to new and better motor cars but more cost effective methods of production. They eventually revolutionized the industry with what seem common methods now, but which were radical then.

Companies, when they do well and establish a lead, gain advantages from economies of scale and brand awareness. Quite often, this comfort zone takes away the pressure that stops them innovating, thus producing opportunities for entrepreneurs. Big companies can seem frightening competition, but as well as their advantages they also have several disadvantages, depending sometimes on the industry or markets in which they are operating.

Whatever dilemma you face there are:

- Always three ways out of it.
- Always three ways to turn it to advantage.
- Always three lessons to be learnt to improve future decision making.

I guarantee the above. If you don't believe me I will run a day seminar for you on the basis that if I don't deliver, you don't pay. Think about the advantage of the above to any company that you know. Those suffering a turndown in their market, those facing overseas trading issues, those with production problems. You only have to look.

Name awareness

When naming your enterprise use care and start by writing down a list of the objectives. Using your name might give your ego a great boost but will it encourage sales? Among these should certainly be something that is memorable and ideally something that tells people what the enterprise does. Look at some of the names out there, for inspiration.

Cash counts

Cash is your top priority; always be aware of present and future movements of cash. Accountants might be more interested in profit and loss, but entrepreneurs know that a sale is real only when the cash has cleared through the bank, and a purchase affects them only when they part with cash to pay for it, not a moment earlier. If you thus keep it simple by planning to maximize the amount of cash in your bank, you will not go far wrong.

Customer service

Progress now

Think of six companies with which you have had dealings in the last year: three from which you had excellent customer service and three where it was awful. This can include local businesses.

Now write down the three things which the three excellent companies did that got them on your list.

Write down the three things which the three awful companies did that got them on your list.

You now have a list of what to do and what not to do when you launch your own business. Interestingly, I have run this exercise with many companies and the answers in both columns are pretty much identical at the end of the exercise. My conclusion is that we all know what we like and what we don't like and, guess what, everybody has much the same opinions. The same companies in both lists do tend to keep coming up. The first list has on it Virgin, Marks & Spencers, McDonald's, Amazon, Disneyland® Resort Paris.

When you have a customer base, you need to develop more customers for what you are supplying or supply more to that market. If you are selling consumables, like soap, your customer will repeat purchase the same item from you. If it is a one-off sell like a CD it may be better to have a series.

A day in the life of Joe Freedom

He wakes up early, raring to go. Passion for the day ahead fills his mind with energy. He owns an executive search consulting firm that is one year old. He has worked hard to get some clients on board. Joe spotted a niche in the market for qualified accountants with fluent second languages and he has set his business up with the name 'Accountants Anywhere'. He employs three members of staff and, although doing well, cash flow is a constant challenge and the much sought for growth eludes him.

The first year was harder than he thought. As a top performer, previously in a leading firm, he never realized the advantages of an established name and a constant flow of candidates and clients. He also never realized how many tasks were completed behind the scenes. His first month was spent entirely looking for offices. His second, designing and ordering stationery, everything from business cards to terms and conditions. His third month he spent getting the website up and running. Yet he was happy, the £25,000 overdraft facility was now just over £10,000 so the pressure was not on yet, he still had plenty of time.

Month four, he focused on recruiting staff so as to get sales coming in regularly. His personal billings were virtually non-existent while he completed all these tasks. Of course, having to establish new clients meant there was quite a time lag to making placements.

By month five he realized that sales were less than he predicted in his budget and the costs more than double. There were so many unexpected things coming up and no system to deal with them. Things like employee liability insurance, registering under the Data Protection Act, installing more telephone lines. He charged for placed executives so he invoiced when they started their new position. He realized just how long 'working three months' notice' meant.

Month six, and sales, while under target, were nevertheless steadily rising. Of course, the staff were paid commission long before it was received. This meant in most cases the invoices were not even out, let alone paid.

Month seven, and his overdraft had reached £24,000 although, on the good side, he had reached breakeven level. This meant that his invoices out and his placements not yet billed totalled £35,000. Debts to suppliers were just £2,400. The landlord of the office had demanded two months' rent in advance as a deposit so technically he had an asset sitting there. He had a 25-year lease, so at least his base was secure.

To build an executive recruitment business he had to look the part, so he had a £10,000 limit on his three credit cards and with them bought two top-quality suits and a new car, nothing over flash but he had to do a lot of travelling and taking clients out to lunch.

In month eight the bank called and wanted to see him. He showed them his accounts and they agreed to maintain the overdraft at £25,000 for a further six months. Joe was expecting them to support him further, but realized now that his house equity would not cover it and this was all they were really interested in. It also came as a shock to him when the bank manager reminded him that they could call in the overdraft at any time. On checking this he found out that banks not only could but often did. Having got his own business he resented the bank manager telling him how to run it.

All the answers to Joe's problems are in this book.

Progress now

What ten things would you do differently from the start if you were Joe?

Entrepreneur culture

The USA is undoubtedly the home of the entrepreneur and continues to lead the world with innovative commercial ideas. Not surprisingly the venture capital industry started in the USA and their ideas are all over our high streets, living rooms and television. The advent of the information age saw many US entrepreneurs, such as Netscape®, Yahoo!®, Google and Amazon, become household names that had not even existed a few years earlier.

I have noticed in Britain that talking about a plan to raise £5million for a venture can meet with doubts from friends, let alone venture capitalists. We perhaps need to learn from the Americans how to dream and think bigger. So many things, for so long, have started in the USA and then five years later arrived here. Why wait? Go there now and fly back in five days with a laptop full of ideas.

Failure: the secret of my success

Plan for how you will react to every possible failure, right from the start. Few entrepreneurs do this, but the great ones nearly all did. Saying 'it will never happen to me' is just unrealistic. If you have dug yourself into a hole, stop digging. Stop when you know you are not progressing and refocus your energies. Learn and move on.

Another bite at the cherry

If you are going off course, don't keep drifting. Your time as an entrepreneur is your company's greatest asset. Staying until the ship goes down can take forever and deny you the next opportunity. Stay focused on your long-term goal. This sometimes means abandoning the direction in which you are going. Entrepreneurs continually reinvent their companies and ideas. The main asset of the business is you, focus on that. If you are the asset, even liquidation cannot stop you from transferring it to your next venture. Set yourself a deadline, targets that have to be reached or you will call it a day and move on.

If something has failed the danger is in kidding yourself. Don't spend years drifting to a slow inevitable end, hoping for that big break. Instead, take all that you have learnt and make a better attempt next time. Each failure is a step to success. Read the biographies of any famous entrepreneurs and you will realize that the secret of mirroring their success is not to be found in studying how they succeeded but how they reacted to their failures. Think of a failure as a consultancy worth £100,000.

Do you own the business or does it own you?

Entrepreneurs tend to think of their businesses as part of them. If it is attacked they react accordingly. Yet the idea never dies; it moves on, learns from mistakes and keeps changing, as you build experience. This experience is a million-dollar asset: don't throw it away. It only needs converting into hard cash. Grow from the knowledge.

As the future unfolds

Traditionally small firms have taken on their bigger competitors by specializing in a niche. For example, Tie Rack competed in one niche against major high street clothing retailers like Marks & Spencer, but only clearly in one line. However, times change and it takes longer for companies to adapt to those changes. Many believe it's the smaller company that moves more quickly to take advantage but this is not necessarily the case. What they notice is that smaller companies can change more quickly if they notice those changes. The arrival of the internet and the continuing developments in its uses and technologies have reinvented marketing. To the internet there are no foreign markets. Small firms can take orders overnight from around the world that previously would have meant setting up local offices.

In the recruitment industry, since the 1970s, there has been the growth of specialist agencies dealing with one profession, accountancy, IT, insurance, engineering, sales, and so on. Before the internet, the value of a recruitment company was its database of candidates, built usually by extensive advertising over a period of time. Now you can set up a recruitment agency from your bedroom at 9am, register with an online CV database, and by 10am have access to thousands of people looking for work in all of the above categories, in any location you want. This is an indication of how much change is going to happen in the one industry.

Once you have got your business established and into profit, you have a choice: to stay small or to go for growth. It depends entirely on your motivation. Growth usually means increased risk. Taking a risk when you have nothing or little to lose is easier than when you have a significant asset to lose. I have noticed that this is clearly where the self-made millionaires and the billionaires part company. The millionaire group are often motivated by insecurity. Therefore their objective when they accumulate wealth is to take it away from risk. The billionaires, on the other hand, were far more prepared to use their capital to leverage to the next level, often meaning taking very high risks.

Many entrepreneurs go for growth. Having worked for a considerable time in the recruitment industry, I have noticed time and time again a company with one branch and a dozen staff make more profits than their competitor with a national chain. More size can mean more problems. Expand only when you are bursting at the seams to supply orders that you already have. If you want to open a branch network, develop a business in that area from your base and set up locally only after you already have a market there.

Complete the journey

Drive will have to be very strong to keep you going. Entrepreneurs have advantages because they are doing exactly what they want to do in their way, and are taking full responsibility. That strength will mean a person who is self-disciplined, confident in themselves and their ideas. This belief must take the knocks of failure. Success is getting up again no matter how many times you are knocked down.

The same risk and fear that stops some people from even trying is the buzz that gets others to go for it. The interviews spread around this book with entrepreneurs show that those who have succeeded have these same fears and have used them to fuel energy and motivation. Some people jump off mountains with a rope around their foot to get an adrenaline rush. Compared with this, the worst thing that can happen in business is that you lose money. Unlike the bungy jump, if the business all goes wrong you can have another go, all the wiser for your experience!

I know that everyone has within them the creativity, drive and all that it takes to be a successful entrepreneur. It takes just three extra things: the motivation, an idea and some streetwise techniques. As James Bond said, 'You only live twice'. Once is your reality and once is the life you imagine for yourself in your mind. If a fantasy is enough for you, stick with it. However, if you want to live your dreams join the cult of being an entrepreneur that boasts beng the creators of nearly everything around you that was not produced by nature. You are sitting on a treasure chest of opportunity: get off, open it up and put it to use!

Develop your future vision by always keeping up to date with the trends and what is happening in your industry. Spot trends and react to them rather than go with the crowd. Going with the crowd makes people feel safe in business, but none of the successful entrepreneurs mentioned in this book succeeded that way. Timing is a key element in business success. All of the famous entrepreneurs whose biographies are listed at the back of this book were in the right place at the right time. This was through luck, through being aware of what was going on in the industry, and seeing where the future could be taken. They also made the most of the opportunity. Remember every single company out there, large and small, was started by an entrepreneur with a dream.

Enterprise Island

A dozen people are shipwrecked on a desert island. The island is in the middle of the Pacific, uninhabited. Some useful debris from the ship washes ashore but no communication equipment. The people consist of four women, four men, two boys and two girls. We join them on the first day as they wake up on the beach after an exhausting night of struggling to survive. They do not know it at this point, but they will become the forefathers of future generations of the island race.

There is no immediately obvious supply of food, no protection against the elements, no protection against wild animals, no medicines should anyone fall ill or have an accident. There is no economy to provide a job! The only option is to use their own enterprise, yet there are no banks to get a loan from. No suppliers to buy provisions and materials from. No resources to live off while developing facilities, food, fresh water etc.

They meet to discuss their priorities. They agree that defence is the first priority against thirst, animals, weather and hunger. The first being the most urgent, they then send four of the party to secure a water supply. A second group concentrates on building a secure shelter, while the third group looks for food, focusing on any fruits that might be around.

By the end of the day, they have found water and a plentiful supply of bananas. The weather is warm and they have found a place of natural shelter to sleep for the night.

They wake on the second day with more energy. Work priorities are obvious so they just work all the daylight hours. By evening they have a clear plan to build a house from various materials that are in abundance. They even manage to make some rudimentary tools. They have collected a heap of fruit. They also have a plan of diverting water from a stream on higher land thorough carved-out tree trunks.

On day five one of the women has a brilliant idea of how to catch fish with minimum effort. She has noticed an inlet cove that was flooded at high tide but emptied later on. Her idea is simply to block the exit with reeds which can be secured in place allow water to pass back out but trap the fish inside. Her husband is an engineer and goes to work on this project with full gusto. After several failed attempts they eventually get it working and have a regular supply of fresh fish.

By the end of a fortnight they are fairly well organized and a different set of needs is coming to the front of their minds: cooking utensils to make their diet more interesting, stronger dwellings, ways to store food for the winter, even schooling provision for the children.

So it goes on, as each new project comes to completion, needs change, things are made more efficient.

Eventually the children arrive in adulthood and seek to take more of a work role. Three of the children are immediately employed on current projects. The fourth though, Harry, has it in his head to do his own thing and develop a device to harness the potential energy from water flowing downstream. While he is developing the project, some of the others feel that he is not pulling his weight with the work to be done. Naturally he still has to eat and his food is being provided by the others. Some of the others, though, decide to share their daily products in return for a share of the spoils should his project eventually work. A barter system had started. Harry feels that the others are jealous of his idea until, of course, he manages to convince them of its viability and they become increasingly supportive of the project. Those who were reticent at the start also begin to consider their position, if and when the project is successful. They will not want to miss out on the benefits then.

Over the years the population grows; the original castaways are elders now. Needs change again. The economy is growing and prospering and a barter system has developed. However, this becomes difficult because the schoolteacher, for example, cannot offer much to those who do not have children. So a rudimentary currency is established which means everybody has to put a monetary value on their services. Market prices are settled by haggling and by the availability of alternative choices.

In the following generations the economy evolves, and thus people and needs constantly changed. The Harrys are always needed whether on their own or working for an established enterprise that encourages ideas. Things fail more than succeed. Yet it is the Harrys who become the richest people in Pacifica.

The above story is not too distantly removed from how the USA was created. The original pioneers were skilled in noticing all the abundance of resources around them. They also had the vision to turn trees into houses, horses into vehicles, furs into clothing, land into crops. You don't need to raise capital to start a business: it is a myth. All the original entrepreneurs started without capital. We are all natural entrepreneurs: it is our natural inclination. You do not have to learn how to do it but uncover the dormant and frustrated talent within.

Imagine you had a field and planted money seeds, and all you had to do is water them and wait, watch them grow, and watch yourself grow rich. Like any valuable crop you need to protect it. Always be prepared for that unexpected storm, make it expected. That way you can have covers ready to protect your crop.

Every time you feel a challenge, read this book – you will find it uplifting, inspiring and with many suggestions applicable to your needs. When your dreams become realities write to me. Your story could be in my next book, inspiring others to achieve the great things that you have achieved.

Entrepreneur – go on I dare you to develop your own enterprise island.

Entrepreneur interview: Homayoon Fassihi

Homayoon constantly comes up with ideas: some have worked and he has sold them profitably, others have failed and he has learnt the lessons. Currently he is MD of DMN Nursing Agency which has clients all over London and East Anglia. Homayoon is 50 years old, originally from Persia, and lives with his wife and three children in Norwich.

Alex: What is your career background?

Homayoon: I always wanted my own business and was constantly seeing opportunities everywhere I looked. I believe that being an entrepreneur is something that is just in me. I have that type of personality where I want to reap a higher level of reward but am realistically prepared to be punished harshly if it goes wrong.

I noticed in the hairdressers that the manager was sending a staff member to the local launderette with a fistful of money for the machine. This to me seemed inefficient. I asked the manager how much it cost him in total to have all his towels washed. He added up the machine cost, but more importantly a staff member's wages for the time they were away from the salon. I said, 'If there was a service that could pick up, clean and deliver back your towels, at less price than what you have just estimated, would you be interested?' He responded, 'Of course.' I said, 'I'll be back'.

My idea was that if I had such a contract with all the hairdressers in Norwich, collection and delivery would be cost effective. I also realized having been to a launderette recently that the place was empty and clearly the marginal cost of running a machine was next to nothing. I had in mind to offer 10% of the retail price for a quantity and a regular deal. There was a profit to be made with minimal investment.

In the end I bought a launderette. I largely ignored the walk-in business. By the end of the year the launderette's turnover, let alone profit, was five times larger than when I had bought it. I literally knocked on doors and gained as many contracts as I could. Hairdressers were an obvious one. Business was booming and there was clearly a need for a dry cleaning service from my clients, so I bought a retail dry cleaners on a prime site with a view to using all of its spare capacity.

In year two I brought in new contracts which included a major London hairdressing chain, Air UK, KLM, Theatre Royal, Anglia TV, two Royal Air Force camps for uniforms, the five biggest hotels in Norwich, Youngs Suit Hire. The machines were literally working around the clock, I was working 18 hour days.

I then sold the launderette together with all the contracts. I later did the same thing with the dry cleaners. During the time there were many challenges on many fronts. I'd also had many other ventures along the way that did not work out or had relatively small success. For example, I developed a TV game called 'Icebreaker' and approached numerous television stations around Europe, later to find that my ideas did appear through somebody else. I launched a free ads newspaper before they were common, to be upstaged by a major group.

It was my wife though that gave my next big idea of a niche nursing agency offering a certain type of service. I set up from scratch and now run this business having personally brought in £1million worth of clients.

I am also currently developing a business plan for a programme of personal security courses, and a web portal focused on Ireland.

Additionally, with my wife Jane we are looking to set up a specialist care home and I am currently finalizing the business plan.

I have been to banks to support me and been rejected many times, but now with a track record of success I find that the bank comes to me. If you have proved you can make money everybody will look at your ideas. The first real success is the hardest, you just have to keep working at it until it works. Having had my fingers burnt has taught me to always be cautious with money. I believe that it is relatively easy to win new business; you need to put far more emphasis on keeping it.

Alex: How do you define success?

Homayoon: Knowing you have created something good and added value from your ideas. It is a feeling of self-confidence, shown by the way you walk and hold your head. Sometimes it is measured in the way other people respond to you.

Alex: What is the secret of success of an entrepreneur?

Homayoon: Think and plan long term and work 18 hours per day on what needs doing now. The payoff comes in say a two-year timescale. Focus on this.

Alex: What advice would you give somebody starting out?

Homayoon:

1 Work hard.
2 Don't give up.
3 Be enthusiastic.
4 Be stubborn.
5 Be honest. People will always accept a shortfall if you are honest and explain.
6 Never blame others, take responsibility for everything.

When you start out you have high expectations and low skills. You don't realize just how low they are and how much you have to learn. So inevitably you experience failure, probably a whole string of them. This mounts up until frustration sets in. You rapidly can find yourself digging out of a hole.

I do not regret a single negative experience because they took me to where I am today. I am very happy, doing what I love and being totally financially free. I advise anyone to cherish their experiences, whatever they are, as signposts to an incredible future. The journey may have a few storms in it but they make you a better sailor!

Be careful of moving too fast. Building a business is like cooking dinner. You want to eat now, but you have to wait for the food to cook properly. Rush and it will be burnt! Be patient, make sure you have all the right ingredients and the recipe for success. Then follow it.

Alex: How do you spot an opportunity?

Homayoon: I just feel that something is right, and this in itself generates an enthusiasm. Even if it does not work out, it becomes invaluable experience for the future.

Alex: What would you have done differently if you could go back in time?

Homayoon: I would be more careful on picking who I work with. I would learn how to say no.

Alex: How do you motivate yourself when things don't go to plan?

Homayoon: Like a boxer, you have to be able to take the knocks and just fight on.

Three tips

1 Visualize your future success, live it now.
2 Believe in magic and miracles.
3 Be unrealistic in your ambition and unreasonable in your determination to succeed.

Two tasks

1 Think about what you would do with £1million to spend.
2 Think about what you would do with £1million to invest?

16

escaping the rat race

In this chapter you will learn:
- how to escape
- to procrastinate procrastination
- the four false myths and one true one
- how to make a smooth transition from employee to entrepreneur
- why you should just concentrate on getting early customers

'Failure is simply the opportunity to begin again, this time more intelligently.'

Henry Ford

'The question is would you prefer to play or watch others play?'

Alex McMillan

A close friend of mine emailed me to point out a major start up event in London. He said it is the main event for entrepreneurs in the calendar.

I disagreed. It is not for entrepreneurs at all, it is for people who want to be entrepreneurs. You won't find Sir Richard Branson or Sir Alan Sugar there, or a million other people who, like them, are busy that day putting their ideas into action. Even the keynote speakers were not entrepreneurs. That is the difference: you need to be a player not an observer.

So are you dreaming of your own business, but still on the commuter train come Monday morning?

The velvet padded cell

Entrepreneurship is not for the faint hearted. That is why so many people with a brilliant idea and commercial skills never launch their ventures. How do those who do escape the rate race, and the shackles and security of employment, make the leap?

For many it is made easy for them: they lose their job. If you're made redundant and over 40, the recruitment market offers fewer and fewer opportunities. You thus have less to lose in going it alone. While resources are dwindling on a daily basis, your imperative is to stop the loss of cash and get earning again. Some people buy franchises, and if they are honest, have done nothing more than just buy a job, recreating the environment they once felt safe in. Nothing wrong with that, though, because they now own a job where they control their own destiny and can enjoy a capital gain.

Another route is by doing something in the evenings and at weekends while keeping the day job. Excellent route as the day job becomes the venture capitalist who claims no interest or share of equity. This is also a good route as it hardens up the 'budding' entrepreneurs for the 100-hour weeks that entrepreneurs work.

You could start with self-employment, especially if you are experienced in something in which it is relatively simple to secure two–three days a week work. It should be reasonably well paid to cover your costs of living, to free the rest of your week to plan, start and build your own business. Self-employment can also get you selling and provide you with a network of useful contacts.

Fighting the fear of failure

Why fear failure? Failure is your best friend. We are so geared to success through our childhood and schooling, sport and exams that life seems to be all about success. I found with my extensive interviewing and research of successful entrepreneurs that asking how they succeeded was the wrong question. Their secrets, ironically, were more in their attitude to failure. They learnt from failure and bounced back, they did not fear failure and therefore did not avoid situations that might mean they failed. They saw failure as the cheapest and fastest form of market research, an essential ingredient to achieve sales.

This is another example of a mindset you have to adopt different from the world where success was good and rewarded, and failure was bad and punished.

So, if you have a fear of failure get over it right now, and now you are over it, learn to look for it. Your failures are your signposts to where you want to be. Changing how you think about failure will help you escape the rat race.

Procrastination – leave it to tomorrow

When are you going to get into business for yourself?

- today
- tomorrow
- end of the week
- end of the month
- next quarter
- next year
- never, just talk and dream.

Commute to the City? Day in, day out? The crush, train delays? Work for a boss, towards their goals? Creativity, innovation, ideas, stifled? Trapped by that monthly salary immediately going straight out on mortgage, rates, credit cards, utilities, food? Frustration building, but not yet taken action? Months, even years of your life just seem like serving time towards a pension? Do you desperately want to work for yourself but don't know how or even what to do? Can't see the sums adding up? Oooh the risks, lose the house, would my marriage survive, would I? Any of above sound like you or someone you know?

I have been working with entrepreneurs for over 20 years and I am yet to meet one in their darkest hour who wanted to get back into the rat race. You just need someone to show you the path.

Once you escape, trust me, you won't want to go back. But you know that don't you? What you don't know is the how. Well actually, it is easy. Much easier than you think. We can show you how, as our club motto goes, make more money in less time with less risk. That is our promise to our members.

Let me dispel some myths.

Myth 1

You need to resign your day job to start your own business, and finance a 'development' period to get off the ground.

It is not necessary to give up the day job to start your own business. In fact, you can leverage your day job into self-employment. There are lots of ways without taking huge risks to make the transition safely to your own business.

Myth 2

You need to raise money, which in practice means securing a loan against your house.

I would not suggest to anyone to secure a bank loan on their house. I would rarely suggest a bank loan even on unsecured terms. There are usually better alternatives.

Myth 3

The main resource you need to start your own business is obviously finance.

Rubbish! The myth goes on to say that there are basically two ways to raise money: loans or issuing shares in your business.

There are over 200 different ways to raise money. More importantly, there are even more ways to avoid the need to raise money at all!

Myth 4

Employees and entrepreneurs think about money, investment and risk in a completely different way.

Totally true. Successful entrepreneurs think about money in a very different way from employees. Learning and then adopting this new 'mindset' is an essential part of setting you up for success before you start. Keep reading this book to change your mindset.

Are employees or entrepreneurs the risk takers?

Employee: I like the security of my monthly salary and the one thing that puts me off being an entrepreneur is the risk.

Entrepreneur: I could not sleep at night if all my eggs were in one basket. My entire life's career could be terminated with one short redundancy notice. Far too risky. I prefer to have several clients, then if one goes I am still OK.

Employee: Look at that Rolls Royce. I wonder what sort of job they have got?

Entrepreneur: Look at that Rolls Royce. There is someone who does not need to work for a living. No doubt they have built themselves a passive income and are now financially and time free.

In employment those earning more than £50,000 per annum are much less than even 1% of the workforce. Even so, after NI and PAYE it won't look that impressive.

In entrepreneurship there are tens of thousands earning more than £50,000 per year, who when they were still employees never even reached half of that! Oh, and they pay less tax and NI on the same income. Many of them no longer have to even turn up to work to receive this!

Entrepreneurs use resources to work for them, employees are a resource.

So stop thinking about escaping the rat race and make a move today, however small. Find something at which you can work evenings and weekends or part time. Something that requires no or little investment and can be slowly built up. A network marketing group, an eBay® business, a membership agent for my club, anything, but get going.

Credit card countdown

One of the essential ingredients of success in your own business is financial discipline. Ensure that you have this before you even plan your escape. Financial discipline means:

- saving for that inevitable rainy day
- living within your means
- knowing the difference between good (invested for a higher return) and bad (luxuries) credit
- not needing to impress others with 'glitz' i.e. a flash car
- borrowing (not money) rather than buying
- buying second hand rather than new
- doing without rather than going into debt
- using cash rather than plastic (this will reduce what you spend all by itself)
- paying all bills before indulging in £1 of luxury.

If you would currently go out with your partner for dinner and pay on a credit card with a hard core balance on it, then you are taking a mortgage out on dessert. That £2 ice-cream will finish up costing you £200. Anyone who pays that for dessert is never going to make it in their own enterprise. If this is you, harden up and change your habits, indulge after you have made it, not before.

The lower you can make your monthly living costs the less pressure you will be under and the sooner you will reach that breakeven point and the profits beyond. You will also increase the likelihood of staying in profit.

Many in starting out see venture capitalists as a way of funding their business and their salary. Investors will not want to pay to you, they will want the money invested in the business. They will also want to see you putting in everything that you have to show commitment and belief in your proposal. Look serious to them and you have far more chance of being funded.

Smooth transitions

Moving from the corporate to the entrepreneurial world can seem like crossing the Atlantic in a canoe: a few strokes in the right direction and one realizes how far the other side is. Enthusiasm is rapidly changed to fear until you finally head back to shore and safety while you still can.

My advice is to stop paddling and ditch the canoe. You are wasting valuable time trying to think of ways to paddle faster. You need to think differently. To continue the metaphor, I would suggest getting on the train to the airport and taking the plane. There is always a faster and safer route. Find it quickly as time is harder to find than money when you start out on your own.

You can make a smooth and safe transition to entrepreneur world, you just have to find a better way rather than concluding that the way is fraught with danger just because you attempted the wrong one.

Ask yourself better quality questions such as: 'How can I get into business for myself while minimizing the risk?

Answers might include:

- starting an evening/weekend online business
- joining a network marketing group
- consultancy part time to your present employer
- buying an already profitable business
- taking in a partner(s)
- finding a mentor
- developing your skills on running a business by joining a course
- buying out your current employer (unless you work for British Petroleum!).

Corporate entrepreneurs

A halfway house to being a true entrepreneur may be to be a corporate entrepreneur. It may be an option worth considering before you make the jump.

A corporate entrepreneur is someone working directly for a company as an employee. In my definition a corporate entrepreneur is someone who has managed to leverage their potential earnings to several times their salary without putting any money in. Someone who saves or makes the company £5million and gets a £5,000 rise has not managed to leverage, that is just a bonus. Someone who is on 10% of the benefit to the company has. Share options are the main way of being a corporate entrepreneur.

The role is a forward-looking one to keep the company ahead of its markets. The expertise can be from any discipline but it requires the entrepreneur attitude already discussed. If you are an innovator, I believe that there is going to be a considerable increase in demand for your services. Quite simply we are going through a phase in economic history of very rapid change. Companies have to keep pace with these changes to maintain their positions, let alone grow. People become accustomed to doing what they do in the same old way. Anyone who can show a company the way forward is going to be highly sought after. Clearly, excellent people communication skills are essential. These roles could be in a staff position inside a company or possibly via an outside consultant.

The internal entrepreneur often picks growth companies, often small usually, but not necessarily, where share options are the key part of the package. Share options are a marvellous and simple mechanism to let employees become corporate entrepreneurs. The formula basically says that they have an option to buy a certain number or percentage of shares at a fixed price left open for say three years. They put no money in but if the company rises in value they can make a substantial capital gain. The company can motivate and tie in key people this way. New start ups backed by venture capitalists usually offer share option schemes to key staff. This way you can still lose your job but not your shirt! In addition, there is potential to participate in the profits. Microsoft® created a large number of millionaires this way.

There is a rising demand for people to bring new ideas into organizations. They might work in any discipline but the roles will be to work on specific projects rather than in line management roles.

If you truly love your work and like creating things then you will never retire or be dependent on somebody else. As a recruiter for many years, I, and most of my colleagues in the industry, have always been frustrated about the preference of the job market for people aged 20 to 35. When people are mid-thirties plus they become sensitive to this and know that moving around is not going to be as easy as it was. There are some good reasons for this, for example the pyramid getting thinner as it reaches the top. This, I observe, means that employees are less likely to take risks in their organization. Their motivation moves from trying to go for promotion to trying to avoid being on the list of any redundancy programme. Let us look at both types of motivation and analyse what expected behaviours would be.

Going for promotion:

• Work hard and long hours.
• Be loyal to boss.
• Produce results.
• Think of ideas that can progress the company.

Avoiding redundancy:

• Do not stick your neck out.
• Go with the crowd.
• Make yourself irreplaceable.
• Be a yes man/woman.

You can be an entrepreneur and an employee of one organization or self-employed working for several. If you wish to be a corporate entrepreneur then your objective must include picking an organization where ideas are encouraged and failure is seen as learning. One of the interesting things about creativity is that if someone is part of the system in any way they cannot not be influenced by it. This is why outsiders to an industry are often the ones who shake it up with new ideas, for example Amazon to the bookselling industry. This equally applies to individuals.

In a corporation anyone in it at any level will have in some way bought into, indeed be part of, the way it is structured now. They will have been influenced by the way it thinks, involved into office politics and informal organizational structure. They also may have axes to grind and a vested interest in maintaining the status quo.

Thus, corporate entrepreneurship can be a very interesting, relatively safe and lucrative way to achieve your goals. If you wish, you could progress it to a full-blown consultancy business. All built from home with no real overheads to get started. If you are also in the post-35 age group where your age can be against you in permanent recruitment, suddenly you have turned this around. They are paying for experience and results more than if your face fits.

I have this idea ...

For me, considering investing in a business, I would value the idea at only about 1%. What I would really look for is the other 99%, the people who can make it happen. So don't get carried away because you have what you think is a good idea until you are sure that you have the skills or you can recruit in the skill to make it happen.

Has someone ever said to you something like, 'You see that product that everyone is buying like hot cakes? Well I had that idea several years ago.' It is usually said with a smug look on their face. These people are 1%ers; 100%ers turn ideas into businesses. You will escape the rat race faster by being an action person than an ideas one.

Employee to entrepreneur mindset

As employees we have all been trained, Pavlov style to work hard and then expect our reward, known as a salary package. The same experience taught you to expect two days off after every five working. Salary thus measures the value of your hard work and thus represents status and recognition level. You learn to judge success by the salary someone receives. If you see someone with an upmarket car or house, you wonder what job they do to have those possessions.

The answer, of course, is that the wealthy receive their unearned income, or not directly earned at least. They have other people or things working for them. Notice how the famous British entrepreneur Sir Richard Branson is always embarking on adventures, balloon trips and the like, and yet his businesses still flourish. He is not on the highest salary in Britain and none of the written works on him suggest anywhere that a high salary was his goal. His wealth does not come through salary.

Imagine a race between you and me right now. The challenge is to see who can dig the biggest hole in one hour.

You go first, pick up the spade and get digging fast, taking no pauses for breath in the whole hour.

I pick up my spade and pass it to ten rather big guys who start digging.

Sorry, I won!

Ridiculous example, showing how ridiculous you are trying to get rich by digging the hole all by yourself. I let you off easy: next time I am going to hire a JCB for each of them. It's a simple business principle that the Americans call leverage. It is why very few people get to be rich before 65, if then, by working for someone else. That is why you should stop digging and make a better plan.

In the world of the entrepreneur, the main measure of success is profit. Having a flash car or a plush office, is not a measure of success, it is the measure of someone who wants to be seen as successful. They are hangover habits from being an employee, a uniform you need to change as you escape.

It can take any adult less than five minutes to register a company online and appoint themselves as Managing Director and main shareholder. I see so many people rush to the printers to have their new status printed on their cards. It counts for nothing and is really dangerous as your thinking is still in a world where titles count for something.

Entrepreneurs are quite like farmers: they till the soil, they plant the seed, they pray for rain and, if all goes to plan, they still know they will have no income for several months. So when they do have a good crop they store some resources to get through the lean periods. They know that work today will be paid several months, even years, into the future.

I am not surprised that, although I did not know beforehand, two of the successful entrepreneurs I interviewed for this book were brought up on a farm. I think that good business lessons, which the rest of us had to learn, were ingrained in them at an early age.

Employees say, 'How can I pay my mortgage, bills, live, while I am building a business if I don't raise finance to cover this?' I am not going to answer that question because it is the wrong question. You need an entrepreneur mindset and when you have this you will stop asking this question. You need to start thinking like someone in business to make a profit and grow capital wealth. You will find ways to cut costs and get sales in fast. You will find ways to make a smooth transition.

You need to realize that the house you live in is not an asset. You need to realize that paying off the mortgage should not be your top priority. Don't you find it interesting that property investors tend to prefer interest only mortgages? Why do you think that might be? Could it be that they are using mortgage finance as leverage and thus want as much of it as possible? See, it is a different way of thinking. Again, 'How can I pay my mortgage off in two years?' is the wrong question.

An asset is something that makes you money, a liability is something that costs you money. Focus on building assets and reducing liabilities and you will do fine in business for yourself. Your house and car cost you money; shares, businesses and rental property make you money. I suggest you read Robert Kiyosaki's book *Rich Dad Poor Dad* to explore this point further.

Like a duck to water

It amazes me how many people I have met who confess that they stayed in the rat race for years, wanting their own business but fearful to make the leap, and then adapted to their new lifestyle nearly instantly. I think it is because when you are actually in business for yourself there is a surge of energy from doing what you really want.

There is always the realization that you are no longer on what Amway (the American network marketing group) calls, 'the 45-year plan') (i.e. leave education, get a job, work 45 years and retire, hopefully with a good pension at 65 finally financially free). People in their own businesses can get financially free in two years. Which means that even if your first venture fails, you could still be able to retire within a two-year timescale and this time you are more experienced.

There is also the realization that while you saw it as more risky and you need more confidence, in practice you are now in charge of your own destiny. Anything that happens, you are in a situation to do something about. In the rat race, you reflect that you could be made redundant in all of 30 seconds and not even see it coming, having no input on the problem.

eBay® – a good start

You can start an eBay® business while keeping the day job and thus avoid the short, sharp, shock of having to go from regular salary to zero income. Even better, you can gain experience of being in business for yourself without risking the house.

eBay® might not be your ultimate plan, just a first step. A step that can provide you with a financial cushion. Even a small amount of profit on eBay® will boost your confidence no end as you are now making profit in your own business. All you have to do now is increase these amounts.

eBay® also offers free and valuable market research. Present and archived auctions will tell you what price and how much interest any particular item attracts. You will also develop your online marketing skills, again free, just use their online tutorials to get going and then learn by your own experience of what works. Look at the listing of 'Power Sellers' in your market sector and see how they do it.

The magic questions here are:

- What can I source regularly at a cheaper price or better in some way than competitors?
- What expertise do I have? What hobbies or interests, that can be turned into a business?

Customers as venture capitalists

To the experienced entrepreneur the last place to go for finance is a bank or a venture capitalist. The first place is a potential customer, because the best source of finance is early customers. Why?

- They charge no interest.
- They take no shares.

The point of business is that customers give you more money than suppliers take off you. So start straight away to think about customers:

- How can you get them to pay before you deliver?
  Theatres, cinemas, football clubs, airlines and holiday companies manage it, why cannot you?
- How can you get them to pay cash quick?
  Discount for cash, or other incentives.
- How can you get them to repeat purchase and keep buying from you?
  Make sure your offer is not a one-off one. Up sell, deliver packages. Amazon will always offer you a two-book deal, why cannot you?

- How can you get them to refer their friends?
  Sky offers £60 incentive? Why cannot you?

- How can you get them to pay an advance?
  Executive search and construction companies manage it, why cannot you?

You see, you can raise the capital with the collateral of the products and services you are about to deliver. That is how an entrepreneur raises finance.

You can even go a step further with customer financing. Did you know that every day companies are bought by individuals like you and financed by the customers of the company being bought? It is called factoring. How cool is that?

Incidentally, if you want to raise finance through banks or venture capitalists you will find them to be much more interested if you have raised finance through customers first. Why? Because it gives them an element of security. Your business plan is no longer a theory, it is a business.

Getting into business for yourself is not about getting up the guts to take the risks. It is about being entrepreneurial to reduce the risks to an acceptable workable level.

Entrepreneur interview: Steve Ball

Alex: What is your career background?

Steve: When I left school I trained to be a mechanic. I left Liverpool at the age of 18 to look for a job – ended up working for a car hire company at Gatwick. Starting on the lowest rung of the ladder I soon fast tracked myself through the business.

I left there and managed the service department of a couple of main car dealers identifying and putting in processes to increase workshop performance and efficiencies.

I had a cycle accident and was unable to drive for a few months and decided to leave the motor trade. I looked for a job that would give me more experience in different fields. I started working in the telemarketing department of a large company and within a few months had progressed through a number of positions to become manager of a £1million trade exhibition in the food and drink industry. Once I had put in place all of the processes and procedures and built the tools for the staff, I became bored and immediately started looking for my next challenge.

An old work colleague called to let me know that the company he worked for was in need of help and was looking for someone to help them with sales and understand why they were having difficulties. I tried to implement change in this business, but they were not ready for it. Frustrated I left after only six weeks.

Desperate to find another challenge I was approached by a major house builder to help to reorganize their Technical Engineering department. It was a challenge I relished. They had rapidly grown by buying up other developers in a short period of time. Every member of staff had a different way of doing things, a different way of filing, different letters and different procedures. It was my job to put new procedure in place and to make sure that all the staff were happy with the new procedures and could implement them. Once I had completed my task and there was no further need for me there, I used my skills in process and procedures to become a product manager for a small company building bespoke software for small businesses.

While at an Enterprise day run by Alex I was fortunate enough to speak about an idea that I had a number of years ago. I announced that I was a 'pillow turner' and asked, 'Are there any pillow turners here today?' To my astonishment over 60% of the delegates said that they were pillow turners too. But what is a pillow turner? Someone who is always looking for the cool part of the pillow when in bed. They, like me, tend to turn or flip the pillow over and over again. We find it difficult to get to sleep and then wake up frequently in the night.

I decided that there was a market for some kind of cooling device for the pillow. On Alex's CD, *Make More Money in Less Time*, one of the key tips is: in business find something that you have a natural passion and enthusiasm for and if you can make money from it then you will be more likely to hit your goal. It was time for me to start my own business. While carrying out research on the internet I found a product in the US called the Chillow®. It was a eureka moment. My prayers had been answered: why hadn't I seen this product for sale here in the UK? Where could I buy one? I contacted the import agent for UK and Europe and within two days had become a distributor for Chillow® in the UK. I decided to call the business 'Pillow Turner'. Early sales came in and I am fast setting up resellers who are also making good profits. It was a simple idea, simple business model and I have a deal with the manufacturer which means I do not have to raise or risk any money or concern myself with production issues. Never looked back.

Alex: How do you define success?

Steve: I think success for me starts with putting food on the table and paying the bills. My philosophy has always been to look after your customers (both internal and external) and the money will look after itself. You do that by ultimately being trustworthy, understanding, responsive, bright and above all organized. If you are missing any of these attributes I believe that you will, in the long run, fail to succeed.

Alex: What advice would you give somebody starting out?

Steve: Write things down. Write down a list of your capabilities and those capabilities of your business. List the type of customer you think you can offer a product or service to. Profile each customer type in detail. What do they want to buy from you? How do they buy something from you? Where do they buy? When do they buy?

Once you have worked this out you can focus your marketing to each customer type and measure your success. Oh yes, always measure where your sales leads come from and where they don't, you can then decide where best to focus your marketing budget.

Alex: How do you spot an opportunity?

Steve: Look for something that you are passionate about and that you know there is a market for, but at the end of the day you have to keep looking and above all listening, and being in the right place to spot an opportunity. Spend time with like-minded people. I am a member of Alex McMillan's Club Entrepreneur. We are always coming up with ideas and help for existing and future entrepreneurs to realize their dreams.

Alex: What would you have done differently if you could go back in time?

Steve: I should have taken time to invent something myself instead of missing the boat and finding someone else had already invented it.

Alex: What made you want to become an entrepreneur?

Steve: I was tired of helping other people to make money, while being paid a wage, and not a very good one at that. The time came when I had enough experience to be able to take a chance and start my own business, a business doing something that I was passionate about and will help a lot of people and should generate healthy income for resellers who work with me.

Alex: How do you motivate yourself when things don't go to plan?
Steve: I have always been optimistic about things. If a customer says 'no', I move on to the next. I do, however, measure why people say no – looking for patterns. Learning what the potential customer's objections are helps you to handle those objections better, and hopefully turn the objections into a sale. If you sell something you have got to understand that not everybody wants or needs your product or service. So therefore you have to be clever and target the customers that do. Profile each of your target customers so you know who they are and where to find them.

Three tips

1 Study people who have been successful in what you are about to embark on.
2 Be a 100%er.
3 Think profit not salary.

Two tasks

1 Start something today, however small, an on-your-own business.
2 Write a business plan and finish it this weekend. Keep it short and simple.

17

exit routes, selling your business

In this chapter you will learn:
- to explore your ultimate goal
- the seven factors that determine what your business will sell for
- the option of buying and selling businesses
- the golden rules of buying a business
- the golden rules of selling a business

'Singleness of purpose is one of the chief essentials for success in life, no matter what may be one's aim.'

John D Rockefeller

'All human actions have one or more of these seven causes: chance, nature, compulsions, habit, reason, passion, desire.'

Aristotle

Having obtained financial freedom (the choice to work or not), you have to consider what to do with your time. Continue what you are doing or to take another direction, perhaps focusing on more personal than commercial goals?

What is your goal after you have reached all your goals?

GOALS to me stands for Go On And Launch Something. Therefore when one goal is reached, another goal should be set, even if that 'launch' is about a new lifestyle rather than being business related.

The biggest error people make with goal setting, in my experience is, going into too much detail when really they need to follow the Michael Bloomberg idea of 'Don't Get it Right Get it Going'. For a business goal, feedback from live prospects is the best form of market research. For a more personal goal you still need to get on with it. This is because planning is not a one-off exercise, it is ongoing.

Planning on the 'exit' should be done at the start. It helps to focus but also fires up the perpetual motivation energies. No journey makes a lot of sense without a start and finish point. So where exactly do you want to get to? When you have a clear focus on where you are going, you will be in a position to keep in the right direction. It will be your benchmark for all decision making along the way.

So the point I am making is that what you want to do with your new business when it is successful is something you need to be thinking about at the start, not when you have accomplished it. Besides there are all the sorts of things you need to do ahead of time. If you are planning to exit your business by a sale, for example, you ideally need three years to groom the business for that sale to get the best possible price for it.

The majority of rich people in the UK are entrepreneurs, the majority of them made it by selling a business. It is usually financially better to go for the capital gain rather than continual profit. Many entrepreneurs I have interviewed, including myself, have regrets at not selling a business when the opportunity presented itself. This route has the lowest risk and the tax rules are more favourable. Even raising finance is a lot easier than for a start up.

As an entrepreneur your mind is constantly challenged, it is very rewarding to build something up. Many entrepreneurs when they have built up a business are so used to working hard, being creative, when they achieve early retirement they soon get bored and desperately want to get involved with something. They may have dreams of travel, of study, or to write a book, but most want to be fully working again. If your success is in self-employment then you will have little to sell unless you translate your expertise into products that then can be sold for a royalty or licence arrangement. Sometimes your client contact list can be sold if your customer base can be transferred easily.

Many choose to sell out in a deal which leaves them running the business they sold with a minority stake. This means that they have their capital gain which is not being eroded at all for two reasons: first, it is well invested, probably in a portfolio of shares or property; second, they are receiving a full salary and their capital base is being added to. The minority stake gives them a good chance of a further and significant capital gain as a bonus from the employment, without the pressure they previously had.

Many entrepreneurs see themselves as talented in bringing something to a small firm, but now probably a different set of skills is needed to develop the business to the next level. Someone offering more structured, process orientated skills and experience can be ideal. Someone perhaps who has been working for a larger company and understands the new paradigm to which the enterprise is heading.

Selling your business

There are seven main things that will influence the price you get for your business.

1 profit level
2 current profit multiples in your sector
3 state of the market
4 premium for branding
5 premium for desirability
6 your negotiating skills
7 size of the enterprise.

Let us look at each of these in turn.

Profit level

The valuation of a small business can be a complex subject. The market, however, like most things in business likes to keep it simple. Thus the initial valuation of your business is a multiple of profits. So if your business is making £150,000 profit per year (after drawing a market management salary cost) and the current multiple is 5 then your business will go up for sale probably around £750,000. Any specific asset, like property, being additional to that.

A buyer will want to see a lot more detail: track record over last few years, market potential, etc. If the profit was higher in the last two years it suggests a declining market.

So as an owner from three years before a sale you want to start manipulating the figures to increase the profitability. This means that major investment, which reduces profit in the short and medium term will reduce the market value of the business. A new buyer will also be looking for ways that he or she can grow the business. So anything that suggests the business can be expanded will fetch a premium.

Current profit multiples in your sector

Multiples are set by the market. They vary probably between about 4 and 12 depending on sector, size of the business and current market conditions. Then they are adjusted for a specific business, depending on the negotiation of other factors to be taken into consideration.

State of the market

Like every other market, that for buying and selling a business goes up and down. It all depends on how many buyers and sellers there are at any particular time, the state of the general economy and confidence levels. One can pick an ideal time when one is ready to sell.

Premium for branding

A good brand can gain not only a premium but a substantial premium because a brand is expandable easily. Much effort should be spent on establishing a clear brand for your business and one that has more than limited market potential.

Premium for desirability

Various other factors can make your business more desirable to a buyer. For example, if a national network of employment agencies does not have an operation in your town, it will probably be cheaper to buy your business than to set up their own operation.

A buyer, whether an individual or a company, can have special skills that as soon as they buy your business they instantly improve its value. They have management skills. A marketing expert may see they can use their talents to grow the business. A computer expert may see an opportunity to make it more efficient and reduce operating costs. They both have a client list or a business that is synergized with yours.

Your negotiating skills

Like anything traded, negotiating skills will determine the final price. If you are not a good negotiator employ one. I suggest a well-chosen professional firm would probably increase the final selling price by more than their fee. Not to mention finding someone who you were not aware of.

Size of the enterprise

As firms grow the multiple they attract grows, mainly due to bigger buyers having bigger pockets and a more competitive market. There is a real incentive, therefore, to merge or acquire as you grow to raise the multiple. In practice, merging two businesses might not now be that easy, if they have different cultures. On the other hand, rationalizations in operating processes might allow some cuts and make them more profitable before increasing sales.

(An entrepreneur, Kevin Uphill of www.avondale-group.co.uk, who has built up a business brokerage is interviewed at the end of this chapter.)

For most entrepreneurs their life wealth is their business and thus their pension scheme. Selling means that at least half of it can be put in the portfolio of investments meaning that your risk is greatly reduced.

The selling and buying businesses option

Let us say you have sold your business and now have a significant capital sum and a lot of free time. Then one serious option is to put at least half of your capital gain into relatively secure investments, to protect from the worst possible downside. The remainder you can have as a facility to buy businesses. This makes a lot of sense because of the following:

- You have considerably more experience now than when you started your first business. You have been there and done it so why not capitalize on that skill.
- Buying a business substantially cuts risk.
- Businesses can be bought for no or little money down. Owners financing, factoring existing invoices, partners.
- Any sort of financing will be much easier for you as you have a proven track record of delivering the goods.
- You can make your hobby and business buying, value adding and selling businesses. It can be great fun and offers very significant capital gains.

If this is a goal then you need to consider:

- How to buy a business while limiting your financial risk.
- How to find and identify bargains.
- How to add at least 10% to the value immediately.
- How to add value to the business on a daily basis.
- How (and when) to sell for a premium.

People who have had an interesting and stimulating career find that although they can't wait for retirement, when it comes it is a disappointment. Not having to work for your living, being able to relax at home, read, do the garden, pursue a hobby, travel is very motivating. Most people, when they take a two week holiday, find that they cannot wait to get back to work.

They need to involve themselves in something fulfilling. However luxurious your house or yacht, it just starts to become boring for most entrepreneurs.

Most entrepreneurs come back into business after a short break. They can now pursue business interests without the financial pressures they were once under. Others really do have a consuming hobby or passion they wish to fulfil, like travelling the world. If this is you, then do it.

There are a few golden rules to success in buying and selling businesses.

- Only buy a business in a sector you know.
- Only buy from a motivated seller (to ensure a discount).
- Use a professional intermediary.
- Have 'something personal' that adds value from day one.
- Focus on developing the branding.
- Build a 'money making machine', i.e. profits are not dependent on you or key staff.
- Work on improving profits rather than sales.
- Find and sell only to motivated buyers (to ensure a premium).
- Each time put 50% of the proceeds into safe investments.

Entrepreneur interview: Kevin Uphill

Alex: What is your career background?

Kevin: I was employed as a Business Development Consultant and I was interested with my father to buy a business transfer franchise. We took advice from the Training and Enterprise Council and they suggested that with our profiles we really ought to start our own business. I believed in taking expert advice right from the start, so that is what we did. I was motivated to be an entrepreneur because I saw it as the biggest challenge, a way to control my own destiny and the only way I could see myself making a million.

My father and I had many complementary skills. However, looking back, we were both arrogant and did not really know very much about running a business. In the first five years we made the mistake of working in the business and not on the business itself. We sell small and medium sized enterprises as a brokerage. This meant that we have and do deal with successful entrepreneurs who are in a position to realize a capital gain on a daily basis.

After we were established and profitable, I was motivated to make some serious money. We asked ourselves some interesting questions determined to develop it into something that would make us a lot of money. Specifically we asked the question, 'How could we develop it so that it pays us a great deal more?' We also saw a potential capital gain as a key objective. As our business meant dealing with successful entrepreneurs, we had a great deal of experience available to us from which to learn.

We decided to grow with an emphasis on installing some very efficient systems and processes. We developed a network of offices around the country, largely on retained earnings, with a programme of continuous improvement. We asked and continue to ask the question, 'How can we make this better?', on every single component of the business at every single point of time.

I was also influenced at the time by the idea that if you cannot be the first in your sector, make your own sector. I saw James Dyson's success as an ideal example of this. So I clarified our market niche within selling small to medium sized businesses and our consultancy approach. We stopped dealing with high street retailers and touched nothing under at least £50K profit. We also recruited very high quality people capable and credible in advising people who, after all, had successfully built up a profitable business. We also invested in training. Our income went up by a factor of five following the enhancements, and we are still growing.

Alex: How do you define success?

Kevin: Health, happiness, fun and balance.

Alex: What is the secret of success of an entrepreneur?

Kevin: To be aware of all the components that make up a business and be receptive to improving them.

Alex: What advice would you give somebody starting out?

Kevin:

1 Listen attentively.
2 Be self-aware of your strengths and weaknesses.
3 Do not believe your own dream. Look at it from an outside perspective and be objective.
4 Work smart before hard.
5 Make business your hobby and make sure it is fun.

Alex: How do you spot an opportunity?

Kevin: Get a raw idea, work out the costs and profits in your head and only get enthusiastic if it has a strong chance of generating a good cash return.

Alex: What would you have done differently if you could go back in time?

Kevin: I would have got more knowledge on marketing and sales issues.

Alex: How do you motivate yourself when things don't go to plan?

Kevin: Winning counts, but if you have done your best, it's fine. Learn from the experience and get going.

Three tips

1 The preferred exit determines the best entry.
2 Know your goals exactly.
3 Stick to what you know well.

Two tasks

1 Plan your exit now. Write down on one sheet your exit strategy.
2 Surf websites to see what price businesses in your sector are going for.

taking it further

Biographies of entrepreneurs

Against the Odds, James Dyson, Texere Publishing, 2000

Autobiography of Charles Forte, Charles Forte, Sidgwick & Jackson, 1986

Bill Gates Speaks, Insight from the World's Greatest Entrepreneur, Janet Lowe, John Wiley, 1998

Bloomberg by Bloomberg, Michael Bloomberg, M Winkler, John Wiley & Sons, 2001

Building a Company: Roy O. Disney and the Creation of An Entertainment Empire, Bob Thomas, Hyperion, 1998

Business as Unusual, Anita Roddick, Thorsons, 2000

Business the Yahoo! Way: Secrets of the World's Most Popular Internet Company, Bob Smith and Anthony Vlamis, Capstone, 2000

Difference between God and Larry Ellison: Inside Oracle, Mike Wilson, William Morrow & Co, 2000

Getty: The richest man in the world, Robert Lenzner, Hutchinson, 1985

Google Story, David A Vise, Bantam Dell, Macmillan, 2005

Grinding It Out: The Making of McDonald's, Ray Kroc and Robert Anderson, St Martins Press, 1990

Howard Hughes: The Secret Life, Charles Higham, Sidgwick & Jackson, 1993

In Sam We Trust: The Untold Story of Sam Walton and How Wal Mart is Devouring the World, Bob Ortega, Kogan Page, 1999

Losing My Virginity, Richard Branson, Virgin Books, 2000

Masters of Enterprise, Giants of American Business from John Jacob Astor and JP Morgan to Bill Gates and Oprah Winfrey, H W Brands, Free Press, 1999

Millionaire Upgrade: Lessons in Success From Those Who Travel at the Sharp End of the Plane, Richard Parkes Cordock, Capston Publishing, 2006

Onassis (Aristotle Socrates Onassis), Willi Frischauer, Bodley Head, 1968

Perfect Store (Inside eBay), Adam Cohen, Piatkus Books, 2003

Pour Your Heart Into It (Starbucks), Howard Schulz, Hyperion, 1998

Q&A: A Sort of Autobiography (Habitat), Terence Conran, HarperCollins, 2001

Real Walt Disney: A biography, Leonard Mosley, Grafton Books, 1985

Rich Dad Poor Dad, Robert Kiyosaki, Time Warner Paperbacks, 2002

Richard Branson, Rob Alcraft, Heinemann Library, 1998

Rupert Murdoch (News International), William Shawcross, Pan, 1993

Screw It, Let's Do It, Richard Branson, Quick Reads, 2006

Simon Marks Retail Revolutionary, Paul Bookbinder, George Weidenfeld & Nicolson, 1993

Story of Henry Ford, Jane Horneshaw, Collins, 1980

Titan, the life of John D Rockefeller Sr, Ron Chernow, Warner Books, 1998

Walking up Brook Street (Brook Street Bureau), Margery Hurst, George Weidenfeld & Nicolson, 1988

Other books by the author

Advanced Selling for Beginners, Alex McMillan, Management Books, 2000

How to Sell a Business for Wealth, Alex McMillan and Kevin Uphill, Thorogood Publishing, 2006

Websites

Sites relating to venture capital

www.nban.co.uk National Business Angel Network
www.bvca.co.uk British Venture Capital Association
www.3i.com

Sites relating to franchising/network marketing

www.british-franchise.org.uk
www.franchise.org
www.franchiseworld.demon.co.uk
www.home-workers.com
www.moneymaking.co.uk
www.pmignet.com

Sites offering advice and support to entrepreneurs

www.ClubEntrepreneur.co.uk
www.sybmagazine.com
www.princes-trust.org.uk
www.fsb.org.uk
www.dti.gov.uk
www.sbs.gov.uk
www.tec.co.uk
www.britishchambers.org.uk
www.WebBigEducation.com

Sites useful for inventors

www.patent.gov.org
www.shell-livewire.org

Businesses of people interviewed in this book

www.pillowturner.com   (Steve Ball)
www.avondale-group.co.uk (Kevin Uphill)
www.bytestart.co.uk   (Emyr Williams)
www.eurodrive.com   (Richard Lowden)
www.achieversevents.co.uk   (Christine Jones)
www.theattunegroup.co.uk   (Christine Jones)
www.wadoryu.co.uk (Sensei Paul Elliott)
www.cbsbutler.com   (David Leyshon)

alternative investment market (AIM) stock market for small growth firms with attractive tax benefits to investors.

business angel wealthy individual looking to invest cash in companies with high growth potential in return for shares. Valuable experience, contacts and other support is also often offered.

business transfer agency agency that sells businesses for a commission.

corporate entrepreneur ideas person within a company who introduces change.

elevator pitch summary presentation of a business proposal.

equity another term for shares in a company.

factoring system that raises immediate cash against sales invoiced as security.

franchising a system that allows each operating unit to be owned and financed by a local entrepreneur in return for access to all the resources and support of the group.

lifestyle business a business where profit maximization and growth is secondary to the owners doing what they love doing. Of limited interest to external investors.

management buy ins external management team buys a controlling shareholding and takes over the management of the company, usually with the backing of a financial institution.

management buy outs current management buys a controlling shareholding, usually with the backing of a financial institution.

National Business Angels Network (NBAN) group of independent agencies around the UK that are introduction services between entrepreneurs and individual investors.

network marketing system that facilitates the selling of goods and services by building up a network of distributors, which, in turn, recruits a network of distributors, and so on. As the network grows so do the long-term passive profits of the distributor.

Opportunity Directional Questions questions designed to help you come up with ideas.

partnership form of business trading which means that the individual partners and the business are one and the same thing legally.

retained contracts money up front before commencing work.

reverse financing instead of getting money into the company, taking the company to the money.

SMILE the five main types of entrepreneur: System, Money, Innovator, Lifestlye and Empire.

street SMARTS the street smart entrepreneur knows which of the five opportunities (Self-employed, Multi-level marketing, Acquire a business, Royalty based, Turnkey or Start up) best suit their personality, goals and situation.

supplier funding credit from supplier organization in return for their long-term potential business from the new enterprise.

SWOT Strengths, Weaknesses, Opportunities, Threats summary analysis of a business which has become a common and expected part of formal business plans.

venture capital investment in a company in return for shares, that is not necessarily looking for security, expecting a risky investment in return for a high-potential return. This can apply to companies at any stage of development. Venture capitalist companies tend to specialize by amount of investment and/or industry and/or location.

wealth reservoir alternative methods of solving the challenge of the capital requirement of a company by relying on the creativity of the entrepreneur.

index

teach yourself ®

From Advanced Sudoku to Zulu, you'll find everything you need in the **teach yourself** range, in books, on CD and on DVD.

Visit **www.teachyourself.co.uk** for more details.

Advanced Sudoku and Kakuro
Afrikaans
Alexander Technique
Algebra
Ancient Greek
Applied Psychology
Arabic
Aromatherapy
Art History
Astrology
Astronomy
AutoCAD 2004
AutoCAD 2007
Ayurveda
Baby Massage and Yoga
Baby Signing
Baby Sleep
Bach Flower Remedies
Backgammon
Ballroom Dancing
Basic Accounting
Basic Computer Skills
Basic Mathematics
Beauty
Beekeeping
Beginner's Arabic Script
Beginner's Chinese Script
Beginner's Dutch

Beginner's French
Beginner's German
Beginner's Greek
Beginner's Greek Script
Beginner's Hindi
Beginner's Italian
Beginner's Japanese
Beginner's Japanese Script
Beginner's Latin
Beginner's Mandarin Chinese
Beginner's Portuguese
Beginner's Russian
Beginner's Russian Script
Beginner's Spanish
Beginner's Turkish
Beginner's Urdu Script
Bengali
Better Bridge
Better Chess
Better Driving
Better Handwriting
Biblical Hebrew
Biology
Birdwatching
Blogging
Body Language
Book Keeping
Brazilian Portuguese

Bridge
British Empire, The
British Monarchy from Henry VIII,
    The
Buddhism
Bulgarian
Business Chinese
Business French
Business Japanese
Business Plans
Business Spanish
Business Studies
Buying a Home in France
Buying a Home in Italy
Buying a Home in Portugal
Buying a Home in Spain
C++
Calculus
Calligraphy
Cantonese
Car Buying and Maintenance
Card Games
Catalan
Chess
Chi Kung
Chinese Medicine
Christianity
Classical Music
Coaching
Cold War, The
Collecting
Computing for the Over 50s
Consulting
Copywriting
Correct English
Counselling
Creative Writing
Cricket
Croatian
Crystal Healing
CVs
Czech
Danish
Decluttering
Desktop Publishing
Detox

Digital Home Movie Making
Digital Photography
Dog Training
Drawing
Dream Interpretation
Dutch
Dutch Conversation
Dutch Dictionary
Dutch Grammar
Eastern Philosophy
Electronics
English as a Foreign Language
English for International Business
English Grammar
English Grammar as a Foreign
    Language
English Vocabulary
Entrepreneurship
Estonian
Ethics
Excel 2003
Feng Shui
Film Making
Film Studies
Finance for Non-Financial
    Managers
Finnish
First World War, The
Fitness
Flash 8
Flash MX
Flexible Working
Flirting
Flower Arranging
Franchising
French
French Conversation
French Dictionary
French Grammar
French Phrasebook
French Starter Kit
French Verbs
French Vocabulary
Freud
Gaelic
Gardening

Genetics
Geology
German
German Conversation
German Grammar
German Phrasebook
German Verbs
German Vocabulary
Globalization
Go
Golf
Good Study Skills
Great Sex
Greek
Greek Conversation
Greek Phrasebook
Growing Your Business
Guitar
Gulf Arabic
Hand Reflexology
Hausa
Herbal Medicine
Hieroglyphics
Hindi
Hindi Conversation
Hinduism
History of Ireland, The
Home PC Maintenance and
  Networking
How to DJ
How to Run a Marathon
How to Win at Casino Games
How to Win at Horse Racing
How to Win at Online Gambling
How to Win at Poker
How to Write a Blockbuster
Human Anatomy & Physiology
Hungarian
Icelandic
Improve Your French
Improve Your German
Improve Your Italian
Improve Your Spanish
Improving Your Employability
Indian Head Massage

Indonesian
Instant French
Instant German
Instant Greek
Instant Italian
Instant Japanese
Instant Portuguese
Instant Russian
Instant Spanish
Internet, The
Irish
Irish Conversation
Irish Grammar
Islam
Italian
Italian Conversation
Italian Grammar
Italian Phrasebook
Italian Starter Kit
Italian Verbs
Italian Vocabulary
Japanese
Japanese Conversation
Java
JavaScript
Jazz
Jewellery Making
Judaism
Jung
Kama Sutra, The
Keeping Aquarium Fish
Keeping Pigs
Keeping Poultry
Keeping a Rabbit
Knitting
Korean
Latin
Latin American Spanish
Latin Dictionary
Latin Grammar
Latvian
Letter Writing Skills
Life at 50: For Men
Life at 50: For Women
Life Coaching

Sage Line 50
Sanskrit
Screenwriting
Second World War, The
Serbian
Setting Up a Small Business
Shorthand Pitman 2000
Sikhism
Singing
Slovene
Small Business Accounting
Small Business Health Check
Songwriting
Spanish
Spanish Conversation
Spanish Dictionary
Spanish Grammar
Spanish Phrasebook
Spanish Starter Kit
Spanish Verbs
Spanish Vocabulary
Speaking On Special Occasions
Speed Reading
Stalin's Russia
Stand Up Comedy
Statistics
Stop Smoking
Sudoku
Swahili
Swahili Dictionary
Swedish
Swedish Conversation
Tagalog
Tai Chi
Tantric Sex
Tap Dancing
Teaching English as a Foreign
    Language
Teams & Team Working
Thai
Theatre
Time Management
Tracing Your Family History
Training
Travel Writing

Trigonometry
Turkish
Turkish Conversation
Twentieth Century USA
Typing
Ukrainian
Understanding Tax for Small
    Businesses
Understanding Terrorism
Urdu
Vietnamese
Visual Basic
Volcanoes
Watercolour Painting
Weight Control through Diet &
    Exercise
Welsh
Welsh Dictionary
Welsh Grammar
Wills & Probate
Windows XP
Wine Tasting
Winning at Job Interviews
Word 2003
World Cultures: China
World Cultures: England
World Cultures: Germany
World Cultures: Italy
World Cultures: Japan
World Cultures: Portugal
World Cultures: Russia
World Cultures: Spain
World Cultures: Wales
World Faiths
Writing Crime Fiction
Writing for Children
Writing for Magazines
Writing a Novel
Writing Poetry
Xhosa
Yiddish
Yoga
Zen
Zulu